English White Water

Foreword

English White Water - the BCU guide is your source of the best white water river trips and 'park and play' spots south of Hadrian's Wall and east of Offa's Dyke.

Everything the paddler might wish for is featured: challenging steep brooks in remote regions, new and unfamiliar options that will open the mind to hitherto unvisited areas, classic trips on classic rivers and the best of an ever-increasing number of 'park and play' spots.

All options featured provide the paddler with an opportunity to appreciate the variety of landscape, flora and fauna that England has to offer… even in the most unexpected of places. Indeed I write this forward having just enjoyed a glorious afternoon's paddle on a featured river run in what many would regard as Middle England's rural sprawl. In its own way as good a day as any spent in wilder parts of the world.

It is a privilege to introduce English White Water as a collaboration of effort. From the involvement of the publisher, Pesda Press and the regional co-ordinators and contributors to the involvement of BCU river advisers and Coaching Service, this guide reflects the collective experiences and knowledge of a network of enthusiasts willing to share their perspective on England's many and varied rivers so that you too may enjoy what's on offer.

As with Scottish White Water, the concept has been to involve as many paddlers as possible in its writing. Paddlers had the opportunity to write up their local river, encouraging the sharing of individual offerings perhaps less known or even unknown, here in England, where the idea of finding or being introduced to something new is often regarded as an impossibility.

Please enjoy their offerings while respecting the trust and responsibility they place on you for ensuring that we and the coming generations of paddlers can keep enjoying them. Particularly bear in mind the growing force of paddlesports, the need to minimise our impact on local communities and the often delicate river environments that we may find ourselves encountering. For our part the royalties from the sale of this book will go towards specific projects that will help gain or protect access to specific sites.

Paul Owen
Chief Executive of the
British Canoe Union

Creek boater, river runner, kayaker or open boater, welcome to the offerings presented here, they are many and varied… Enjoy.

Contents

English White Water
The BCU guide

Pesda Press

www.pesdapress.com

This guidebook was produced by

BCU Coaching

The royalties will go towards specific projects that will help gain or protect access to specific sites.

For further details, membership, etc., please send an S.A.E. to:

British Canoe Union
John Dudderidge House
Adbolton Lane
West Bridgford
Nottingham
NG2 5AS

Front cover - Salmon Leap or Dog Leg Rapid, River Tees
Back cover - Marlow Weir
Pandora's Box, Upper Dart
Lower Irthing
Boulters Weir

First published in Great Britain 2003 by Pesda Press
'Elidir', Ffordd Llanllechid
Rachub, Bangor
Gwynedd
LL57 3EE

Design and artwork HappyBoater@hotmail.com
Printed by Cambrian Printers - Wales
Copyright © 2003 British Canoe Union

ISBN 0-9531956-7-8

Contents

Important Notice

Paddlers should need no reminding that white water paddling is an adventure sport involving an element of uncertainty and risk taking. Guidebooks give an idea of where to access a river, where to egress, the level of difficulty and the nature of the hazards likely to be encountered.

Conditions vary considerably with changing water levels. Erosion can block a river with fallen trees or change a rapid by moving boulders and even collapsing bedrock.

This guidebook is no substitute for inspection, personal risk assessment and good judgement. The decision on whether to paddle or not, and any consequences arising from that decision, remain yours and yours alone.

White water paddling is a popular and rapidly growing sport, which is amazing when you consider that paddlers have agreed access to only 3% of the rivers on which permission should be sought to satisfy the letter of the law. Despite lobbying by the BCU, the recently introduced Countryside and Rights of Way Act 2000 does not specifically cover waterways, though there are some signs that the situation may change in the future.

The Legal Situation

Most inland waters in this country, especially the smaller and upland rivers, are privately owned and to canoe on them without permission could constitute an act of trespass. There are a few rivers where there is a right of navigation. Where there is no public launching point, or a public footpath to the water's edge it is necessary for the paddler to get permission to cross private land to access the water.

Simple trespass is a civil offence, not a criminal offence. It is not a police matter unless a criminal offence is committed; this would only be if wilful or malicious damage was done, there was a conspiracy to commit trespass, there was behaviour likely to cause a breach of the peace or it was a case of aggravated trespass.

Aggravated Trespass (under criminal law) should not be confused with ordinary trespass, which is a civil offence. To commit aggravated trespass you must first be trespassing; whilst trespassing you must also have the intention of obstructing or disrupting a lawful activity (such as hunting, shooting or fishing) or intimidating those engaged in such lawful activities. Canoeists should not fall foul of this new law if they canoe in a peaceful and considerate manner.

What Can a Landowner Do?

An owner is entitled to ask trespassers to leave his land. He may use reasonable force to eject them if they refuse, or to deny them entry on to his land. Once on the land, the owner can ask the trespassers to leave via the shortest or an agreed route to the highway. In doing so he can't insist that they take an unreasonable route or a route over other private property. In practice, if you are challenged, behave reasonably and politely and leave as requested; that is usually the end of the matter.

A bailiff acting on behalf of the owner can do similar, under the powers given to him by the owners. An Environment Agency Bailiff has the powers of a constable for the enforcement of Salmon and Freshwater Fishery Act related offences, in relation to poaching or damage to spawning beds. (Spawning beds are usually gravel banks and damage occurs if your feet, paddles or canoe make contact with the river bottom during spawning periods).

Damages or a fine *may* be awarded against the trespasser. An injunction *may* be granted to prevent repetition of trespass, or even to restrain threatened trespass. Failure to adhere to, or ignoring the terms of an injunction would be in contempt of court. This could lead to a fine or imprisonment. For damages to be awarded or for an injunction to be ordered, that case will have to go to court. In practice this is costly, and both damages and the intention to trespass in future are difficult to prove, so landowners rarely resort to the courts.

What If You Are Challenged?

If you are challenged whilst paddling, please be courteous and polite whatever the situation. Avoid anything that could be interpreted as a breach of the peace, conspiracy to trespass, or risks causing damage to spawning beds (i.e. criminal offences). If you are challenged by an Environment Agency official you can be obliged to give your name and address. If you are accused of trespass and genuinely believe you are exercising a public right of navigation or are paddling within the terms of an access agreement, you should say so and refuse to admit trespass. There is no case if you can prove that you are within your rights or have permission. Where you have a legal right the law requires you to exercise the right reasonably with due consideration for others.

River Advisers

The national organisations forming the BCU have a team of voluntary 'Local River Advisers' who donate their own time, skill and patience into improving access for canoeing.

River advisers provide information and advice on the access situation that is currently in force on 'their' river. The Access Team is divided into regions, with rivers within that region having a specific Regional Access Officer. It is essential that you contact the river adviser for the river well in advance of your trip. By doing so you may avoid conflict, preserve the terms of an agreement, and even gain knowledge of the best places to eat and drink in the local area after your trip. Please adhere to the advice that you are given. Details of whom and how to contact the correct person are listed in the BCU Yearbook or are available from the website bcu.org.uk.

Access Agreements

The BCU can only advise individuals on when and where to paddle a river if an access agreement exists. If no specific information is available, i.e. there is no access agreement, river advisers will pass on any information they have, but the decision on whether to paddle or not rests with the individual concerned.

For those such as youth groups, who are unable to *risk* paddling without specific permission, access agreements are a lifeline. It is *vital* that the precious agreements we have are maintained. Therefore, please respect the terms of those few agreements that do exist. They are highlighted in the guide by a 'tick' symbol in the thumbnail guides.

The work of the access committee in establishing such agreements should be recognised in the context of licence agreements with the Environment Agency and British Waterways which, for those of us paddling the 'park and play' spots of England, provide benefit through BCU membership. The River Thames was added this year.

The Future

The help of members is needed to achieve the BCU's objective of securing new legislation to give canoeists an equitable share of scarce and finite waterway resources. Members can help by making sure that their own MP, local councillor and local press, radio and TV are aware of the very difficult situation faced by canoeists. The changes we need will not come about until the public understands our problems and supports our aims; this is the pressure that will encourage our legislators to cast their votes in favour of fair shares for canoeing. We also have to demonstrate the need for change; therefore we are compiling a file identifying access problems all over the country and recording specific details, such as dates and locations. Any member encountering an access problem is urged to provide details to the Local River Adviser or Regional Access Officer concerned and to the Access and Facilities Service at the BCU, e-mail access@bcu.org.uk.

Code of Conduct

All canoeists should remember that they are ambassadors for their sport. England's rivers, lakes and the sea are a precious natural resource, enjoyed by a variety of recreational users and providing a workplace for many more.

On the Land

- Observe the Country Code
- Drive and park considerately, not obstructing gates, lanes or passing places
- Avoid damaging fences, gates, walls or river banks
- Use recognised access points where possible
- Keep noise to a minimum
- Be discreet and don't cause offence by changing or urinating in public
- Respect private property and if in doubt, ask for permission to cross land or drive on a private road
- Take your litter away with you

On the Water

- Respect all other water users
- Co-operate with anglers to avoid lines, friendly communication can reduce potential conflict
- Do not linger in pools already occupied by other river users
- Keep numbers in your party consistent with safety, the nature of the stretch of water and the impact on your surroundings
- Have special regard for inexperienced paddlers in your group
- Offer assistance to anyone in genuine need, on or off the water, but do not put yourself or fellow paddlers at risk
- Follow the general rules of navigation and local byelaws

In general, treat others as you would wish to be treated, respect the environment and follow safety recommendations. Make sure you have Public Liability Insurance (this is an automatic benefit of BCU membership). Assist the BCU in promoting the concept of equal rights of access and enjoyment of England's waterways for all by adhering to this code and explaining it to other paddlers and the general public.

Grading

Each river section in this guidebook is given a grade, based on the International Grading System which is expressed as a number from 1 to 6. If a second grade follows the first in brackets, e.g. 3(5) this usually indicates a harder rapid or rapids on the section which can be portaged if necessary. Individual rapids are often graded too. If a river is at the easier or harder end of a grade this may be indicated with a plus or a minus, e.g. 4+. Where a river may vary in difficulty depending on water levels, this may be indicated by showing the two grades divided by a forward slash, e.g. 3/4.

The International Grading System

Grade 1 - Moving water, unobstructed and without technical difficulties. There may be small waves and riffles to wobble the boat.

Grade 2 - Waves, small stoppers and other minor obstructions which are simple to avoid. Eddies and cushion waves may be strong.

Grade 3 –Distinctive waves, stoppers and technical difficulties. There may be drops and powerful constrictions. The main distinguishing feature of Grade 3 water is that the paddler will have to follow a distinct route to avoid obstacles and hazards.

Grade 4 - Severe waves, drops, stoppers and other obstructions. The route is not easily recognisable and will usually require careful inspection from the boat or bank. Grade 4 encompasses a wide range of rivers, from those with pool-drop rapids to those with extended continuous rapids; so there is a huge variation in difficulty. It is common to distinguish easier grade 4 rapids by grading them as 4- and harder rapids as 4+.

Grade 5 - Extremely difficult rapids with precise and technically demanding routes to be followed. Stoppers, currents and waves will be powerful and inspection is essential.

Grade 6 - All of the above carried to extremes. Grade 6 usually means fiendishly hard or seemingly unrunnable rapids, which may just be possible in certain conditions.

Contributor:
Mark Rainsley

Rivers change, water levels change, different individuals find different kinds of water harder or easier than the guidebook writer. The grading system is of necessity vague and imprecise. Use the guidebook grade as a starting point. Inspect the rapids as you see them, make your own decisions.

This can only make us better and safer paddlers.

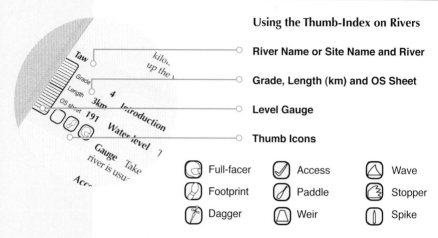

Using the Thumb-Index on Rivers

River Name or Site Name and River

Grade, Length (km) and OS Sheet

Level Gauge

Thumb Icons

Full-facer	Access	Wave
Footprint	Paddle	Stopper
Dagger	Weir	Spike

Grade Ranging from 1 to 6, allowing for +/- grades.

- 4/5 indicates that the run has rapids of both grades shown.

- 4 + or – indicates that the author feels the run is at the harder or easier end of the grade.

- If a river contains one or two rapids which are harder than the rest of the run, but the trip could feasibly be tackled by someone intending to portage the harder sections, this is shown by using brackets. For example 3 (5).

Level Gauge The majority of English rivers will vary greatly in their severity at differing water levels, many are only runnable after heavy rainfall. The white area in the gauge gives a rough indicaton of suitable water levels. The top of the scale denotes flood or sustained heavy rainfall, the bottom, drought. *Attention must be paid to actual and forecast weather affecting the watershed.*

Thumb Icons *Full-facer,* this is a short boat run of a rocky or precarious nature, best to come equipped with full-on gear. *Footprint,* the approach to this run requires a significant walk-in. *Dagger,* this section is not a tried and tested milk-run, the authors may have only run it once or twice, or the rapids may be subject to periodic change, proceed with due caution. *Access,* indicates that there is a formal access agreement. *Paddle,* indicates that the river is suitable for open canoes. *Weir,* indicates that much of the white water action is provided by weirs; ensure you can distinguish between killer weirs and fun weirs. *Wave,* this indicates that there is a surfable green wave at the site, though it may not be present at all water levels. *Stopper,* this indicates that there is a retentive stopper at the site, though once again it may not be present at all levels. *Spike,* this indicates that there is a need for caution due to the presence of underwater debris.

The guide breaks down into 5 geographical areas: The South-West, The South and East, The North-East, The North-West and The West, with each of these areas being further divided into sections grouping rivers of the same locality. Generally these sections are based around the river basins of the larger rivers but we have made exceptions to this in an effort to ensure that the rivers appear in the book in the most useful order to the reader.
Put-ins and take-outs are given for each trip along with the relevant directions for finding them by road and by foot. In some cases an access point may be described which, although not necessarily the shortest or easiest way to or from the river, avoids conflict with landowners or local people.
Distances are generally given in miles when travelling by car and in km's when on foot or afloat. Most of the time a road atlas will suffice for finding your way to the river but having the relevant Landranger OS map to hand will often make the task much easier. Six figure grid references are often given with a location. Directions on the river are always given from the paddler's point of view. So river left is always that seen when on the river and looking downstream. Playboaters however, spend much of their time facing upstream when surfing or playing on a wave, so when describing playspots we often refer to surfer's left or right. Surfer's left is the same as river right.
Sizes of drops and falls are given in metres.

Using the Maps

Symbols and Icons

River (numbered beneath) ○————○ ⑤

Road identifier ○————○ **A390**

Significant Town ○————○ ● Liskeard

Significant Peak ○————○ ▲ **Scafell Pike**

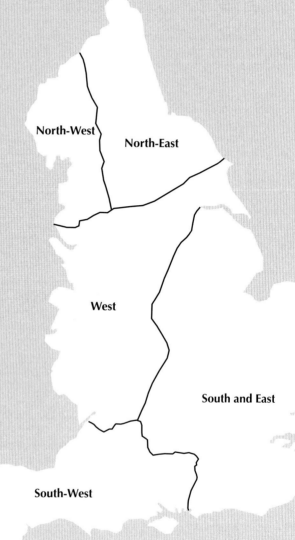

North-West

North-East

West

South and East

South-West

The South-West

Contents

Cornwall

Exmoor and Somerset

North Dartmoor

South Dartmoor

Other

Introduction

'It was broken water, little falls between rocks, swirls under the wooded banks…all the way down for five miles, nearly to New Bridge' - An early canoe descent of the River Dart, from 'Rapid Rivers', William Bliss, 1935

The best white water trips in the South-West are arguably the best in England, and rival their equivalents in Scotland and Wales.

Between Hampshire and Land's End, there is a huge and active paddling population, joined at weekends by almost every paddler in the South-East of England. People crammed onto the River Dart on Saturday morning might assume that absolute saturation of the South-West's paddling resources has been achieved.

The good news is that they'd be completely wrong. The River Dart, along with the 'Riverdart Adventures' Country Park (and accompanying bar), is undoubtedly the communal centre of South-West boating. However, the region offers many alternatives to suit paddlers of all abilities. Despite a lack of mountains, the geology of Dartmoor, Exmoor and Bodmin Moor create numerous steep creeks whilst the lowlands produce many easier touring white water trips. When all runs dry, the nation's finest surf beaches await nearby.

The only mystery is why the vast majority of the region's rivers see very few paddlers. Next time you squeeze into a full eddy on the Dart, ask yourself a few frank questions. Is it possible that other similar quality rivers lie empty nearby? Could you be missing out? Are you going to explore something different next weekend …or will you just be joining the Dart queues again?

Access is very much a live issue in the South-West. The BCU SW Region Access Team are hardworking and enlightened in their approach, and have had notable successes with some rivers. Inevitably, many rivers in the South-West have no agreed access and a few are nothing short of conflict zones. How rivers without agreements are approached is down to the individual. All I can note is that the South-West section of this guidebook has been researched by paddling in small proactive groups, choosing discreet times and taking an environmentally sensitive attitude to the surroundings. With this approach we have not encountered a single objection or caused any offence that we are aware of. The rivers are there if you know how to claim them.

Mark Rainsley

South-West Regional Coordinator for the Guidebook

'I found myself going through what seemed very private grounds, and went as fast as I could and dared' – William Bliss.

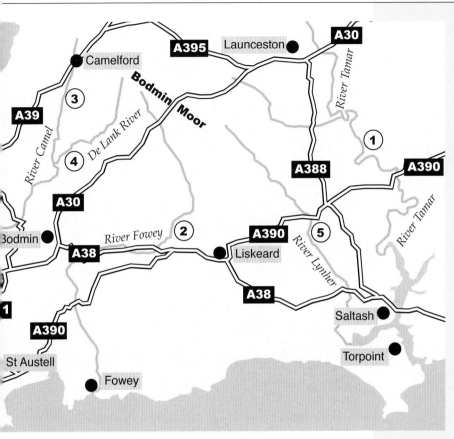

Cornwall

Tamar (Upper - Greystone Bridge to Horsebridge)

Grade **2**

Length **12km**

OS sheet **201**

Introduction   A pleasant combination of flat water touring and easy white water. Few major rivers will offer you the solitude and silence you'll experience downstream of Greystone Bridge.

Water level   The Tamar will be paddleable throughout the access season, being a major river with a huge drainage. However, very high levels are best avoided as some of the weirs will become dangerous and difficult to avoid.

Gauge   It should be clear if the river is too high for comfort; take a look at the weirs directly below the put-in.

Access   You need to access the river 300m upstream of Greystone Bridge on river right (Cornwall!) where there is an unmarked track down to a water extraction building (367805) beside the river. There is no worthwhile parking here and your vehicle will not be welcome parked near the entrance of the quarry a little way up the hill.
At Horsebridge (400749), there are several options for parking, of which the best is on the river right side of the river. There is an agreement permitting paddling from 15th October to 28th February, weekends only. Details from the river adviser, www.bcu.org.uk/access/riverinfosouthwest.

Description   Much of this long section is flat, but there are numerous small weirs which have runnable slots in the centre and pools with defined waves and eddies below. These make great training spots. There is only one weir with a significant drop, the rest are all under a metre in height.
Open boaters and touring kayaks will be in their element here; the wooded valley is almost eerily quiet and the only sign of civilisation comes when the river passes through Endsleigh Gardens. The only natural rapids are found just past the Endsleigh House.

Contributor:

Mark Rainsley

Other important points   Worth combining with the following section for a long day out.
On the Lower Tamar, those with an interest in the region's industrial heritage will want to keep an eye on the river right bank.

Tamar (Lower - Horsebridge to Gunnislake)

Introduction   A great touring section which has more white water interest than that upstream. The 'Rock Garden' rapids and shorter distance make this a better proposition for novice white water paddlers in short kayaks.

Grade	**2**
Length	**9km**
OS sheet	**201**

Water level   The Tamar will be paddleable throughout the Access season, being a major river with a huge drainage. This section is not recommended in high water due to the large weirs.

Gauge   Use your discretion in judging whether the river is high.

Access   At Horsebridge (400749), there are several options for parking of which the best is on the river right side of the river. This trip finishes directly below Gunnislake new bridge (433723) where it is possible to egress on the river right bank up to a quiet lane.
There is an agreement permitting paddling from 15th October to 28th February, weekends only. Details from the river adviser.

Description   A more serious undertaking than the section up-stream, as well as the smaller channelled weirs like those found on the upper section. There are two large weirs which will require inspection and possibly portage: 'Coffin Weir' and 'Broken Weir'. Both are easy to inspect or portage by stopping on the river left bank as soon as you spot the ominous horizon line.
In the penultimate kilometre, the highlight of the trip is found; the 'Rock Gardens'. Long, successive natural rapids provide endless chutes and eddies; the perfect training ground.

Contributor:
Mark Rainsley

Fowey

Introduction   The Fowey drains the east side of Bodmin Moor, Cornwall. Cornwall's grade 4 trip looks like an improbably small stream at the put-in bridge. Don't be put off... within a few hundred metres it is a sizeable white water river well worth attention in high water conditions.

Grade	**3 (4)**
Length	**5km**
OS sheet	**201**

Water level   Save this for a very rainy day. The river upstream of the put-in parallels the road as it meanders across open moorland

and is frequently overgrown. It should ideally be filling or even spilling its banks on this section.

Gauge   You need a minimum of enough water to ferry glide bank to bank at the put-in, but the more the merrier.

Access   The put-in is the Golitha Falls car park (228699). Launch below the bridge from the footpath.
This section finishes where there are two bridges close together, called Treverbyn Mill (206675).
The Fowey sees few descents and there have been no recorded objections.

Description   The whole venture looks unpromising at the start. The first few hundred metres involve ducking and weaving tree branches on what is essentially flat water. Persist! After the river bends right and the tourist path ends, the trees clear and a good section of rapids and falls begins.
Things kick off with a long grade 3+ rapid where the river narrows into a flume. This is closely followed by two successive grade 4 drops. These will need inspection on river right and may well merge into a single monster rapid in very high water. The river loses a surprising amount of height on this section, known as Golitha Falls.
A third longer grade 4 rapid is the end of the harder difficulties, but the river chunters on with a noticeable gradient and continuous grade 3 rapids until a stream enters on river right.
From here to the take-out the river is grade 2. Two footbridges marked on the OS Landranger map do not exist, having been swept away in floods. One has been replaced by an unlikely looking slippery log, and the second can be seen smeared along the river left bank.
The last hazard is a small weir just before the take-out.
There is reported to be 'pleasant cruising' if you follow the Fowey further to the sea.

Other important points   If you aren't convinced on arrival, walk the path downstream from the car park on river right and take a look at Golitha Falls... these begin just after the good path ends.

Contributor:
Mark Rainsley

Camel

Grade **3 (3+)**
Length **5km**
OS sheet **200**

◯ ◯ ◯

Introduction   A small but continuously entertaining river, the Camel offers grade 3 creeking! The Camel drains the western edge of Bodmin Moor, and is best known for a notorious pollution incident in 1988 when 20,000 tons of aluminium sulphate accidentally found its way into the river and the water supply of nearby Camelford. Thankfully, today the secluded river valley is a pleasure to visit and paddle. I won't forget watching a brown trout throw an impressive wavewheel over the lip of a fall.

Water level   Rain is needed to bring this section up. The Camel seems to hold an acceptable flow of water for a few days after high water, perhaps because it drains boggy moorland.

Gauge   You need a minimum of enough water to float under the bridges at the start. High water would be jolly, but care would have to be taken regarding low tree branches.

Access   The Camel joins a sizeable stream at the bridge near Trecarne (097805), where there is limited parking near a ford which offers a good launching point. Egress at Penrose bridge (089764). One of the main owners objects to canoeing on the Camel.

Description   The Camel is challenging at the grade and needs respect. Trees are a tad irritating... there are several across the river on this section, all of which can probably be ducked or paddled over with care.

Right from the start, the first of many bedrock ledges forms a small drop. The river has non-stop small rapids interspersed by these small drops. Some of them may form backlooping stoppers in high water, and stopping to portage/inspect could be tricky as eddies are limited. Some of the drops feature undercut pools. Towards Tuckingmill Bridge, there is one long, harder rapid where the drops come thick and fast and the river loses height quickly. Tuckingmill Bridge is a possible finish point. Directly downstream of the bridge a barbed wire strand across the river tries to discourage you from carrying on, but it's worth it; numerous grade 2 rapids help you wind down from the fast and frantic paddling above. The river opens out and you pass through gardens and a fishing resort before Penrose Bridge. Not a place to linger, perhaps. It is recommended that you go no further. The river directly

Contributor:
Mark Rainsley

below is truly awful, choked with low bridges, fallen trees, barbed wire and piles of garbage.

De Lank

Grade	**5**
Length	**5km**
OS sheet	**200**

Introduction   Grade 5 in Cornwall. What could possibly go wrong?

Water level   You need some recent rain to bring the river up. The De Lank drains a large boggy plateau (called Bodmin Moor) and seems to retain its flow for a day or two after rain.
Note that a significant amount of water is extracted halfway down, at the quarry. If you are only doing the bottom section from the footbridge, then you want as much water as possible.

Gauge   At the put-in you need just enough water to float under the bridge. Much more than this might not be a great idea for the top half, due to the gradient!

Access   The river above Delford Bridge is paddleable but very overgrown. Put in at Delford Bridge. If you want to 'wuss out' of the river's hardcore sections, walk in a few hundred metres along a footpath to the nearby footbridge (101749).
Take out at the bridge near Tregaddick (089738) or paddle a kilometre of flat water down to the River Camel and take out at Merry Meeting Bridge (089732).
The only access problem I encountered was a few funny looks from quarry workers. The farmer who owns the land through which the De Lank flows from the quarry onwards welcomes paddlers, being one himself.

Description   From Delford Bridge, the river is flat for about a mile and there are a number of tree blocks to duck or portage. Trees continue to be a pain throughout the trip, but these were the only blocks in October 2002. The river then loses 100m in height in the following kilometre!
When you see quarry workings appear above you on river right, be on your guard. There is one bouldery fall to warm you up, and then suddenly the river falls off the edge of the world! Tight back-to-back drops provide plenty of excitement as the river loses an impressive amount of height in a short distance. It is all paddleable, but depending upon water level and how shiny your boat is, you'll

probably make a portage or three. 'Eighties' throwbacks who get excited about Spuds and full face helmets will be in their element. However... sharp-edged blocks of quarried rock and old metal industrial junk start appearing in the falls; not very nice. Then, when the quarried blocks begin to outnumber the rocks put there by nature, the river flings the ultimate insult at you... it simply disappears. The river has sunk under the masses of discarded blocks of stone heaped into the gorge by generations of quarrying. You are left with the humiliation of shouldering your boat up the river right bank and carrying it down past the quarry buildings to a track which carries on along the bank of the (missing) river. You need to select a spot to climb back down to the river, but don't be fooled... the river resurfaces and disappears again more than once. When you put back in, you'll find some more steep falls. Note the large pipe on river right which appears to have taken a significant amount of water out of the river. You reach a footbridge (101749) which is a great starting point if the river is high, or if you want to miss the gruelling adventures above.

From the footbridge onwards, the river eases to continuous grade 4 and eventually grade 3 just before the bridge near Tregaddick. This section would be a great place to be in spate.

Contributor:
Mark Rainsley

If you've started from Delford Bridge, you'll probably collapse from exhaustion at the take-out.

Other important points   Cornwall's grade 5 river... who would have thought it? If you do this at all, I guarantee that it'll just be the one time. Leave the playboat at home and take your elbow pads.

Lynher

Grade	**1/2**
Length	**15km**
OS sheet	**201**

Introduction   A lovely unspoilt river. The river features are small but defined and this is a great place to enjoy your first white water.

Water level   This is a sizeable river, paddleable for much of the winter months. High water is not recommended as the rapids and eddies will wash out.

Gauge   An ideal level at Kerney Bridge would be to have enough water to float, but a few rocks exposed in the river bed.

Access   Kerney Bridge (319709) has reasonable parking and launching.

Newbridge (357680) is a good spot to break up the trip, with access to the river from a lane on river right below the bridge.

Notter Bridge (384608) allows egress on the river right bank. There is an access agreement allowing boating from16th October to 28th February. Prior permission is required, contact the river adviser, www.bcu.org.uk/access/riverinfosouthwest.

Description   The Lynher has only occasional grade 2 rapids and those seeking major action should look elsewhere. The Lynher's real strength is as a touring or coaching river.

The best section is the 5km from Kerney Bridge to Newbridge. This has many miniature rapids with natural waves and eddies almost purpose-built for learning basic moving-water skills. There is one weir to inspect on this section.

A longer trip can be had by continuing to Notter Bridge, the tidal limit. This section has more sporadic rapids and Pillaton weir which can cause pins in low water.

It is possible to make a longer expedition still by paddling on down the estuary, but then you'd have to grasp all that confusing tidal stuff.

Contributor:
Mark Rainsley

Other important points   Do you have any non-paddling friends who want to sample white water? They might still be talking to you after this trip.

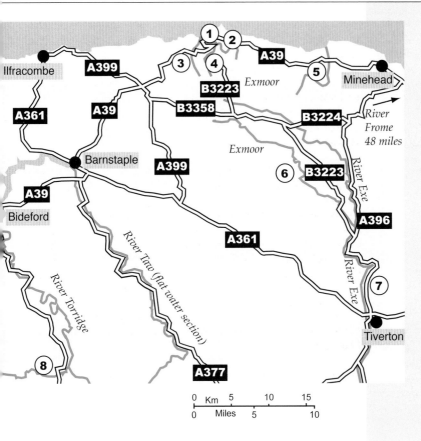

Exmoor and Somerset

East Lyn (Watersmeet to the sea)

Grade	**4/5**
Length	**3km**
OS sheet	**180**

Introduction   Creek boating that invites comparisons with Ecuador and California. Look up 'boof' in your BCU Handbook! The East Lyn is superb.

Water level   The East Lyn is very 'flashy' and rises fast after rain. High levels are to be avoided and it is recommended to catch the Lyn 'on the drop'. The river stays paddleable for up to a week after rain and is thus the most reliable difficult trip in the South-West.

Gauge   Upstream of the bridge in Lynmouth there is a long stony island. If it is possible to scrape either side of this island, the trip is still on; the more channelled river upstream will be grade 4. If you can paddle comfortably past the island the grade will be 4+ and if the central rock slabs directly above the bridge are all covered you are looking at grade 5. With the long island nearly covered the East Lyn is frankly, scary. Levels beyond this are best avoided (Gd 6).

Access   This section begins at Watersmeet (744486) where the Hoaroak and East Lyn rivers merge. There is plenty of parking on the A39 from where you carry your boats down the zigzag path to the river. In Lynmouth, the take-out is obvious. It's called the Bristol Channel.
The Lyn has an agreement allowing pre-arranged access with the river adviser, www.bcu.org.uk/access/riverinfosouthwest.

Description   Between Watersmeet and the sea, you are going to fall 110m, most of it in one short gorge! Within sight of Watersmeet, the river slides over a 2m angled ledge. If you find this challenging, call it a day. A section of bouncy grade 3 follows.
After you pass a house on river left, the East Lyn narrows into Myrtleberry Cleave and the drops begin. A technical series of falls with a footpath directly beside on river left make a telling warm-up for the main gorge. In low water there is a line down the left, in high water the central line is…memorable.
Count the bridges across the gorge as the rapids pile up. The second bridge is the point of no return for the main gorge where things get steep. Take out on river right above the bridge and clamber up to the path. Inspect the gorge from this path high above but remember to compensate for Shrinkavision™! There's no shame in portaging along this path. We're all friends here.

Carrying on? Things get chewy right below the second bridge. The first few drops lead to a fall with nasty rock formations in the centre. 'Crux A' follows...a sticky natural weir leading straight into a waterfall, complete with dodgy shallow plunge pool. Watch out for those siphons. More drops and slides follow, with good eddies allowing you a chance to get your breath back. These lead down to 'Crux B'. Boof for your life! The river thunders down a channel to the left and dumps you into one of the stickier holes around, walled in by the cliff behind. Allow space in your itinerary for time spent in this hole.

Contributor:
Mark Rainsley

A low water pinning involving emergency services happened on the rapid directly below the gorge. Be careful here. After this you can afford to relax a little and enjoy the continuous grade 4 down into Lynmouth. If the gorge is too high, this section offers a chunky blast right to the sea.

Upper East Lyn (Brendon to Watersmeet)

Introduction   Paddled along with the section of the Lyn below Watersmeet, this makes up one of the best wet days out in the UK; source to sea in a series of beautiful gorges, with no end of white water interest.

Grade	**4(5)**
Length	**4km**
OS sheet	**180**

Water level   Amazingly, this section is almost always paddleable in the winter. The river stays paddleable for up to a week after rain and is thus the most reliable difficult trip in the South-West. On the other hand, high water makes for a fantastic experience and this can still be manageable when the East Lyn's gorge below Watersmeet is becoming too high.

Gauge   As long as there is enough water to float in Brendon, the upper East Lyn offers a worthwhile trip.

Access   Access at the village of Brendon (766482). There is a car park with a small toilet block to park behind, beside the village hall. Arrive changed and ready to go to minimise disruption in this small community. Don't forget to put a coin in the car park fee box. Walk behind the village hall and through a small gate to the river. This section finishes at Watersmeet (744486) but you'll almost certainly want to continue down the following section. *The catch? Paddling is not permitted on this section of river. Unfortu-*

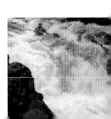

nately, if you paddle this section you may endanger the access agreement on the downstream section. If you haven't done so already, please read the chapter on access.

Description   Environmentally, the upper East Lyn is stunning. It is only suitable for small groups and not for those who need to inspect at every corner. Minimise your effects on the surrounding undergrowth by staying in your boat. The hardest fall can be inspected/portaged over bedrock, thankfully.

About fifty yards downstream of the put-in, the river begins to descend through small, steep boulder rapids. The road is nearby, above on river left. The first significant rapid appears around a right-hand bend; a series of ledge drops form worrying horizon lines! The second drop is known as 'the hole from hell'! It's a deep and sticky pour-over backed up by a large rock. Swims here give ample opportunity to visit the 'green room'.

Further steep, bouldery rapids eventually take the paddler away from the road to a beautiful green gorge. There are a number of small drops and blind corners to keep you guessing. A blind horizon line below a sharp 'zigzag' in the river hides a 'gnarly' 3m drop. Vertical pins have happened here in low water and the rock formations are hazardous.

It's not far to the hardest drop. The river backs up behind a major horizon line. The following rapid, probably grade 5, is often portaged on river right. It's a tight two-tier waterfall, with an intriguing choice of a 'safer' line or a 'necky' line.

The most difficult falls are done, but the fun is far from over. The East Lyn eases off to grade 2 for half a mile or so, before steepening again in the final mile to Watersmeet. A long series of drops, wave trains and rocky reefs keep your paddles flailing right down to Watersmeet. In high water these are an incredible rollercoaster slide!

Next you pass the National Trust Cafe on river right; staying close to this bank will make you less obtrusive to the tourists there. You are now at Watersmeet and the lower East Lyn awaits you. Perhaps the best is still to come...

Contributor:
Mark Rainsley

Other important points   Let's wish for a better access future on this superb section of river.

West Lyn (Barbrook to Lynbridge)

Grade	**4**
Length	**1km**
OS sheet	**180**

Introduction   The River West Lyn is one of two channels which drop steeply from northern Exmoor into the Bristol Channel at Lynmouth. It joins the regularly paddled East Lyn shortly before reaching the sea.

Water level   This rises very fast after rain, having a steep catchment. You need to paddle just after rain as it drops quickly.

Gauge   Most rocks down in Lynmouth should be covered to make a journey upstream worthwhile.

Access   Access at Barbrook (715476) where you will have to climb down to the very canalised river.
This section finishes at a pub a kilometre downstream where there is a footbridge.
If you are going to attempt this, it is recommended that you pick a quiet time and minimise your presence.

Description   This short section begins with continuous grade 3, walled in by the canalised banks. Passing behind some houses, the river steepens to grade 4. There is one fall where the river narrows between confining rocks and forms a challenging drop.
You then pass through a caravan park on river left, with the river passing over small ledges. A footbridge looms and this is the end; you need to get out above it on river right. Don't miss! A path leads across the bridge and up to a pub car park.

Other important points   What happens downstream of this takeout? Well, 'nothing good' is the agreed consensus. The river loses over 150m in height in the final kilometre. From the road you get glimpses of falls landing on rock, man-made weirs and sharp jumbled rocks. Chris Wheeler attempted this section sometime back in the 80's and only recalls walking out in despair. Is this the last great challenge in the South-West? There has to be something worth paddling in that epic final mile!

Contributor:
Mark Rainsley

Hoaroak Water (Hillsford Bridge to Watersmeet)

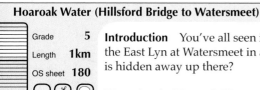

Grade **5**

Length **1km**

OS sheet **180**

Introduction   You've all seen it…the waterfall creek which joins the East Lyn at Watersmeet in a series of crunchy waterfalls. What is hidden away up there?

Water level   Hoaroak Water can be and has been bashed down in low levels as a slow and very conspicuous stunt. However, maintain some environmental sensitivity (and personal dignity) and wait until there is a reasonable flow after rain.

Gauge   Upstream of the footbridge at Watersmeet there is a sloping waterfall which divides around a slabby rock in low water. It has been suggested that the river becomes worthwhile when this central slab is covered. High flows not recommended.

Access   It is possible to climb down to the river at Hillsford Bridge (741478). Parking is available here. You will want to walk down to Watersmeet first on the river right footpath to inspect. Hoaroak Water ends at Watersmeet (744486) where it joins the East Lyn River. There is plenty of parking on the A39 up the zigzag path, but carrying on down the East Lyn makes more sense. There is no agreed access to Hoaroak and you are on National Trust land. Extreme care is advised in order to paddle this river without causing offence to locals or damage to the pristine surroundings.

Description   The Hoaroak consists of tight grade 4+ rapids interspersed with waterfalls. Several dangerous siphons are formed by the rock formations. Although most of the individual rapids are 4+, it is serious enough to merit an overall grade of 5. Clambering around inspecting from the river could cause damage to the gorgeous surroundings; you should strongly consider inspecting the river thoroughly beforehand from the footpath.
Grade 4+ rapids commence right from Hillsford bridge, including one nasty siphon. Things quickly become tight and steep; one chicane will stick in your mind and is grade 5. After the halfway point is reached, you will encounter Pencil Falls, a 4m waterfall with a dubiously narrow lip. The final waterfalls visible from Watersmeet are the biggest drops and are not too difficult; mind your ankles though.

Contributor:
Mark Rainsley

Other important points   If you have water in the Hoaroak, the following section of the East Lyn will be a better experience.

Horner Water

Grade	**3**
Length	**5km**
OS sheet	**180**

Introduction   If you can bring yourself to take it seriously, Horner Water offers an entertaining run in spate. Despite being very steep and fast, there are few technical difficulties… simply hang on and keep an eye open for eddies! Do not be deceived by the grade; this is fairly unforgiving when it's running.

Water level   Horner Water has a small catchment and a small dam impedes its flow; very heavy (and current) rain is needed to turn this tiny stream into a credible paddling adventure.

Gauge   There is a gauging weir visible beside the road, a little way upstream of West Luccombe. There are three gauges along-side and below the small weir; the third gauge should read '1' as an absolute minimum; ideally you want much more. The river should be overflowing its banks at the put-in.

Access   Epic steep lanes bring you to the highest road access (875447). The take-out is 175 vertical metres below, anywhere before the village of West Luccombe, as the river flattens out alongside the road. There are plenty of parking opportunities. Horner Water is rarely paddleable and has seen too few descents to generate any access difficulties. Horner Wood is part of a Na-tional Nature Reserve and care should be taken not to damage the surrounding banks, as always.

Description   Horner Water is a true ditch at the access point; be assured that it quickly picks up some volume and becomes wider en-route downhill!
If you don't like the rapids you see at the start, don't bother; what you see is what you get all the way to the bottom of the hill, with constant even gradient. There is only room for a small group and they need to be awake; there were only two tree blocks in October 2002 but you didn't want to miss the eddies above. If the river is running at the spate levels it requires, you'll arrive at the take-out about five minutes before you started!

Contributor:
Mark Rainsley

Other important points   Somewhere to consider if the East Lyn is too high.

Barle (Simonsbath to Withypool)

Grade **2**

Length **10km**

OS sht. **180/1**

Introduction   This unusual section offers undemanding but continuous white water high upon some of the bleakest moorland imaginable. It is only recommended to those who want a bit of real exploring; the paddling is not great but it offers a unique view of Exmoor.

Water level   Recent rain is necessary. The more the merrier, although you will need to be alert for the sheep fences in high levels. Paddling this in low levels could cause damage to salmon spawning beds (a *criminal* offence).

Gauge   It should be clear whether you have enough water to paddle from Simonsbath. All stones in the river bed should be well covered.

Access   This section begins at Simonsbath (773392), high on Exmoor. There is limited parking near the bridge, access the river about 500m downstream.
This section finishes at Withypool (844354) where there is a small car park 100m up the road, river right of the bridge. Landacre bridge (817362) offers a quieter alternative finish point, which misses out several kilometres of flat water.
There is negotiated access much further downstream at Tarr Steps, but not on this section. Paddlers should be very aware of the importance of the gravel beds for salmon spawning, and should take every precaution to avoid disrupting the river bed. You are unlikely to encounter any company whilst paddling this.

Description   The first 500m are best avoided and portaged on river left along the 'Two Moors Way' footpath; the river flows through two sheep fences and an awkward bush. After this poor start, the river winds away from farmland and enters a long section of open moorland. There are continuous small rapids with several mini-ledges. In high water the river is quite fast and bouncy.

Contributor:

Mark Rainsley

There are two more sheep fences to duck or dodge before you reach Landacre bridge which makes a possible take-out point. Below Landacre, the river is flat down to Withypool where there is a safe weir under the bridge. Take out on river right below the weir.

Triple Drop, River Dart

Upper Walkham

Webburn

Teign

Lower Walkham

Barle (Withypool to Tarr Steps)

Grade	**2(3-)**
Length	**7km**
OS sheet	**181**

Introduction   This lovely section offers perhaps the best white water on the Barle. The river is quite sizeable and is in no sense a 'tree ditch' like the section above from Simonsbath.

Water level   The Barle below Tarr Steps needs to be at a good level.

Gauge   If there isn't quite enough space for a paddler to squeeze under the Tarr Steps, there is a good flow for this section.

Access   Begin at Withypool (844354) where there is a small car park 100m up the road, river right of the bridge.
Finish at Tarr Steps (867321). There is no parking beside the river; use the large tourist car park up the hill.
There is negotiated access from Tarr Steps, but not on this section upstream of the steps.

Description   In Withypool village, you launch beside the miniature weir under the bridge. Downstream the water is flat at first, but gradually steepens to simple, bouldery rapids. The river gets progressively trickier and has a 'slow build' feel to it which will appeal to the hung over. The adventure culminates in a very long rapid taking you right down to Tarr Steps; this is perhaps grade 3. Watch out for a cable bridge low over the river lurking somewhere in this final kilometre.

Contributor:
Mark Rainsley

Other important points   Continuing on past Tarr Steps makes for one of the longest sections of quality grade 2 paddling in the country.

Barle (Tarr Steps to Dulverton)

Grade	**2**
Length	**10km**
OS sheet	**181**

Introduction   Here in Somerset lurks the South-West's most popular and perhaps best grade 2 trip. There are numerous rapids and they are impressively long and continuous at the grade.

Water level   Its upland characteristics mean that the Barle falls pretty fast. It is often runnable for weeks after rain, but low water trips can be a bit like hard work and are best avoided. The Barle is best in medium levels after a recent top-up. High levels increase the speed and danger out of proportion to the grade.

Gauge   If you can float under Tarr Steps (an ancient stone footbridge beside a ford), you have enough water for the whole section. If there isn't quite enough room to duck under, you have an ideal level. If the river is up to or over the bridge, then this trip (whilst not especially harder) will be a dangerous 'mare' for those normally comfortable on grade 2.

Access   Put in at Tarr Steps (867321). There is no parking beside the river, use the large tourist car park up the hill.

It is possible to finish at Marsh Bridge (906289), but parking is pretty limited and there is still plenty of interest in the final 2km to the usual egress at Dulverton (912277). At Dulverton, use the public car park and not the limited parking by the river.

There is an access agreement for this section. Paddling is allowed October to March, or April below Marsh Bridge. Details from the river adviser, www.bcu.org.uk/access/riverinfosouthwest.

Description   The River Barle drains the opposite side of the hill from the much harder River Lyn. The river is custom built for those learning white water skills and you will usually find Tarr Steps car park chock-full of canoe trailers, bearded coaches (steady! – Editor), open canoes and similar horrors.

The very first kilometre from Tarr Steps is the best of the Barle. A group will have to be organised as anyone not previously briefed on the concept of 'eddy-hopping' will rapidly fade from view! There is even a solitary stopper hidden on river right around a zigzag bend; a foaming boat-eater or an inviting playspot? It's all about individual perspective. The rapids continue but inevitably become more spaced. Even so, it's a great section for those wanting to hog every breakout and surf every wave.

Directly after a sharp bend 5km into the trip, a rock ledge on river left upstream of an old bridge forms an enjoyable playspot. 3km further on you reach Marsh Bridge which is the first possible finish point. Continuing towards Dulverton, still water and a horizon line herald the town weir. This will need inspecting as some of the boulders in the base of the weir carry a risk of entrapment and boat damage. Below the weir a long braided rapid offers a final reminder of the natural rapids upstream. Take out river left directly before Dulverton town bridge.

Contributor:

Mark Rainsley and
Steve Balcombe

Other important points   The best open canoe trip in the region?

Barle (Dulverton to Exebridge)

Grade	2
Length	6km
OS sheet	181

Introduction   This run is the rather plain sibling to the more popular and interesting Tarr Steps trip, but that is precisely where its attraction lies, as an easy but worthwhile first moving water trip, an open boat trip for the less adventurous, or a pleasant April evening paddle when all the rivers around are closed for the summer.

Water level   Recent rain is ideal to speed things along, although this will be paddleable through much of the winter. For the less experienced, high water is best avoided.

Gauge   There is a concrete ramp just above the bridge at Dulverton. If the river just laps onto the bottom of this, you have low but sufficient water. A foot above this is a pleasant medium level, and if the river is running reddish-brown you have a more interesting trip ahead of you!

Access   The usual start is at the aforementioned concrete ramp in Dulverton (912277). Use the public car park, not the very limited parking beside the put-in. It is also possible to start at Marsh Bridge (906289), 2 km above Dulverton, but parking is limited and this is not an easy spot to put a less experienced group on the water. Finish your trip at Exebridge (930245) on the River Exe. At Exebridge the Anchor Inn don't mind you using their car park but ask permission… and consider a post-trip beer or two.
There is an access agreement for paddling from Marsh Bridge to Exebridge from October through April. Note that this is a month longer than the section from Tarr Steps. Details from the river adviser, www.bcu.org.uk/access/riverinfosouthwest.

Description   An alert group leader will find numerous places for his/her charges to learn or practise basic moves. It seems that every white water feature is here, but always on a gentle scale and forming an ideal introduction to the sport.

Two weirs are encountered. The first will be portaged by beginners but adds extra interest for those who want to run it. Take care in higher water; the left-hand run down the steps forms some nasty stoppers. The second weir is easy, but needs care, as a rather large hole has recently appeared in its face. Not long after the Barle and the Exe converge, there is an enjoyable surf wave lurking on river right. 1km on the Exe and you reach the Anchor Inn.

Contributor:
Mark Rainsley and
Steve Balcombe

Exe (Bridgetown to Bolham Weir)

Grade **2**

Length **26km**

OS sheet **181**

Introduction   The Exe at this point is a small river with natural rapids and some interesting weirs. The white water is often similar to the nearby Barle, but tends to be more infrequent.

Water level   Here near its Exmoor source, the Exe is paddleable through much of the winter. However, recent rain is recommended to make the rapids entertaining and the flat water bearable. Very high water levels are not recommended as the danger from trees and weirs outpaces the technical difficulty to an uncomfortable extent.

Access   Bridgetown (923332) offers opportunities to launch. This long section could be broken up at Exebridge (930245) where the Anchor Inn are tolerant of paddlers who make use of their hospitality.

The finish is at Bolham Weir (948153) where parking is possible in a lay-by near to some water authority buildings.

There is an access agreement allowing winter paddling. Details from the river adviser, www.bcu.org.uk/access/riverinfosouthwest.

Description   From Bridgetown the Exe is narrow and winding; watch out for low branches or trees in the river. This section forms a good introduction to moving water but should not be underestimated in high flows. There are numerous small, natural rapids and some small weirs. About a mile above Exebridge, the Barle enters from river right and shortly after there is usually a fun surf wave on river right. Consider a finish at Exebridge.

Below Exebridge, there are few rapids but the river winds through more pleasant scenery. When you reach Washfield Weir the river bends to the left and slides over a broken shelf offering plenty of route choices. There are some nice surf waves lurking below this weir and it's not a bad spot to stay and practise skills. Only a short way below is Bolham Weir, a very nasty affair with a *deadly* towback. *Portage on river right* when you see the horizon line, then paddle across the river downstream of the weir to the road to take out.

Contributor:
Mark Rainsley

Other important points   Paddled along with the adjacent River Barle, this offers a great weekend of easy white water.

Exe (Bolham Weir to Bickleigh)

Grade	**2**
Length	**9km**
OS	**181/192**

Introduction   This is a popular trip which has plenty of interest stemming from both natural rapids and notable weirs. This is probably the best white water trip to be had on the Exe.

Water level   This is possible through most of the winter. However, it is recommended to save this trip for medium to high levels when Exmoor has received a recent deluge.

Gauge   Make a judgement about the level at Bickleigh bridge, the take-out. In particular, check that the weir stopper below the bridge is manageable for your group.

Access   Bolham Weir (948153) offers parking in a lay-by near to some water authority buildings. Finish at Bickleigh bridge (937075), where there is a picturesque weir and pub.
There is an access agreement allowing winter paddling. Details from the river adviser, www.bcu.org.uk/access/riverinfosouthwest.

Description   Launch below Bolham Weir. It is horrible if you have any flow in the river, and has already claimed a paddler's life.
The next landmark is Salmon Ponds Weir. This is well-known as the start line of the Exe Descent Race, and sees awesome carnage in high water race years. The weir face is unusually long and makes the equivalent of a humping grade 3 rapid in high water. In low water you are forced to paddle the river left of fish steps, a less dignified but equally enjoyable option.
If the Exe is flowing well, the following stretch into Tiverton is constantly exciting with small drops and bouncy rapids. Town Weir, in Tiverton, has two distinct sections, again giving the impression of a long natural rapid. The smaller Walronds Weir ('Tivvie Two') follows as you exit Tiverton and can form a reasonable playspot.

Contributor:
Mark Rainsley

Grade 2 rapids continue for some distance to Broken Weir, which is a simple shoot but (as the name suggests) is in poor repair; inspect first. From here it is a short distance to the final stunt, Bickleigh Weir. Break out on river left above the bridge and watch your group members pass under the bridge and disappear from view one by one… intimidating!
Break out on river left directly below the weir and take out.

Exe (Bickleigh Bridge to Haven Bank Quay)

Grade   **1**

Leng. **7-21km**

OS sheet **192**

Introduction   The Exe flattens out en route to Exeter with what little gradient there is absorbed in a series of massive weirs. These weirs are nobody's idea of fun in high water. Conversely, they still provide serviceable white water when absolutely everything else in the South-West is dry. This is because many of the big weirs have channels or ribs on their faces which focus the water into jets and flumes. Playboaters may enjoy this trip.

Water level   This is not a high water trip, unless you wish to spend your day portaging monster closed-out stoppers. It is possible with care in medium flows, but the Exe higher up the valley will be much more fun. This is best saved as a fall-back option for when Dartmoor is dry and the river very low.

Gauge   Park at 'The Mill on the Exe' pub (914923) beside Blackaller Weir (also known as 'Flowerpots') and take a look. If the weir is showing some dry patches on the weir face, the Exe is very low but can be paddled. If the river left chute is forming a stopper at the bottom, then you have a reasonable medium level. If this chute is washing out into a wave, the Exe is high and the tow-back on the main weir face should persuade you to go elsewhere.

Access   This section starts at Bickleigh bridge (937075), where there is a decent pub where you can ask permission to park. The full trip from here will be a slog in low water.

To cherry-pick the best white water, a small quiet group can park at Stoke Woods car park (923962) outside Exeter on the A396. Carry your boats up the road and along a track to launch just upstream of the railway bridge. Seek up-to-date info from the river adviser on where to launch.

The trip finishes at Haven Bank Quay (922919) in the centre of Exeter; park near 'AS Watersports' paddlesport shop.

There is an access agreement allowing winter paddling. Details from the river adviser, www.bcu.org.uk/access/riverinfosouthwest.

Contributor:
Mark Rainsley

Description   Start directly upstream of Bickleigh bridge and run the weir below. The following section is flat apart from Thorverton Weir (935019), and this section has little to commend it to white water paddlers.

Most paddlers will wish to launch from Stoke Woods near Four

Pynes Weir, making for a much livelier 7km trip. Directly upstream of Four Pynes is a low railway bridge. The weir below
is a huge sloping face, unsurprisingly forming the mother of all
stoppers when the Exe is high. In low water, the diagonal 'rib'
across the weir makes a great powerful 'chute' to slide down or
play in at the bottom. In medium levels, this 'chute' takes you into
a formidable closed-in stopper, and is best avoided.
2km below, the river splits into two channels. If you head right,
the river meanders for a mile or so before rejoining the main channel, with a nasty boulder dam to portage. This route is recommended for less experienced paddlers. If you head left, directly
below is Cowley Steps, which you should have inspected from
Cowley road bridge beforehand. You can just about get out and
inspect/portage on river left using an old tunnel, but this will not
be an option if the water level is high. The weir consists of three
channels, with the main centre channel flowing over a series of
steps, each with its own individual stopper. The three channels
lead into a pool and there are two more steps (i.e. river-wide stoppers) that will certainly require you to move out of first gear. The
steps deserve respect, but are quite playable in low water levels.
Downstream of Cowley bridge, the two channels converge and
the river enters Exeter, passing some huge flood defence works en
route. Eventually you reach two large weirs, collectively known
as Flowerpots Weir. The first step is known as Head Weir. The
river right route usually supplies a good surf wave. The second
much bigger weir is Blackaller Weir. This can form a dangerous
towback on river right, inspect on the same side.
All that remains now is to paddle through Exeter under the main
road bridges until you reach Haven Bank, getting out on river
right where there are various launching ramps.

Contributor:
Mark Rainsley

Other important points   There are further weirs downstream
towards the estuary which can be serious in high water.

Torridge

Introduction   The Torridge meanders across north Devon to meet
the sea at Bideford. Its rapids are small and undemanding but
ideal for those wanting a long trip on moving water. The Torridge
is highly recommended as a river on which to practise your open
canoe expeditioning skills.

Grade   **1/2**

Length   **30km**

OS sheet **180**

Water level   The Torridge is paddleable throughout the access season. Medium to high water levels are recommended to speed the flow and enhance excitement, but care must be taken as some of the weirs become dangerous.

Access   The Torridge can be canoed from Sheepwash bridge (486058) in high water. Starting at Hele bridge (540063) and finishing at Rothern bridge (480198), both on the A386, makes for a simpler shuttle journey, which can even be made by bus.
At Hele bridge, park in a nearby lay-by and get to the river upstream of the bridge on river left. At Rothern bridge, the Puffing Billy pub provides parking opportunities and sustenance.
There is an agreement allowing paddling from 1st October to 28th February. Written permission from the river adviser is compulsory, www.bcu.org.uk/access/riverinfosouthwest.

Contributor:
Mark Rainsley

Description   The Torridge below Hele bridge is certainly not for white water junkies, but has charms of its own for those willing to soak up the river's slow pace and mild currents. Lady Palmer Weir (portage right if needed) and Taddiport Weir (portage left) are the only significant drops. In high water however, the current is constant with swirling currents and small waves.
Rothern bridge is just below Taddiport Weir. It is possible to carry on until you reach the tidal river near Bideford. Note however that the dangerous Beam Weir is not far downstream and can be awkward to portage. Check it first.

Frome

Grade   **1 (2)**
Length   **11km**
OS sheet **172**

Introduction   Hidden away in a quiet corner of Somerset, the Frome is essentially a flat water river, but few flat water paddlers would enjoy it. The Frome is crammed with a weird and wonderful selection of man-made weirs and rapids; a trip is always fun.

Water level   The Frome should be paddleable throughout the winter. It can be paddled right up to high levels, with appropriate care at the weirs. The river is not recommended out of its banks.

Gauge   It is worth looking at the possible take-out on river left below Iford bridge. If it looks particularly difficult for an inexperienced group to stop here, you have high water!

Access   Access the river from the A36 at Shawford bridge
(793535) near Woolverton (halfway between Warminster and
Bath). There is hardly any parking here; shuttle excess vehicles to
the take-out. Take out either at Iford bridge (801589) opposite the
gorgeous Iford Manor or 2km further on at Freshford Inn bridge
(791599). Both take-outs involve leaving the river on river left
below the respective bridges.

There is an access agreement permitting paddling outside the
fishing season, subject to a complex list of rules, including seeking
prior permission from various parties. Full details from the river
adviser, www.bcu.org.uk/access/riverinfosouthwest.

Description   It hardly needs to be spelled out that the weirs on
the Frome, whilst usually enjoyable, deserve respect and caution.
The first of many comes shortly after Shawford bridge. Scutt's
Mill Weir offers a straight drop with a sticky walled-in hole in
high water, or a rather solid boat-breaking ledge in low water.
Hence, this weir is often portaged on river left.

Rode Mill Weir comes next, this can be a scrape to get over due
to the very wide ledge. If you're already 'weired out' you'll be
happy to know that things now improve vastly.

Langham Farm Weir has had its flow diverted through an intimidating looking tunnel bridge perpendicular to the river's flow.
This requires a proactive approach and many paddlers will want
to inspect from river left. In high water, the tunnel is impassable
and water flows over the weir. Below the tunnel is a channelled
chute of water which is a great training spot. Tail squirts galore
below the tunnel and in two small jets nearby.

Tellisford Weir is a small sloping weir, an easy shoot. A HEP
project takes water from above the weir and makes the following
100m of the river very dry (except in high water) and irritatingly,
a portage down the river bed may be required in low water levels.
Next on your itinerary is the infamous Zoom Flume. Once paddled, never forgotten! The river is accelerated down a unique
concrete gutter with a memorable wave waiting at the bottom.
This makes for a notable play wave in high water, but be aware of
the sharp rocks beneath.

You've now done the best of the Frome, but there are more entertaining weirs to keep you guessing. There are three weirs before
Iford bridge and one more beyond if you finish at Freshford. The
final weir is large and makes for a memorable finish.

Contributor:
Mark Rainsley

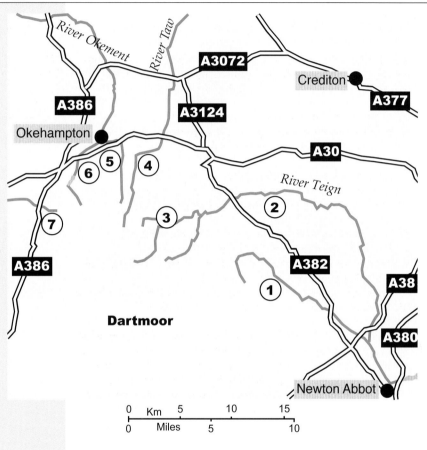

North Dartmoor

Bovey

Grade	**4**
Length	**6km**
OS sheet	**191**

Introduction   The Bovey is a small river with plenty of interesting rapids formed by rounded green boulders. It flows through the glorious woodlands of Lustleigh Cleave, straight through.

Water level   The Bovey drains a wide area of bog. Once this is fully saturated after a long wet period, only a moderate amount of rain is needed to make it paddleable.

Gauge   The level is difficult to judge at the put-in. What looks like a reasonable low paddleable level is actually too little; much of the water drains under boulders in the steeper sections.

Access   Put in at Clapper Bridge (753828), which actually isn't a clapper bridge. There is some space to park here.
Take out at the next road access, Drakeford bridge (789802). There is a sizeable parking area here.
No access problems have been reported here. The river flows past some private houses near the start, exercise discretion.

Description   This has the makings of a good trip, but is somewhat spoilt by numerous obstructions, mostly green and made of wood. The first kilometre is flat and involves paddling under or over two wire fences. The river then narrows to form a small rapid leading down to a low clapper bridge which may need portaging in high levels. Directly below are a series of small bouldery drops which give some idea of the river's character; the boulders are jumbled loosely and much of the water siphons underneath them. The following section picks up pace and steepens to grade 4. The river drops away alarmingly beside a house on river left. Don't worry… it's just the river sinking underground. Basically a huge pile of rocks blocks the river and the water gradually percolates through it rather than over it. This is harmless enough, simply climb out and carry your boat down to the pool below.
The following section is the best of the Bovey. The river narrows and flows down a series of steep flumes. This is also where the trees become a problem. From this point on, expect to portage around a great many fallen trees, not always in convenient places. The rest of the Bovey is continuous grade 3 with several steeper grade 4 sections. In addition to the trees, you'll find yourself por-

Contributor:
Mark Rainsley

taging a low footbridge.
Towards the end, watch out for a huge undercut boulder on river left. You'd have to be a moron to paddle under it, but knowing some paddlers... After this, you pass under another bridge and it's just two more tree portages to the take-out.

Other important points   Worth doing once. Honestly!

Teign

Grade   **2(3-)**
Length   **12km**
OS sheet   **191**

Introduction   The Teign is a large river which is, oddly, little paddled. It provides an excellent alternative for those who want an easy paddle, but are sick to death of the Dart Loop; it's slightly easier but more adventurous.

Water level   The Teign has the second largest catchment area on Dartmoor, after the Dart. However one of its two tributaries, the South Teign, is dammed. Hence, heavy rain has less effect than one might imagine. Medium flows after recent rain are best. High water is fun, but care has to be taken regarding low tree branches.

Gauge   The weir at Steps Bridge needs to be paddleable on river right as a minimum. If it is all covered the river is high.

Access   There is very limited roadside parking beside the A382 bridge (713893). Access the river through a gate from the footpath on river left. It is also possible to start several kilometres upstream for more grade 3 (see the North Teign descriptions).
This section finishes at Steps Bridge at (804883). Take out directly below the bridge on river right and walk up a path to the road. There is a decent car park 100m up the hill from here.
Other possible take-outs are Fingle bridge (743899) or Clifford bridge (782898).
There is no access agreement. This is a popular fishing river and discretion is advised.

Description   An enjoyable, quiet trip through scenic woods. The first half is best, but grade 2 rapids appear all the way to the end. Just below the put-in bridge, the flat river passes below an old metal bridge, which has loose metal wires trailing in the river; be careful.

A kilometre from the put-in, the hills close in on either side and the river squeezes between two big, rounded boulders... this is the dramatic point of no return for the 'Teign Gorge'. Unless of course, you walk or paddle back upstream again.

Just downstream, the river backs up behind a rather gnarly stepped weir. This can be run by the fish steps on river left or portaged easily on the same bank.

Between here and Fingle bridge is the best of the Teign, enjoy it. Continuous grade 2 paddling with small drops and boulders to negotiate. Two steep technical rapids require a fair bit of manoeuvring, so they are probably grade 3. The only flat water on this section is where another weir pools the current. This can be run anywhere, but has a convenient chute on river left. Not long afterwards you reach Fingle bridge, which is another possible access point. It also has a pub serving decent food!

The river flattens out below Fingle bridge for a while. This lasts until a sloping weir is reached, easily paddleable. Between here and the take-out, infrequent grade 2 rapids keep the interest up. Clifford bridge is a possible finish point. Otherwise, complete this pleasant trip by carrying on to Steps Bridge and running the small weir above the bridge.

Contributor:
Mark Rainsley

Other important points   The best open boat trip on Dartmoor?

North Teign (Upper)

Introduction   Most definitely one for masochists, involving a slog across open moor, very steep, bouldery drops and some rather strenuous wrestling with trees.

Grade	**4+**
Length	**2.5km**
OS sheet	**191**

Water level   Recent or even current heavy rain is needed to make this happen. You are right on the moor and not far from the source; expect it to run off quickly.

Gauge   It is difficult to judge what the water will be doing once you arrive at the start of this section, but a glance at the gauge rocks for the following section of the North Teign is the best clue you'll get, that and the amount of rain falling.

Access   This trip starts 370m above sea level on open moorland, where a popular footpath crosses the North Teign at an ancient

clapper bridge (654871). You need to drive up the south side of the valley from Chagford to reach the end of the road at Batworthy. There is good parking outside a farm entrance. Wondering where the river is? It's a mile away on the other side of the hill. Walk up the boggy track beside the farm. Once past the farm, the track veers right and heads downhill to meet the river at the aforementioned clapper bridge.

A take-out is possible up a footpath from the bridge (671875), but if you've made it this far, you'll certainly want to carry on down the vastly better following section of the North Teign.

It is highly unlikely that you'll encounter access problems (or for that matter, anybody) on this remote section of river.

Description   Directly from the clapper bridge, the river is steep and boulder strewn. Things are clearly heading downhill, so full spate might be a suicide mission. This is pure pinball paddling where elbow pads and a sense of humour are essential equipment. Sadly, this section becomes increasingly arduous as you descend into the valley. You will find yourself making portages around, over and under trees on several occasions. By the time you reach an old footbridge (not marked on maps), the gradient eases and the tree hazard becomes silly; every rapid will involve an element of tree dodging. Although the rapids at this point are not technically hard, mistakes are likely to result in a beating from an 'Ent'. Eventually you reach the second, newer footbridge, which offers a possible egress. Things get vastly better from this point and pushing on is recommended.

Contributor:
Mark Rainsley

North Teign (Lower)

Grade **4+(5)**
Length **3.5km**
OS sheet **191**

Introduction   Steep creeking around and over large boulders and natural ledges with few opportunities to stop and reflect. This section is reminiscent of the upper Plym. The lower half of this section is a bouncy grade 3 jaunt which may be worth considering by itself.

Water level   This will be paddleable for around twelve hours after heavy rain. The North Teign has Dartmoor's second largest catchment after the Dart itself. Spate conditions would make for continuous grade 5…after you Sir, I insist.

Gauge   Directly downstream of Chagford bridge are several rounded boulders close to the bank on river right. These should be nearly or completely covered for a 'non-scrapey' trip. Note that the steep and flashy catchment means that something totally different may be happening up the valley!

Access   This section starts at a footbridge hidden from the road. From Chagford, follow the road up the south side of the valley from Chagford. At a sharp left-hand bend in the road (the last before the road ends) a footpath leads steeply downhill to the footbridge, (671875). Parking possibilities are limited. The carry is no longer than 400m.

The take-out is at Chagford bridge (694879). Leave the river directly downstream of the bridge on river left; this is a public footpath. There is a good lay-by here for parking.

No access problems have been reported on this section of river but you do pass through the grounds of some very exclusive looking property. Discretion is advised so that no offence is caused.

Description   The first thing that anybody completing the tree-strewn section upstream of this will notice is that the tree blocks vanish once the footbridge is reached. Presumably this section is managed and cleared.

The first kilometre drops 50m. Don't expect a warm-up! The river is effectively walled in by dense woodland and rhododendron bushes so inspection or portage is awkward. The paddling is frantic with stacked up drops, slides and slots. This is creek boat territory with some shallow landings and tight manoeuvring to keep you alert.

A vertical weir pops up as a reminder that you'll shortly be entering civilisation and below this, the gradient begins to ease. The banks open out and you pass the immaculate grounds of the Gidleigh Park Hotel.

When you reach a submerged set of stepping stones (683878), where a footpath leads up to the river right road, the river enters a kilometre of continuous grade 3. This is worth considering in isolation. You first pass the confluence of the South Teign* on river right. The bushes then close in again and there are pleasant bouncy rapids. One thing which will wake you up is a large tree across the river. Thankfully this can easily be bypassed using a small river left channel.

Once the gorgeous Holystreet Manor is seen on river right, the

river flattens out and 500m of flat water take you to the end at
Chagford bridge. Anybody choosing to continue downstream to
the A352 bridge will find 2.5km of flat water with two weirs.

Other important points   *This has seen descents of the last few
kilometres but almost never carries enough water due to the dam
up the valley.

Taw

Grade	**4**
Length	**3km**
OS sheet	**191**

Introduction   An adventure in true Indiana Jones fashion.

Water level   This is only viable in spate.

Gauge   Take a look at the river from the bridge in Sticklepath. The
river is usually almost dry; you need to see it filling the banks at least.

Access   The river is accessed from the village of Belstone. Find
somewhere appropriate to park on the narrow lanes and carry
your boats up a track out of the village until you reach a sheep
pen (622926). You are now at the river but carrying on further up
the hill is recommended, choose your start point.
The trip finishes at a weir (637939) where there is parking up a
quiet road outside Sticklepath. If you carry on into the village
500m below, it is hard to find a good take-out.
This has seen too few descents for any access problems to develop.

Description   The Taw is a small river with frequent small falls
and technical rapids. It begins promisingly with steep drops in
succession. However it is soon enveloped by trees which choke
it from end to end. Expect to do a lot of ducking and weaving,
and portages will be necessary. No fun at all compared to its near
neighbour, the East Okement.

East Okement

Grade	**4+**
Length	**5km**
OS sheet	**191**

Introduction   One of England's more adventurous paddling
trips, the East Okement combines trekking, steep slides and technical drops to make for a memorable day out.

Water level   The East Okement requires masses of rain to come into condition. Ideally the moors will already be saturated and you will set off on the epic journey to the put-in whilst heavy rain falls. It will only stay up for a short period.

Gauge   It should be easy to decide whether the river is in spate in Okehampton. There is also a gauge beside a lane beneath the A30 road bridge (603947). This should read a minimum of 0.4m, ideally it should read 0.55 or higher.

Access   You have to earn the East Okement. Drive through Belstone and park at (616934). Carry your boat past the gate, along the track up and over the hill. Along the 2km route march you will get tantalising glimpses of the river to ease the pain. Eventually the track meets the river at Cullever Steps, (605922). Finish the trip at Okehampton College (589949) where there is plenty of parking. Access problems are unlikely.

Description   There is no warm-up. The East Okement squeezes between some bushes and then suddenly a worrying amount of open space opens up below you. The East Okement loses an impressive amount of height in the next kilometre, sliding down long granite slabs. This is great fun and mostly harmless, but watch out for the slide which slings you unceremoniously into a coffin slot. Sadly, this can't go on forever. The river changes character to bouldery rapids and over the following kilometre trees encroach to an awkward extent. Whilst these are quite bearable (compared to, say, those on the nearby River Taw) you may wish to retain your enjoyment of the river by portaging for a few hundred metres.

The river regains interest when the character changes once more. A long section of bedrock ledge drops commences with a nasty 6m waterfall. This has been run, but the paddler landed upside-down on rock. The portage is easy enough on river right. Not long after the portage, be on the lookout for a nasty little slot drop that may require a short portage. Otherwise, the next section is splendid with many drops and small holes to keep you busy. The river only winds down when you float under the A30 and pass the gauge. Grade 3 water takes you into Okehampton through canalised banks. There are small weirs and footbridges through a park before the finish at Okehampton College is reached. Take out on river right. If you continue, finding a take-out in town is difficult.

Contributor:
Mark Rainsley

West Okement

Grade   **3(4-)**
Length   **5km**
OS sheet **191**

Introduction   A good intermediate level run which offers entertaining technical paddling in a quiet corner of Dartmoor.

Water level   The flow of the West Okement is impeded by the dam of Meldon Reservoir. The dam does not usually fill until late winter and this is unlikely to be paddleable before then. Water flows from the dam after plenty of rain; this can remain in condition for some days after the rain has passed. This may still offer manageable paddling when other intermediate rivers are too high.

Gauge   It should be easy to gauge whether there is sufficient flow to paddle by taking a look at the take-out.

Access   There is a large car park near the dam at (563917). From here, carry your boats several hundred metres down the footpath to access the river through a convenient gate.
Take out just above the footbridge (585944) where there is a car park which serves Okehampton Castle.
The West Okement sees few descents and no access problems have been reported.

Description   The West Okement begins with continuous grade 3 which is enjoyably technical. There are one or two low trees to duck but this is an enjoyable section of water. After the bizarre looking railway bridge is passed under, be on the lookout for three ledge drops in succession; these mark the start of a grade 4- rapid with two tight slots needing inspection.
Be on the lookout for a portageable barbed wire strand across the river directly below the A30 bridge. The river now eases to continuous grade 2 which can be enjoyed right down past Okehampton Castle to the take-out.
If you carry on into Okehampton the river becomes canalised over small weirs, and finding a take-out is difficult.

Contributor:
Mark Rainsley

Lyd

Grade   **4**
Length   **3km**
OS sheet **201**

Introduction   The Lyd is a spate ditch with sharp variations in difficulty and quality.

Water level   The Lyd is a tiny river with limited catchment requiring very heavy rain to be paddleable.

Gauge   There should at least be enough water to float at the start but as much as possible is needed to make this worthwhile.

Access   The Lyd can be accessed by driving up a track beside the Fox and Hounds pub (526867) on the A386 north of Tavistock. From the end of the track there is a 300m walk to the river. Egress is above or below where the Lyd flows under the A386. Parking is limited and you may have to carry your boat up the road some way.
Few paddlers have been on the Lyd and no objections recorded.

Description   The Lyd is a tiny river with room for only a couple of paddlers. The river winds calmly through gorgeous scenery for the first kilometre. Things then change drastically; the bottom drops out of the river and there is a series of continuous, small, rocky waterfalls with only micro-eddies to break up the gradient, very unusual on Dartmoor. This is fun!

As the last significant drop is reached, trees suddenly encroach on the river and spoil the fun. A short portage is needed but things are a bit messy from here on. You have a choice. There is soon a footpath on river right, which will take you to the finish 800m away. If you choose to paddle on there are a few more small drops but more tree dodging is required and a combined wire fence and tree block has to be portaged. Be careful as you approach the A386 bridge. Take out well above on river right and walk to the road. As you get nearer to the bridge, the sides and gradient steepen and you are forced inexorably into the tunnel. Assuming that the tunnel is clear of trees, you get to experience something akin to the start of the River Erme gorge… in darkness.

Carrying on further is not recommended. More wire fences encroach on the river; there are few good egress points and before long, the Lyd enters the awesome Lydford Gorge. This potholed nightmare is lethally unpaddleable. The bottom half can be paddled at grade 3+. Requests for access to the gorge and lower river have been refused in the past.

Other important points   An adventurous experience for a small group when the nearby Tavy is too high?

Contributor:
Mark Rainsley

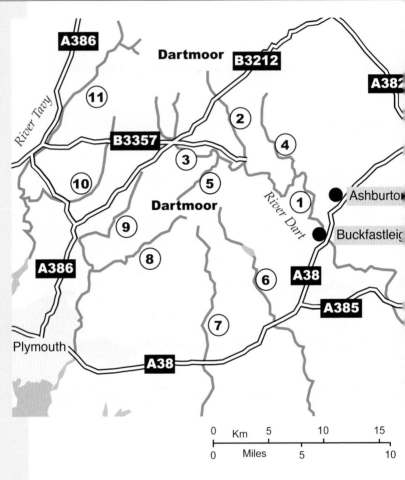

South Dartmoor

Dart (Upper - Dartmeet to New Bridge)

Grade	**4**
Length	**7km**
os	**191/202**

Introduction   The upper Dart can offer all things to all men (and women) looking for a challenging trip. Club groups looking to stick their necks out and seasoned hair boaters will both find their personal nirvana on the Dart; or if the water level is wrong for their needs, a personal hell. This is the best grade 4 river in England, but it needs to be appreciated that this grading encompasses a very broad spectrum of difficulty and character.

Water level   After heavy rain the Dart rises rapidly. It drains off gradually, remaining paddleable for at least the following week.

Gauge   See the Dart 'Loop' guide for details of how the New Bridge ledge relates to the Waterworks Bridge gauge, viewable on the internet. At the New Bridge ledge, the water needs to reach the lowest part for the upper Dart to be worthwhile. At this level, expect very technical slaloming through rocks, grade 3 and 4. As the ledge gradually covers, the Dart becomes less technical but more demanding. The 'primo' level is when the ledge is mostly covered (medium-high), offering stunning, continuous but manageable grade 4 paddling. With the whole ledge covered, the Dart is high and bank full, stopper-filled grade 4+. Higher levels still at New Bridge (water flowing through the third arch) begin to enter the 'big water zone'. Experts only.

Access   Dartmeet (672732) is a fittingly atmospheric start point. The car park is right beside the East Dart, but the access agreement dictates paddling from below the confluence with the West Dart. Carry boats across the road from the car park, across the boggy field up to a stile and along the footpath into the next field. New Bridge car park (712708) is the finish.
You are on your own in a wild valley during this trip; if you need to walk out, your best option is probably to follow a path close to the river left bank.
There is an access agreement requiring pre-booking many months in advance. Full details from the river adviser www.bcu.org.uk/access/riverinfosouthwest.html or www.dartaccess.com.

Description   For the first kilometre, a series of pool drop grade 3 rapids offer a perfect warm up. You pass Coombestone Island via a long, technical rapid, and after a series of grade 3+ boulder

gardens, the first of many bedrock rapids is reached, a sticky diagonal ledge leading to a fun slide down a slab. More boulder gardens follow, with the first grade 4 rapid among them; it has a distinct horizon line at the top, and huge boulders 100m below on river right to avoid at the end.

A grade 3 boulder rapid on a left-hand bend leads to a small ledge drop. Below is Luckey Tor, where the river divides around a narrow island and Venford Brook falls in from river right. Avoid the boulder chokes on river right. Close to either side of the island is the way to go, dropping you into a bedrock sluice complete with sticky hole at the end. Things are hotting up now. Local expert Stuart Woodward notes that this is the place to cut your losses and walk out if your group is struggling.

You now enter the 'mad mile' of grade 4 drops, all of which merge into a single mega-rapid in spate. The 'mile' begins with a series of bedrock ledges, leading into a long chicane rapid between rock walls. This finishes with some decent surf waves, and then the river begins to bend right above an island. Get out and inspect, a sneaky ambush lurks below. A series of four natural sloping slabs are harmless enough in low levels, but carry increasingly impressive stoppers as the level rises. There is usually a sneak route through or past them, but I do know that missing it in spate is a bad thing...

After the slabs, the Dart narrows to form several hundred metres of superb rapids and falls. When another island is reached (694720), the river right channel leads down to the horizon line of Euthanasia Falls. Despite the daft name, this is quite runnable and no more difficult or dangerous than anything else on the river. It's an unpleasant no-brainer in low levels, when a rocky chute forces you down into (and past) a facing rock wall. At higher levels, this can be simply avoided by paddling a different line.

There are many more ledge drops and rapids in the following 500m, but your mind will be focussed on the rapid that finishes the 'mile'. Sharrah Pool is its proper name, but paddlers know it as 'Surprise, Surprise' or 'Pandora's Box'. The river splits around an island; get out and inspect above. Sadly, this nasty rapid is more dodgy than difficult and has led to numerous injuries. The river left channel is technically easiest, although it feeds you down towards a claustrophobic narrow slot. River right of the island opens up a tricky but painless sneak-route to the far right at certain water levels. However, missing this will mean that you wind up in the awful centre channel. The river gurgles over and under an evil boulder choke with pinning rocks pointing upstream. These rocks shift around regularly. This is one rapid where high levels are far more appealing.

The last significant rapid now follows, a steep boulder jumble. Note a ledge drop and cliff on river right halfway down. In spate, Zambezi river guide Jonno Church spent two hours trapped here being annihilated by the ledge's stopper but unable to escape the eddy feeding it. He eventually solo-climbed the overhanging cliff, lugging his creek boat. Respect!

You can relax now; the only real hazard from here on is trees. The river braids around Bell Pool Island and after the channels rejoin, enjoy a straight kilometre of bouncy grade 3. After Wellsfoot Island is passed, the Dart becomes 'pool drop' in character for the final run-out to New Bridge. Carry your boat up the steps to New Bridge car park.

Contributor:
Mark Rainsley

Dart (Loop - New Bridge to Waterworks Bridge)

Introduction   The Dart 'Loop' is arguably the finest introductory grade 3 trip in the UK. With its varied, forgiving and reliable high quality rapids, the Loop seems purpose-built for club trips and white water coaching. Budding playboaters will also find many places to hone their skills. The recent development of facilities for paddlers at the River Dart Country Park, (the bar in particular), has transformed the culture of Dartmoor boating. The flipside is that you are unlikely to find solitude (at least at weekends) on the Loop.

Grade	2(3)
Length	6km
OS	191/202

Water level   The Loop is paddleable for most of the access season. Whilst it is still a good trip in low paddleable levels, its features and rapids are at their best in medium levels. In very high water or spate, the river does not exceed continuous grade 3+, but the lack of eddies and the increased tree danger make for a hazardous undertaking.

Gauge   There are two ways to assess the flow: the lowest part of the bedrock ledge upstream of New Bridge, and also a gauge on river right 100m upstream of Waterworks Bridge, helpfully monitored by a web camera, www.riverdart.co.uk/webcam.
Do not paddle the Loop if it is a scrape to get past New Bridge. Preserve your dignity.

If the water is below the lowest wooden slat (4'6") on the gauge, the Loop is low. It is paddleable down to about six inches below this slat. This corresponds to the water being below the New Bridge 'ledge'.

The lowest three slats (4'6" to 5'6") measure from medium to high levels on the Loop. This corresponds to the New Bridge ledge being from partly covered to wholly covered.

Above the third slat, and with the ledge wholly covered, the river is high and obviously more challenging for a group. If water is flowing through the third arch at New Bridge, it is in spate; consider adapting your plans.

Access   New Bridge car park (712708) is always a bustling hive of paddlers. Some of the area is marked off for non-paddlers, respect this. You may alternatively be able to acquire a shuttle up to the start from the Country Park.

Finish just upstream of Waterworks Bridge (735698) on river right. Carry your boat several hundred metres through the Country Park grounds to the car park. Until recently the egress was at Holne Bridge. This is no longer permitted.

There is an access agreement requiring pre-booking many months in advance. Full details from the river adviser www.bcu.org.uk/access/riverinfosouthwest.html or www.dartaccess.com.

Description   From New Bridge, it is 50m to a small wave which is excellent at high levels, offering a breaking wave which can be cartwheeled, blunted and suchlike.

The river bends right and drops over a tiny ledge producing a small stopper across most of the river. Below this is a long grade 2 wave train leading to a left bend in the river. The river mostly flows right of an island and overhanging trees should be watched out for. The river leads down to a small rapid before a right bend... this is the spot to attempt tail squirts. From the bend, an easy series of rapids leads down past another island and a footbridge to where the river widens and the River Webburn enters from river left, producing a miniature play stopper.

All of the trickier rapids are still to come, and it's not too far downstream that the river opens out into a wide pool above an island. Most water flows to the right of the island and forms the Washing Machine rapid. This somewhat dubious name describes a 1m ledge which forms a towback. The stopper can be easily avoided by staying close to the island... but why? At low levels, the ledge provides a good introduction to running drops. In high levels, the hole is genuinely formidable but is again easy to avoid. A series of steep grade 2 rapids follow and you will recognise some sloping rock slabs on river left which offer a painful seal launch. The river continues flowing fairly straight until you reach a right bend and a calm pool. Below, the Dart steepens into a very long rapid, this is Lover's Leap. This name describes the cliff at the very end of the rapid which the inexperienced will find tricky to dodge. There are several stoppers and rocks to negotiate in the rapid, which is an enjoyable introduction to grade 3.

Lover's Leap is followed by a series of wide and rocky rapids. After the river flows right of a long island, keep your eyes peeled for the horizon line that marks the approach of Triple Falls (Gd 3). There are three small rapids here, and only the first qualifies as a fall, being a small ledge that washes out in anything other than low levels. This is a good spot for cartwheeling. The second 'drop' is a chute through a flushy wave and the final fall is a longer rapid with some small waves and stoppers to negotiate. This section merges into an impressive wave train in spate.

Flat water gives a chance to mellow out before a left bend leads into the Spin Dryer. This is an eddy on river right beside a good wide surf wave. The eddy tends to be tricky to escape for the inexperienced, surfing the wave out is the key! Directly below the eddy on river right is a small play stopper that works well at some levels.

A wave train provides a lively bounce down to Holne bridge (731706) where the 'Loop' as such ends. Carry on 200m to Holne Weir. This can always be simply shot by a convenient 'chicken' chute on the far river left. Anywhere else will require extreme caution and just isn't worth the hassle. You are now in the grounds of the Country Park and you may encounter rafts.

Around the corner, a smaller weir has been recently modified into a great playhole, portentously named 'The Anvil'. This is of competition quality and works from about 4'6" up, the higher the better. Those paddling down from above have the choice of a wide sneak on river left or a 'boof' direct into the far right eddy. You are then unceremoniously carried under a shower of water from a seal launch ramp, and the take-out steps are on river right upstream of Waterworks Bridge. If you've completed your first Loop trip, you'll feel eight feet tall.

Contributor:
Mark Rainsley

Dart (Lower - Waterworks Bridge to Buckfastleigh)

Grade   **2**

Length   **5km**

OS sheet **202**

Introduction   This stretch, taking the Dart right to the border of the National Park, is the most popular open canoe trip on Dartmoor and also sees heavy use by coaching groups. There are several good rapids but this is forgiving and friendly.

Water level   This should be paddleable throughout much of the access season. High levels are enjoyable, but employ caution if you use this as a fall-back option in spate conditions.

Gauge   There is a gauge on river right 100m upstream of Waterworks Bridge. The lowest wooden slat corresponds to the normal winter 'background' low flow. Six inches below this will still be possible as a minimum.

Access   Launch just upstream of Waterworks Bridge (735698) on river right. This is in the grounds of the Dart Country Park, who offer parking and other facilities.
Finish at the 'Little Chef 'on river left outside Buckfastleigh (745666). 'Little Chef' tolerate us using their car park, despite past incidents of paddlers changing in front of their windows. Don't spoil their customers' breakfast, and eat there after your trip. There is an access agreement requiring pre-booking. Details from the river adviser www.bcu.org.uk/access/ riverinfosouthwest.html or www.dartaccess.com.

Description   Below Waterworks Bridge there are a number of widely spaced grade 2 rapids to enjoy. The most memorable are where the river funnels right past a small ledge, and where it drops steeply through waves and stoppers to the left of a big island. Eventually Buckfastleigh Abbey comes into view on river right, heralding the approach of Furzeleigh Weir. Get out well above on river left to inspect or portage this hefty dam. If the water level is high, the main weir face can be slid down, followed by running the ledges and waves below. Do not be tempted to run the fish steps on river left. In recent years they have eroded to form spacious undercuts, hidden in all but the lowest water levels. Lethal!
Below the weir, the river speeds through narrows, with micro-eddies to attempt and at least one excellent surf wave to enjoy. It's all too short however, and when you pass water-carved caves on

Contributor:
Mark Rainsley

river right, the end is nigh. Float under the bridge and break out at the beach immediately on river left. 'Little Chef' is hidden in the trees above.

Dart (Lower - Buckfastleigh to Totnes)

Grade	**1/2**
Length	**14km**
OS sheet	**202**

Introduction   This long section is mostly flat and bears little re-semblance to the various sections of the Dart upstream. However, it has reliable access and flow and sees plenty of use by novice groups and open canoes.

Water level   This can be paddled throughout the access season. It offers an easier (but not necessarily safer) alternative for when the rest of the Dart is too high for your group's taste. It is difficult but not particularly essential to gauge the flow precisely. If the river looks high you may wish to inspect the portage route past Kilbury Weir, also known as Salmon Ponds Weir (747662) beforehand.

Access   Launch behind the 'Little Chef ' on river left directly downstream of the stone bridge leading into Buckfastleigh (745666). Change discreetly, 'Little Chef' are very patient with people using their car park but remember to eat or drink something there afterwards!
A useful access point which bisects this section is Staverton bridge (785637) where there are mill buildings offering parking. Ask permission and don't park in loading bays or obstruct the locals.
The take-out is in the centre of Totnes on the now tidal Dart. A car park on river left is useful, but there are numerous options.
There is an access agreement requiring pre-booking. Details from the river adviser www.bcu.org.uk/access/riverinfosouthwest.html or www.dartaccess.com.

Description   Directly downstream of the put-in, you encounter Kilbury Weir. This complicated construction consisting of small steps and chutes is currently *very dangerous*. Sections of the weir have eroded under water leaving metal rods and loops hidden under the water. If you really have to paddle this, *very* close inspection is recommended. Portage on river left.
The following kilometres are pretty much flat until Hood Weir, which is partly collapsed. This is paddleable with care, mind out for tree roots. Shortly below is Staverton bridge which is a popu-

lar alternative access point, given the lack of excitement on this stretch so far.

Below Staverton there is little more white water interest but at least, more 'oomph' in the current. A weir shortly below Staverton bridge has breached on river right, making for an enjoyable fast chute and training spot. Be alert for concrete junk. Portage should be easy on either side.

The river is now mostly flat as it winds towards Totnes. As the river bends left entering Totnes, an imposing horizon line appears; Totnes Weir. Inspect and possibly portage on river right. In low water the huge weir face can be shot, with the salmon steps offering an exciting alternative. In spate the stopper and wave at the bottom are truly monstrous.

Below the weir, the Dart is now brackish salt water. For those who have experienced the Dart in its varied moods right down from the high plateau of Dartmoor, this will be a poignant spot. A small rapid lurks under a bridge and then you are in the centre of town with the take-out car park on river left.

Other important points   For the true Dart addict, things don't end here; the estuary leads for another 16km down to Dartmouth and is a delight to paddle.

Contributor:
Mark Rainsley

East Dart

Grade   **3**
Length   **7km**
OS sheet **191**

Introduction   In appropriately high water conditions, this is an enjoyable small river with continuous white water and a chance to enjoy Dartmoor at its quietest.

Water level   Although this can undoubtedly be paddled lower, it should be saved for high water conditions, partly to bring the rapids in condition, partly because paddling at low levels might affect spawning beds.

Gauge   All rocks should be covered at Postbridge. Most or all rocks should be covered at Dartmeet.

Access   There are two possible starting points. Postbridge (647788) is the higher access point, with good parking beside a National Park Information Centre.

The second option is a start at Bellever bridge (658774) which is a

quieter spot and misses out the awkward first kilometre.
This trip ends at Dartmeet (672732), which is better known as the
starting point for the classic Upper Dart run.
*At time of writing, there is no permitted access to the East Dart, and
paddling this could have an adverse effect upon the access situation for
the separate River Dart.*

Description   Shortly below Postbridge, a strand of barbed wire
across the river makes for a dubious warm-up. In the following
100m you are then strained through some awkward tree branches
and under a low footbridge whilst negotiating steep grade 3 falls.
The river soon overcomes its poor start and eases to grade 2 rapids interspersed with small weir ledges. The last makes a notable
stopper and is just upstream of Bellever bridge. If what has been
described so far isn't your idea of fun, this is a good place to start
the trip.
The river now flows through open moor on one bank and oddly,
dense forestry plantation on the other. The continuous rapids
frequently reach grade 3- and, once the plantation is left behind,
the river has more gradient and some great waves and stoppers
to thrash through. A second plantation is reached, again on river
right. The river enters its steepest section with fast and furious grade 3. The good news is that this carries on, although the
river widens and loses gradient just before the end. In December
2002 a single tree had fallen across the river 100m upstream of
Dartmeet.

Contributor:
Mark Rainsley

West Dart

Introduction   This sizeable river meanders tranquilly across the
high plateau of central Dartmoor for some distance before gradually picking up gradient.

Grade	3+
Length	10km
OS sheet	191

Water level   The West Dart can be bashed down at low levels,
but it would be dull and possibly detrimental to spawning beds.
Save this for spate conditions. This is best enjoyed when the Upper Dart becomes too high for comfort.

Gauge   The West Dart should be filling or spilling its banks.
Looking upstream from the confluence with the East Dart at Dartmeet, no rocks should be visible.

Access   Two Bridges (608750) has good parking and forms
the upward road limit of the West Dart. A quieter put-in which
cuts out a lot of flat water is the bridge near an outdoor centre
(626738).
The West Dart terminates a short distance downstream of Dartmeet
car park (672732) where it converges with the smaller East Dart.
*At time of writing, there is no permitted access to the West Dart. Pad-
dling this could have an adverse effect upon the access situation for the
separate River Dart.*

Description   Below Two Bridges, the river has intermittent
easy rapids and a lot of flat paddling. This 3km section is often
bypassed by starting near the Dartmoor outdoor centre, described
above.
The river has plenty of grade 3 rapids below this point, but also
lots of flat meandering. The river is overgrown in several places,
but a channel can always be found which offers a clear path
through the trees. It is worth looking out for the confluence of
the River Swincombe on river right when you reach some stepping stones (which should be well covered); paddlers have been
known to detour up the bank of this small stream. Past this point,
the river gradually acquires more gradient. Once you are under
Hexworthy bridge, you are into continuous big and bouncy grade
3+ all the way down to the East Dart confluence. This section is
excellent in spate and the 'tiddly' West Dart suddenly feels like a
much bigger river. Get out on river left of the newly formed River
Dart and walk back up to Dartmeet car park.

Contributor:
Mark Rainsley

Webburn (Ponsworthy to Dart Confluence)

Grade   **3+**

Length   **4km**

os **202/191**

Introduction   A very steep, bouldery creek through secluded
woodland. What could be finer? Unfortunately the Webburn actually turns out to be a masochist's paradise!

Water level   The Webburn needs recent rainfall, but anything above
a medium-high level would probably be *lethal*, due to the *trees*.

Gauge   The best way to gauge the flow is where it flows into the
River Dart 'Loop' (716717). It should be obvious whether a boat
can float freely down this stream or not.

Access   Access the Webburn in the vicinity of Ponsworthy (702738). You will probably have to cross farmland downstream of the village bridge to access the river, use discretion.
Stagger out at the bridge where the Webburn joins the Dart, (716717). There is a car park nearby.
There is no permitted access to the Webburn, and paddling this river may impact upon the Dart agreement.

Description   The first (and best) kilometre is actually on the West Webburn. Directly below Ponsworthy, your chosen ditch drops sharply away with continual small falls and bouldery rapids. Eddies are few and small; there is barely room for a group of three. This is splendid stuff! So, what is the catch?
The Webburn suffers from numerous tree-blocks that require ducking or portaging. This is bearable in the steepest early section of the river. However, after joining the smaller East Webburn tributary, the river enters a long gorge that looks inviting, but is usually blocked end to end with trees. The portage is really gruelling, high up the bank through brambles and rocks. To add to the jollity, I once nearly fell down a disused mineshaft here.
Back in the water below the gorge, fast grade 3 continues all the way down to the Dart.

Contributor:
Mark Rainsley

Other important points   Some paddlers have had great portage-free runs on the Webburn; clearly the trees move around from season to season.

Swincombe

Grade	**3+**
Length	**3km**
OS sheet	**191**

Introduction   A novelty trip high on the moor which offers an alternative start to the West Dart.

Water level   This is only possible in spate.

Gauge   The West Dart should be out of its banks.

Access   Find your way by road to where tracks lead off to the left and right from the road (652726). There is no sign of the river here; it's hidden a kilometre away up the track to the left (west). Unload and carry along the track which will be mostly under water if the Swincombe is up. The Swincombe is reached at a bridge

(642725). It is possible to walk another kilometre up to a dam, but the section above is mostly flat.

The Swincombe flows into the West Dart; see West Dart guide for details of the take-out.

This is a wild paddle that is rarely possible; a group venturing out in the lousy weather required are unlikely to meet anybody.

Description   From the start, you are propelled down a narrow tunnel of bushes. The water is bouncy but the main difficulty is staying clear of the bushes. The river flows under or ideally, over a small footbridge (take care) and just below is a road bridge near some houses. After the bridge, the bushes are supplemented by a few low hanging trees and the river drops over several steep drops before entering the West Dart.

Contributor:
Mark Rainsley

Other important points   There aren't any eddies, so the ability to break out is unnecessary!

Avon

Grade	**4(5)**
Length	**4km**
OS sheet	**202**

Introduction   Further proof that South Dartmoor has some of the finest creek boating in the UK. The Avon drains the watershed between the Dart and the Erme. It is harder than the Erme at a similar water level but often similar in character.

Water level   The headwaters of the Avon are captured by a dam, so it needs loads of rain to come into condition. The Avon is not usually possible until the spring when the dam has filled. This is a good river to check when the Dart and Erme are high. The Avon is stomping in rare high levels, but the gorge section becomes a portage.

Gauge   You will see the falls upstream of Lydia bridge during the drive up. If a rock 'spur' is visible on the lip of the second drop, the river is too low.

Access   The start is at or upstream of Shipley bridge (681629). There is a convenient car park there. From the take-out in South Brent, head for 'Avon Dam'. Be warned… those fun-loving Devonians have turned some of the signs to point in the wrong direction.

Lower Walkham

Pandora's Box, Upper Dart (Note the pinned kayak!)

Pandora's Box, Upper Dart

Lower Tavy

Upper Dart

For the take-out, you have plenty of choice within the small town of South Brent. A convenient spot is a parking area near a garden centre beside the railway bridge, with a convenient track down to the river (697603). Some finish their trip earlier at Lydia bridge (695606) but the parking is not great here.

The access situation is troubled. Some residents close to Shipley bridge apparently prefer not to see canoeists on the river. You are recommended to minimise offence by arriving changed and leaving quickly.

Description   There are a series of steep drops beside the car park at the start. These are only possible in low levels as they are obscured by rhododendron bushes. Below Shipley bridge, the river doesn't give much warm-up and your group needs to be awake. Weave through some tree branches and run a one metre drop with a sticky hole. *Immediately*, get out on river left. Don't get out on river right, as it is a private garden, but trust us on this one, *get out!*

The river disappears without warning off a big drop into a sheer-sided gorge, with a grabby towback that will annihilate those who missed the sketchy eddy. The gorge is a tough undertaking, with the first fall followed by plenty more drops in increasingly confined surroundings. At the narrowest point, a river-wide hole can close out the river with huge towback, so the gorge is a portage (river left) in high levels.

This is an impressive start! Thankfully, the river has less nasty surprises after this. You can now enjoy continuous grade 3 and 4 paddling all the way to the take-out. Your group needs to be switched on, as eddies are few and far between and getting out to inspect isn't always an option. A detailed description will spoil all the fun, but you will wish to be aware that a couple of broken weirs need care.

The falls at Lydia bridge make a fitting climax to a superb river. Upstream of the bridge in the village of Aish, a steep double drop with chewy stoppers will need inspecting. You can get out on river right just above it and portage if necessary. Shortly below the bridge, you see the railway viaduct loom up and it's time to get out upstream of it on river left and walk up to the cars.

Contributor:
Mark Rainsley

Erme (Upper - Above Harford Bridge)

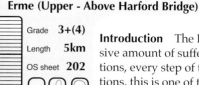

Grade **3+(4)**

Length **5km**

OS sheet **202**

Introduction   The Erme above Harford bridge requires an impressive amount of suffering to reach but if you pick the right conditions, every step of the carry-in is worth it. If you have spate conditions, this is one of the most intense and continuous trips in the region. Do not be deceived by the moderate grade; this is as full-on and committing as any high water Dartmeet run. Splendid!

Water level   Spate conditions are ideal and you need to time this right as the Erme will rise and fall in a matter of hours. Expect the level to change dramatically whilst you paddle.

Gauge   Look upstream of Harford bridge. If all rocks are covered and the river is full, perfect. If a few rocks are showing, a shorter trip is worth considering.

Access   Drive up to the water treatment works (630613) where the staff have not previously objected to small, quiet groups using the car park at the end of the road. Do not however impede the works traffic. Shoulder your boat and follow the track around the hill. After 1500m, you reach the river. If there are rocks showing, launch at this spot for an enjoyable 2.5km of grade 3+. If everything is covered, the river is grade 3+ above and solid grade 4 below. Ignore your group's whinging and force them to keep marching. The track takes you up to a hut and weir (640632). This section ends at Harford bridge (636596), which is the standard start point for an Erme trip.
This trip happens in wild places and wild weather. You are highly unlikely to encounter an access difficulty.

Description   On launching, you will be surprised by how fast things happen. There are few distinct drops. However, the gradient is considerable and there is absolutely no let-up right down to Harford bridge.
You will notice a change in character once the track is left about halfway down. The gradient increases, more stoppers lurk and your route choices are somewhat reduced by the appearance of trees along the banks. In spate, there is no stopping now! As you approach the final bridge, a series of natural ledges make surprisingly solid stoppers and you need to be able to think up good lines on the hoof. Break out below Harford bridge and take a long deep breath.

Contributor:
Mark Rainsley

Other important points   At optimum water levels for this section, the Erme below Harford bridge may not be everybody's 'cup of tea'.

Erme

Grade	**4/5**
Length	**5km**
OS sheet	**202**

Introduction   The Erme is among the finest grade 4 paddles in the UK, it is a narrow bedrock creek dropping steeply through gnarled, ancient woodland. Every kind of rapid is here (okay, except for Zambezi-style monsters) crammed into a remarkably intense and varied trip. The final 2km descends 100m; expect to become very familiar with the bank on your first trip!

Water level   The Erme is regularly in a paddleable condition, usually being possible within twelve hours of heavy rain. Once as I climbed off the river after a low water run in pouring rain, an elderly local told me that the run-off took three hours down to Ivybridge. Sure enough, the water level then rose dramatically, exactly three hours after the rain began…

Gauge   Look at the ledge falls in the centre of Ivybridge. The top rocky ledge is your gauge. The degree of 'scrapey-ness' here will give you an indication of what the whole trip above will be like. If the ledge is well covered, the trip will be quite intense with grade 5 in the gorge…perhaps not ideal for a first run down. Consider a run on the upper Erme. If the ledges are all *washed-out*, go elsewhere.

Access   This section starts at Harford bridge, (636596). There is space for a few cars beside the bridge. The locals at Harford have always been patient with canoeists; don't abuse this by blocking the narrow lane.
The trip finishes in the centre of Ivybridge. Take out just upstream of a weir beside the leisure centre (635560); there is plenty of parking. There is an access agreement. Paddlers must notify the river adviser of their intention to paddle. Check out the river adviser's details online at www.bcu.org.uk/access/riverinfosouthwest.html.

Description   Directly below Harford Bridge, the Erme drops away in a series of grade 3/4 ledges and bouldery falls. The river quickly loses gradient and mellows to grade 2/3 with the occasional small drop. There are several trees in the river in the

following section, which can usually be 'snuck' around with care. After 2km of this easy water, rhododendron bushes encroach in several places. Be on the lookout for a 50cm river-wide ledge... directly downstream of the ledge the river narrows without warning into an undercut narrow slot. This is paddleable at low water levels. In higher water, a huge back-tow appears and *this innocuous looking slot becomes unpaddleable*. Portage/inspect on river right. Now you find what the fuss is all about! The river quickly cranks up to continuous grade 4 drops, with sticky holes developing in high water. An old weir needs care... the tempting flume on river left has caused vertical pins. Below the weir there are two steep rapids in quick succession, and then you find yourself breaking out sharply upstream of a massive railway viaduct. You've reached the Erme Gorge. Those who have had enough can easily walk out now. Either way, the gorge must be inspected for trees from the river right path. The gorge is long and intense, with several crux moves to nail. It is fast, narrow and committing. A swim would be long and probably lonely.

The gorge opens out and somehow you are in the centre of Ivybridge. Approaching the town bridge, the ominous horizon line beneath will remind you that the fat lady hasn't sung yet. These final falls are surprisingly big and have pinning potential; don't forget to dodge the chomping stopper at the end.

The take-out is directly below, when you reach a footbridge. Beware of carrying on over a dodgy weir beside a sports centre.

Contributor:
Mark Rainsley

Plym (Upper - Cadover Bridge to Shaugh Bridge)

Grade   **5**
Length   **3km**
OS sht. **201/2**

Introduction   The upper Plym is the hardest trip on Dartmoor, and a contender for England's best grade 5 creek. The river starts deceptively mildly, but once it kicks into gear, it never stops.

Water level   Catching the right water level for the Plym is notoriously tough. It rises fast after rain, often being the first Devon river to bear the brunt of incoming south-westerly fronts. It drops equally fast when rain stops; assume that the level will change whilst you are paddling. Catching the Plym on the drop is safest.

Gauge   Look below Cadover bridge. If it is possible to paddle around or between the pebble banks the river is a rather bumpy grade 4+. If you can comfortably float over these stones the river is at an optimum grade 5 level. If the Plym is filling or spilling the banks at these points the Plym will be absolutely relentless, maybe grade 5+. In any conditions, you are advised to walk upstream a few hundred metres from Shaugh bridge to be clear about what you're getting into.

Access   Launch from the bleak parking area beside Cadover bridge (555646), where the river is an unconvincing meandering ditch. Shaugh bridge car park (533637) is the finish. One option to prevent your car becoming yet another crime statistic at this spot is to shuttle further and do the lower Plym too.

There is no access agreement, but paddling is never obstructed. Locals quietly run this all year round.

Description   The Plym begins with several forgiving pool drop falls which offer a chance to loosen up and quell the nerves. If you are struggling at this point, quit. You will recognise certain distinct rapids early on: a series of reef slides, a boulder rapid leading right under a large rock, a river-wide ledge fall with a shallow landing. A detailed description of the Plym from this point would put a dent in the Amazonian rain forest and be largely futile.

To summarise: more reef and boulder rapids, as the rapids gradually merge into one. High boulders obscure the route ahead and things become completely manic as the river literally falls away. Anybody on the bank inspecting at this point will be confused; at what point does the rapid actually end?

It's no macho hype to say that the Plym is powerful and deadly. Although everything can be walked and inspected easily, your 'hazard radar' needs to be switched on and turned up. There are many siphons and pin spots lurking, and a tree in the wrong place could spell catastrophe. A creek boat is recommended.

A glimpse of the high Dewerstone cliff on river right will tell you that you're within sight of the end. The river zigzags and then spills over the last major rapid, a series of slides and falls through sticky stoppers, with siphons to avoid at the bottom.

Contributor:
Mark Rainsley

Break out at Shaugh bridge and indulge in a bit of mutual congratulation. You probably didn't even notice the amazing, ancient, gnarled wood that the Plym flows through.

Plym (Lower - Shaugh Bridge to Bickleigh Bridge)

Grade   **3+(4)**

Length   **3km**

OS sheet   **201**

Introduction   The lower Plym is short but crammed with entertainment. Those who have previously been scared away by the upper Plym's reputation may be surprised by this relatively friendly, bouncy blast.

Water level   The Plym runs off amazingly fast so you need to be here during or directly after rain. It is possible but rather dull to paddle when the upper Plym is at a low, paddleable level. This is best saved for high or spate water levels when the upper section is too high.

Gauge   If all rocks upstream of Shaugh bridge are covered, you have an acceptable level. If all rocks downstream of the bridge are covered, that's just splendid. Hang on tight!

Access   Launch upstream of Shaugh bridge (533637) where the smaller River Meavy joins the Plym. Shaugh bridge car park is unfortunately notorious for car crime.
Finish at Bickleigh bridge (529618) where there is only room to park one car. Use discretion here and don't test the patience of the locals. There is no access agreement, but paddling has not been hindered with these access and egress points being used. Access is not permitted downstream of Bickleigh bridge.

Description   The lower Plym commences with a bang, so be warmed up. The rapid leading around the corner from Shaugh bridge is the most intense on the trip. It is possible but considered 'wussy' to launch below this on river right!
If you survive this first rapid, things ease to pool-drop with many large rapids testing your hole-dodging skills. There are a significant number of low tree branches and fallen trees lurking in these rapids, so stay awake.

Contributor:

Mark Rainsley

The further you go, the more spaced apart the rapids become and by the time you see the take-out bridge, the adrenaline released by the first rapid will have dispersed. The locals prefer paddlers to take out on river right at a beach 200m above Bickleigh bridge; this should have been identified beforehand.

Meavy

Grade **4**

Length **1.5km**

OS sheet **201**

Introduction   A short but pretty river that offers an alternative start to the lower Plym when the upper Plym is too high for comfort.

Water level   The Meavy is dammed upstream, forming Burrator Reservoir. Prolonged rain is needed to ensure sufficient flow overtopping the dam. There are also a number of feeder streams which help to bring the Meavy up more quickly. When the upper Plym is high, the Meavy tends to still have moderate flows.

Gauge   Walk a little way upstream of Shaugh bridge and look at the last bouldery rapids; will you scrape on these?

Access   Put-in is at Goodameavy bridge (529646). There is some parking beside the bridge.
Take-out is at Shaugh bridge (533637) or better still, continue down the lower River Plym. Car theft is common at the car park at Shaugh bridge.
The Meavy sees few descents and flows through pristine surroundings; there is only room for a small sensitive group.

Description   Paddling is certainly possible upstream of Goodameavy in very high water. Below the dam there is 500m of grade 4 ruined by tree jams, and then allegedly (I have not seen this) several kilometres of easy water complete with wire fences and bushes.
From Goodameavy, the first section is flat. After a grade 3 rapid on a left hand bend, the river becomes continuous grade 3 and 4 until Shaugh bridge. The difficulties consist of manoeuvring through steep boulder gardens with the odd tree-avoidance tactic making for the trickiest moves. There is plenty of wood in the Meavy but it can usually be ducked and dodged safely.
This is a very narrow river and flows through lovely natural surroundings; tramping up and down the banks inspecting would not be appropriate.
At Shaugh bridge, you are strongly recommended to continue straight on to the lower Plym (see guide).

Contributor:
Mark Rainsley

Other important points   Entering the lower River Plym with its bigger volume and gradient, is like hitting 'fast forward'... be warned!

Walkham (Upper - Merrivale Bridge to Huckworthy Bridge)

Grade   **5**

Length   **5km**

OS sheet **201**

Introduction   Despite what you might suspect at the put-in, this is no godforsaken tree ditch. This is a fantastic river offering some of the steepest creeking in England; there are no big falls, but no flat bits either. Non-stop frantic paddle flailing is the BCU approved method for descending the upper Walkham!

Water level   This will only work in high water conditions. Expect to paddle this during or after heavy rain as the put-in is high on the moor and runs off fast. Spate conditions provide an utterly continuous grade 5 'scarefest'.

Gauge   There is a gauge directly upstream of Huckworthy bridge on river left. It is however on private land and can only be accessed by paddling a short distance upriver. It should read at least 0.7 for this section. I have paddled this up to 1.4 (full-on!), but something around 0.9 would probably be ideal. A simpler gauge is to take a look around at Merrivale bridge. Is the river filling its banks? Is the rain hissing down?

Access   Merrivale bridge (550752) is on the main road crossing Dartmoor from Ashburton to Tavistock. Turn off for the inn there and follow the road down to a smaller bridge. There is parking for a few vehicles here. The first kilometre is very dangerous so the best idea is to carry your boat along the track on river left. This can be found 100m from the river up the road and is a public right of way. Follow it until you pass through Longash Farm. Then go through gates down to join the river (546744). The carry is no more than a kilometre. This misses the first few rapids of the steepest section and you may wish to climb back upstream a bit. The take-out is the bridge (532705) in the lovely, quiet hamlet of Huckworthy. There is room for a single car below the bridge on river left where you climb out.

No access objections have been encountered, so let's keep it that way.

Description   If you choose to paddle the first kilometre, you will find yourself repeatedly strained over, under and through bushes and trees. This can be done (with a few portages), but is a miserably dangerous experience.

The river changes character dramatically when it reaches a sudden rocky waterfall. The trees simply disappear and you are

Contributor:

Mark Rainsley

presented with an astounding vista; the bottom falls out of the
Walkham and all you see looking downhill is a long series of
horizon lines. Lovely.

The paddling for the following 2km is relentless, endless small
drops with sticky stoppers and must-make micro-eddies. In
normal levels this is very technical grade 4+ and 5 eddy hop-
ping; in spate the eddies become infrequent and you are forced to
'straight-line' some very chewy holes. The amazing thing is that
there are no obvious portages and no significant tree hazard.
Finally, the river eases in gradient and just before Ward bridge,
there are a couple of portages around fallen trees. Carrying on
past the bridge is recommended; directly downstream of the
bridge the Walkham picks up pace again, with a kilometre of
grade 4 drops. Towards the end of these rapids, the river narrows
into a tunnel of rhododendron bushes and then flattens out above
a sticky weir. The last kilometre eases down through the grades
and includes a second portage around a fallen tree before Huckworthy bridge is reached.

Walkham (Middle - Huckworthy Bridge to Bedford Bridge)

Introduction This section is unlikely to appeal for its own sake,
but makes a reasonably enjoyable warm-up for the lower Walkham.
A look at the map will suggest flat water, but don't be deceived;
there are notable rapids to enjoy, both natural and man-made.

Grade **1/2(3)**
Length **3.5km**
OS sheet **201**

Water level If the much harder upper Walkham is in condition,
this is perhaps too high, due to the weirs and the barbed wire hazard described below. Low to medium paddleable flows are best,
and recent rain is necessary for this.

Gauge All rocks in the river downstream of Huckworthy bridge
need to be covered.

Access This section begins at Huckworthy bridge (532705).
There is parking for one or two cars but discretion is advised in
this small friendly village.
The section described finishes at Bedford bridge (504704), but it's
better to carry on into the lower Walkham.
Few paddlers use this section and no objections have been
recorded.

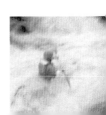

Description   Launch at Huckworthy bridge. The first obstacle is a weir forming a simple slide. The second weir is partly collapsed making a technical grade 3 rapid. The third weir is surprising, a slide direct into a long grade 3 rapid. This rapid is in a strange miniature gorge with mossy green walls and has a shock waiting at the end...a closed in slot drop! Thankfully it is *usually* harmless enough. The fourth weir comes as you enter Horrabridge. It is a small drop with a grabby stopper. Directly downstream some maniac has dangled loops of barbed wire from a private footbridge. This is no problem to dodge in low water levels, but use extreme caution whilst approaching this.

You now enter the Weir Park in the centre of Horrabridge. The weir here is shallow and sticky, but it is safe enough to paddle in low levels. Easy water leads out of the village down to Bedford bridge. It is possible to stop here, but it is strongly recommended that you keep going to enjoy the excellent grade 3 section below.

Contributor:

Mark Rainsley

Other important points   Enjoyed along with the lower Walkham and Tavy, this forms a long and varied grade 3 trip.

Walkham (Lower - Bedford Bridge to Tavy Confluence)

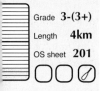

Grade **3-(3+)**

Length **4km**

OS sheet **201**

Introduction   If you don't enjoy the Walkham then you don't deserve this sport. Both grizzled hair boaters and hairy grizzly open boaters are catered for in the various sections of the river. This lower section forms a unique training ground with numerous small drops, micro-eddies and mini-waves to test a group. This is the best of the easier Dartmoor trips other than the Dart Loop.

Water level   The Walkham below Bedford bridge needs rain to make it possible. Enough water to float comfortably from the launch point will be sufficient for the sections downstream, but more is preferable. In spate this is still possible with care, becoming a sumptuous feast of bouncy grade 3.

Gauge   Check the weir upstream of the bridge in nearby Horrabridge. The sill and weir face should all be well covered.

Access   Launch from Bedford bridge (504704). There is some parking here. Take-out is at Denham bridge (477678) on the River Tavy, which this trip ends upon.

Paddlers have not always been welcomed by some of the land-owners downstream. Small and quiet groups do not tend to encounter objections.

Description   Below Bedford bridge, occasional grade 2 rapids attempt to keep you awake. The scenery is pleasant, a wooded valley with little evidence of civilisation.

After you pass under a bridge with helpful *'No Swimming'* signs all around, the river moves up a gear. It steepens over a series of small ledges and forms a long grade 3- rapid which finishes with a sudden one metre drop. Collect your wits, as the rapids are now pretty much continuous from here to the Tavy. This is a remarkable bit of boating at the grade. The river narrows and is confined by bedrock banks, forming numerous eddies along the banks; this section is perfect for a small group learning to eddy-hop down a river.

The only naughty bit is near the end, where the valley opens out with fields on either side. Much of the river disappears down an unconvincing looking slot leading into a twisty rapid. This will make a few folk practise their roll!

Contributor:
Mark Rainsley

The river now leads down to the Tavy where further entertainment awaits in the 3km to Denham bridge.

Tavy (Upper - Tavy Cleave to Hill Bridge)

Introduction   A high moorland adventure, with an epic walk-in over open moor. The upper Tavy is often referred to as 'Tavy Cleave' after the central feature of this trip. The river is small initially but builds and falls rapidly as it spills off the granite plateau that is Dartmoor. A true mountain stream, giving adventure of a kind not often found in the UK.

Grade	**4+**
Length	**7km**
OS sheet	**191**

Water level   The Tavy Cleave run can only be considered when all else is off the scale and the rain is still falling. Quick to peak and as rapid to drop off.

Gauge   If the river is flooding at Hill bridge, the Cleave awaits. Otherwise, the upper Tavy can be run from the Willsworthy car park access point in normal high levels. At these levels the Tavy below Hill bridge will be dangerous because of trees.

Access   Hill bridge (532804) is best known as the start of a

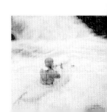

popular grade 3 trip. However, in this case it is actually the finish point. From Hill bridge, return to the Peter Tavy road but turn left up the valley. Park at the gate at the road end (546805). Carry your boat up the track past a firing range hut and into the wilds. Follow the track around the valley head and right over Standon Hill, a carry of at least 4km with 150m of ascent. The track gradually fades into a path and eventually, a boggy, high plateau. You are aiming to reach the river in the vicinity of a firing range notice board (567833). You'll need a map, a compass and plenty of 'attitude' to survive in the weather needed to bring the Cleave up. There is a way for softies to experience the upper Tavy, although this misses the Cleave and reduces the trip to 4.5km. From Willsworthy car park (537823), carry for 1km along a track towards the river until you reach a leat stream. Float your boat in this and tow it up the valley for 1km and launch at the leat stream's source (550830).

Access to the upper section is across a military firing range; do not venture out when the red flags are flying!

Description   After all your walking, you encounter a relatively flat and narrow stream winding its way through a steep-sided valley. Do not be down-hearted young Jedi. Numerous streams join to swell the watercourse and soon after, the gradient drops away with several long, narrow rapids.

Rapids are characterised with an unusual element of sharp rocks, perhaps indicating their relative geological youth. The run itself contains mainly large bedrock features within a shallow yet wide sweeping watercourse. Numerous entertaining features are found in the run through the Cleave, of which the Coffin, a narrow slot within a broad ledge, is the most prominent drop before the leat stream (alternative access) takes off on the right.

Past the leat, the last of the sweeping bends awaits and then you drop beneath the tree line. The valley squeezes the river into a narrower channel. Rapids are more bouldery in nature now and lead to a host of differing problems, including eddy finding and tree ducking. The tree canyon soon gives way to open fields and a lessening in gradient before the take-out at Hill bridge.

Contributor:

Mark Rainsley and
Simon Westgarth

Tavy (Middle - Hill Bridge to Tavistock)

Grade	**3+**
Length	**9km**
OS sheet	**201**

Introduction   This is an excellent white water trip, offering one of the most intense paddles at the grade in England. The Tavy flows around many blind corners and drops which make leading a group effectively and safely a real challenge.

Water level   The water level needs to be selected carefully. This will not be possible more than twelve hours after rain. Low paddleable levels are to be avoided as the river is constantly rocky. On the other hand, the tree hazard quickly becomes dangerous when the river is high. Careful study of the weather forecast will increase your chance of catching the rather flashy Tavy at a level in between these extremes.

Gauge   If all concrete in the weir at Hill bridge is completely covered, the Tavy is too high. The rapid beside the road below the weir will tell you if there is enough water to paddle without scraping. Don't fool yourself, things only get rockier downstream.

Access   Hill bridge (532804) offers parking for a few cars. There are two possible take-outs; Harford bridge (505768) is the most popular after 5km. The second possibility is to add the enjoyable but much less continuous stretch down into Tavistock to your itinerary. *The take-out options need checking beforehand.* In low paddleable levels it is possible to take out directly upstream of the Tavistock Town Weir by breaking out on river left immediately below the bridge. This allows you to cross the bridge and use the large car park (482743) just downstream on river right. In higher water levels or with an uncertain group, it is best to egress through a small park 100m upstream on river left.
There is no formal access agreement for the Tavy above Tavistock, however objections have almost never been encountered. The Tavy also sees discreet use in summer spate by locals. The Environment Agency have (perfectly reasonably) asked paddlers to avoid scraping down the river in low levels.

Description   There is a weir directly below Hill bridge which usually has a safe route available. A blow by blow description of the following 3km would be meaningless. The paddling consists of non-stop technical manoeuvring around rocks, stoppers, islands and low trees. It can all be 'read' from the eddies by a

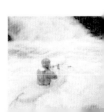

capable group, but be alert for trees which lurk at head height in some channels.

The first distinctive rapid comes where the Tavy narrows over a one metre ledge fall. There is little that stands out for some distance after this, until you reach a pool above an island where the river splits and the gradient increases noticeably. At time of writing (Spring 2003) there has been a tree blocking much of the river above the island for some years. The rapid below needs inspecting on river left and is grade 4 at higher levels. A series of natural weirs lead down into a narrow slot with a grabby stopper. Note that there are bits of metal sticking out of the river bed hereabouts. After gathering your group in the pool below, special care needs to be taken. The following several hundred metres is quite frantic and contains numerous ledge stoppers. More crucially, there are several fallen and low trees which need real caution to avoid. There was a tragic paddling fatality here in 2000. Some of the most dangerous trees have since been cut back but others remain. The river now gradually becomes less technical but the waves and stoppers increase in size all the way down to Harford bridge. If you are taking out here, egress immediately on river right below the bridge. The eddy is small and somebody always drifts off downstream looking sheepish…

Below Harford bridge, the river lacks the quality enjoyed so far. Occasional grade 2 and 3 rapids continue, with one memorable chute below a metal bridge sometimes producing a playspot. A particularly gruesome hazard is Kelly College Weir, *portage on river right*. You are now entering Tavistock and the river becomes increasingly man-made.

The first bridge after the weir portage is long and tunnel-like. It has a weir above it which is runnable with care by a tiny chute close to river right, and a long rapid underneath it. All manner of playspots lurk about here in high river levels.

Contributor:
Mark Rainsley

Be on the look-out for your chosen take-out, which you should have scoped out previously. The last-gasp escape option is the eddy on river left directly below the town bridge and above the nasty Town Weir. A mixed group will want to be off the river before this.

Other important points   The Tavy should not be underestimated and is arguably more challenging than a low water trip down the Upper Dart.

Tavy (Tavistock to Denham Bridge)

Grade	**2+(3)**
Length	**11km**
OS sheet	**201**

Introduction   The section described here has some enjoyable rapids and is regularly paddleable. It has similarities to the Dart Loop and offers an easier alternative which is ideal for coaching. Local experts rate this section for its playboating in flood.

Water level   Paddleable for two or three days after heavy rain has brought the upper Tavy into gear, this trip is possible when the upper sections are too low. On the other hand, it remains fun and relatively safe in full flood (continuous grade 3) when similar sections such as the Dart Loop are flowing through the trees.

Gauge   If it is possible to paddle down the rapids beside the car park in Tavistock, the rest will be fine.

Access   This trip begins in the centre of Tavistock where there are all sorts of parking possibilities. Best option is a large car park (482743) on river right just downstream of the town weir. Also consider beginning on the upper Tavy. Take out on river left at Denham bridge, (477678). There is good parking here.
There is no access agreement for this section of the Tavy. Objections were received from a landowner in the past. However, in the winter of 2002-3 he confirmed that he has no objections to sensible, unobtrusive groups outside the fishing season.

Description   Launching below the town weir, fast easy rapids take you out of town. Watch out for a stopper lurking under one bridge in high water. As you pass the last houses, a series of small drops form a grade 2 rapid.
The Tavy now winds through woodland away from civilisation and roads, with frequent grade 2+ rapids and drops (and some great surf waves in high water). Groups inexperienced on white water will love this. The enjoyable River Walkham enters from river left and shortly after the river bends sharply left and then right below a cliff with a house on top. This is the hardest rapid on the river, a grade 3 slalom through big rocks.
The next hazard is a weir which can be run in most water levels. Inspect and portage if necessary on river left. You are now back in civilisation and houses line the banks. Just before Denham bridge is a tiny sloping weir which produces an enjoyable play wave at all water levels.

Contributor:
Mark Rainsley

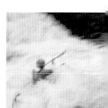

Playboating in the South-West

The South-West is blessed with some of England's finest white water touring; it could be argued that paddlers visiting the area for park'n'play posing have missed the point somewhat. However, there are a number of reasonable playspots which are worth a visit and save the trip along the M4 to the Thames Valley. The best are probably the 'Anvil' weir in the River Dart Country Park and Flowerpots Weir beside the 'Mill on the Exe' pub in Exeter. Info on the Anvil can be found in the Dart Loop river guide, or at www.riverdart.co.uk. Flowerpots (see River Exe guide) is actually two weirs, working throughout winter; a great surf spot on river right on the top weir, and a good playhole on river left on the second weir. Avoid the gnarly tow-back on river right of the lower weir at all costs.

The entries below give some of the possibilities in the region outside the more familiar white water areas.

Woodmill Weir, River Itchen

Playspot

OS sheet **196**

Woodmill Weir (439153) on the River Itchen in Hampshire is a purposely developed concrete ledge which works year-round and depending upon water levels, offers a grippy cartwheel stopper or a spinnable surf wave. Affectionately known as the 'Itchen Death Gorge', this tiny weir is tidal and begins to work from about three hours after high water. The weir is beside Woodmill Outdoor Centre in Swaythling, reached from Junction 5 on the M27. Call the Outdoor Centre's Canoe Shop for further info, telephone 023 8055 5993.

Spetisbury Weir, River Stour

Playspot

OS sheet **195**

Spetisbury Weir (911031) on the River Stour in Dorset has a sluice producing a tiny surf wave that is ideal for beginners. It works through the winter months. The weir is accessed via a footpath from the A350 amongst private property and the locals are very friendly. This will only be maintained if groups are small and quiet; there is no room for more than 6-8 paddlers. If you arrive and there are already paddlers' cars parked, then you will have to try elsewhere. Surfing at Kimmeridge?

Hayle Sluice, River Hayle

Playspot
OS sheet **203**

Hayle Sluice (556374) in Cornwall is a tidal stopper. It works from three hours before high water local time, being best on springs. Two tunnels feed into a large pond over a concrete sill. This creates a beast of a stopper! Both Penzance and Hayle Canoe Clubs use it for training and hold rodeo competitions there. You`ll find it behind Jewsons! Some pictures at www.pzcc.net.

The following are also worth considering:

East Mills Weir near Fordingbridge on the River Avon in Dorset sometimes produces an amazing wave in spate conditions, similar to Hurley's middle gate. However paddlers are not welcome and will receive abuse.

Some paddlers swear by the playspots on many **small weirs on the River Frome** in the centre of Bristol (launch at Frenchay Bridge, (640772) for a 2km trip). Others describe it as a polluted dull ditch.

Some work has been done on **Saltford Weir** on the Bristol River Avon to try to develop a playspot there. At time of writing, the plan is 'on hold'.

Contributor:
Mark Rainsley

Surfing in the South-West

Where - The north coast catches swells with a 6,000 mile fetch from Brazil! In general, the size of the swell decreases heading east from Lands End to the marginal surf breaks of Somerset. There are an almost infinite number of high quality spots to choose from, both reef and beach breaks. Paddlers tend to congregate at extremely popular spots like Newquay in Cornwall and Croyde in Devon, but only a little imagination is needed to avoid the crowds. The south coast breaks are often of dubious quality, with a much smaller fetch across the Channel. Notable exceptions are Bigbury Bay in Devon and the reef breaks at Kimmeridge in Dorset. A useful guidebook to breaks can be found at www.beachwizard.com.

When - Accurately forecasting surf is about as easy as nailing jelly to the ceiling. The north coast is relatively reliable, always having long periods of swell when fronts come in from the Atlantic. The south coast usually requires foul local weather to come into condition, and catching the brief time-span where the wind drops and the waves remain is a frustrating exercise. However, the range of information on weather and conditions available to surfers has improved massively in recent years; in particular, beach web cams allow you to ascertain conditions at a glance. A site that offers tons of forecasts, web cams, and local reports with a distinct South-West bias is www.A1surf.com.

How - Surfing is far more than just a fallback option for when the rivers are dry; it is a sport in its own right, with its own culture, rules and etiquette. This has too often been forgotten by whitewater paddlers and as a result, we have a poor reputation among board surfers. They call us 'Goatboaters'; their stereotyped kayaker shows up by the minibus load and then spreads out all over the break, dropping in on and wiping out others at leisure. Ring any bells? Please remember; we're still just tourists out on the waves. Board surfers have been there longer and do it better. If we are to have any hope of being respected as equals out there, we need to learn some basic etiquette for starters. The BCU Handbook has good advice on this, also try:

Contributor:
Mark Rainsley

www.the-watershed.co.uk/bcusurf.roadrules.htm and www.bodyboardinghq.co.uk/html/etiquette.htm.

A final thought: never, under any circumstances, refer to boardies as 'speed bumps'. They get upset.

The South and East

Contents

Introduction

Look at a map of England and what do you find? To the north and west… mountains, moors and white water rivers. To the south and east… cities, motorways and flat countryside. So what place does the region have in a guide to English white water?

In practice, this is the region where most of England's white water paddlers are based and where they do most of their white water paddling. This has always been the case, from the golden days of slalom paddling to the latter-day era of playboating and freestyle. It's no coincidence that the BCU is based in the region, previously at Addlestone near the Thames, and now at Holme Pierrepont in Nottingham.

Man-made weirs have transformed natural rivers in the region into large, pool-drop rivers with controlled, calm flows interspersed with weirs. These weirs create fast, powerful white water conditions, with waves, holes and wave trains that provide excellent conditions for playboaters and slalomists.

Over the last 20 years we have seen a further remarkable development - the man-made white water course - with the creation of the Cardington, Holme Pierrepont and Nene artificial white water courses.

Small wonder that playboating and white water paddling have become so popular, with playboating venues available all year round. The sport has been taken to the cities and to the people. For many paddlers today, the short drive to the local playspot is a very tempting option when river running in the UK entails a 3-4 hour drive in the hope that the rivers will be at the right level, when most rivers are at their best for only 6-7 weekends each winter.

The following pages are inevitably dominated by the well-known Thames weirs and artificial courses, however, they also contain numerous lesser known venues that are less crowded and provide ideal training grounds.

Finally, what does the future hold? Close co-operation now exists between the BCU and Environment Agency. As a result, there is every chance that the second edition of this book will feature a longer chapter on the South East, East Anglia and East Midlands, to include further new venues. Let's hope so.

Chris Wheeler

South and East
Regional Coordinator
for the Guidebook

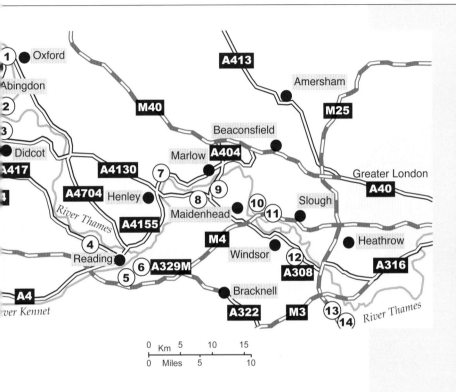

Thames Valley

The Thames Valley

The Thames has been the focal point for white water paddling in the South East over the last 50 years and for the sport generally for longer still. Slalom developed at Hambleden, Shepperton and other weirs and over the years the number of canoe clubs has multiplied, offering everything from slalom, playboating and river running to sprint and marathon. In the mid 1980s, the advent of short plastic boats sparked off the craze for playboating and the popularity of Hurley Weir. Today, every weekend throughout the year, you will see playboaters driving around the Thames Valley in search of white water, Chertsey in the summer, Hurley for most of the year, and as the Thames gets higher and higher, Shepperton, Boulters and Mapledurham.

There is a right of navigation on the Thames and Kennet. However all craft require a licence from the Environment Agency. Fortunately this now comes free with BCU membership.

Thames Valley Weir Comparison Chart

The weirs are listed in the order of which is likely to be working from flood at the top to summer low at the bottom.

River level (no. Hurley gates)	0	1-	1	1+	2-	2	2+	3-	3	3+	4-	4	4+	A	B	C
11 Jubilee																■
4 Mapledurham														■	■	
9 Marlow													■			
10 Boulters												■				
14 Shepperton											■					
8 Hurley					■	■	■	■	■	■						
7 Hambleden							■	■	■	■						
1 Double, Oxford							■	■	■	■						
3 Sutton Courtenay						■	■	■	■	■						
5 County							■	■	■							
6 Blakes						■	■									
12 Old Windsor				■	■											
2 Abingdon	■	■	■	■	■											
13 Chertsey														■	■	

	Not Running		A	High 4 gates
	OK		B	In stanchions
	Ideal		C	Washed out

The Double Weir, River Thames

Location   54 miles north-west of Central London, in South
Oxford, on a backwater just south of Donnington Bridge Road
(522043).

Playspot
OS sheet **164**

Characteristics   A small, double radial (hence the name) that
creates a small, clean, green wave. The wave crests, making it
slightly retentive when the level of the weir pool is not too high.
In short playboats various moves are possible including front and
back surfing, flat spins, low blunts and wave wheels.

Introduction   The Double is perfect for introducing people to
moving water. It's where Chris Wheeler first experienced moving
water, swimming 6 times one Sunday afternoon!

Water level   Medium winter levels, when Hurley is on 2 or 3
gates. Any higher and it washes out.

Access   Head for the southern side of the Oxford Ring Road. At
the roundabout situated between the A34 and A423, follow the signs
northwards for the City Centre, onto the Abingdon Road. After 400m,
turn right at the second set of traffic lights, into Weirs Lane, which
becomes Donnington Bridge Road after 100m. The weir is on the
right, also after 100m. It is possible to park up on the right, off road,
close to the weir. However, parking is limited. An alternative is to
continue along Donnington Bridge Road for a further 300m, taking
you over both the backwater and main river. Take the first left after
you descend after crossing the river and left again and park in the
car park. From here you can walk back to the weir by carrying your boat
over Donnington Bridge and continuing for 200-300m. Alternatively,
you can access the main river from the Riverside Centre's slipway,
then paddle upstream for 400m, turning left into the old Long Bridges
open air pool, heading left then right over the small 'Lasher' weir and
then heading on downstream for a further 300m. It's vital that you
do head right and over The Lasher, because if you go straight on you
will end up approaching the lethal 'Treble' radials. Beware! When the
river is high, relatively little water flows over the Lasher; most of the
flow heads towards the 'Treble' which is to be avoided at all costs!

Description   Looking upstream from the weir pool, and from left
to right, there are 2 walled-in radial gates, with the right-hand

wall protruding about 6m further downstream than the left-hand wall. At the right level, with both gates open, a nice little breaking green wave forms. The right-hand wall creates a very clean eddy line, good for tail squirts. Talking of squirts, it is possible to mystery move here in a squirt boat, but this has its hazards; this is shopping trolley territory.

Other important points   Important! Do NOT mistake The Double for The Treble (the set of 3 radials situated to the right of The Double looking upstream). Here, the weir pool has been scoured out, creating a lethal tow back.

Contributor:

Chris Wheeler and Rob Yates

Hide all valuables if you use the car park behind the Riverside Centre; theft here is rife.

The Riverside Centre is well worth a visit. It contains one of the best canoeing and outdoor shops in the Thames Valley.

Abingdon Weir, River Thames

Playspot

OS sheet **164**

Location   50 miles north-west of Central London and 7 miles south of Oxford, Abingdon is located upstream of the main Thames weir playboating venues. The weir is situated just to the east of the town centre, 200m upstream of the road bridge over the Thames in the town centre (505972).

Characteristics   A steep, high concrete ramp with 10 small radial gates in a row at the top, that generates a retentive stopper that provides an excellent blasting zone.

Introduction   Abingdon provides locals, particularly members of Abingdon's Kingfisher Canoe Club, with a good alternative to the long drive to Chertsey. The weir is however, very much a one-move wonder, the move being the 'blast'. No wonder that the club calls its annual fun rodeo, tongue in cheek, the KCC 'Blast-a-thon'.

Water level   Abingdon is usually at its best from May to July, at about the time that Hurley is dropping from 2 to 1 gates and playboaters are threatening to 'slash their wrists'; in other words, when the Thames is at summer levels, but not too low. Any earlier and the stopper can be very sticky, you will be too busy surviving to pull any controlled moves. Any later, and you may find that all 10 gates are closed.

Access   From Abingdon town centre, follow the signs for Oxford. This will take you off the inner one-way system, north up 'The Vineyard'. After 100m, after traffic lights, at a mini-roundabout, head right following the signs for Radley. After 100m, turn right at the next mini-roundabout into Audlett Drive. After 200m, once the road has gradually veered to the left, take the second right, where there is a community centre and car park. Don't park in the car park, drive past it, turn left and park up just before the entrance to the Territorial Army centre, taking care not to cause an obstruction, and carry your boat from here. Head 20m back towards the community centre and take the footpath to the left. Follow this for 50m as it curves to the right until you reach a small backwater. Go over the small footbridge, turn left and walk a further 50m until you reach the weir.

Description   Looking upstream at the weir from the weir pool, looking from left to right, you will find the playboating venue, followed by two dangerous walled-in radial gates and then a walled-in row of sluice gates, followed finally by the lock. When the river is at the right level, you will find between 1 and 5 gates open. Expect to find alternate gates open (as opposed to two in a row) thanks to a helpful lock-keeper. Each gate forms a small stop-per at the base of the weir, each less than 2m wide, with a thin film of water flowing down over a ramp that is about 30 degrees off hor-izontal, resulting in an excellent venue for blasts. Abingdon may be a one-move wonder, but in the latest 2m long playboats a lot of fun can be had pulling just about every version of the blast imaginable. Stable forward blasts, reverse blasts, blast transition 360s, clean spins, hands only spins and finally the no hands clean spin.
The weir pool is only 2-3 ft deep and is awash with debris. Hand rolling at Abingdon, you run the risk of cutting your hands; it's safer to sit upside down for a while and wait for the boat to stop moving, then gingerly feel the river bed and push off a boulder.

Other important points   The other hazard at weekends con-sists of anglers, who also like the weir pool. However, if you are relaxed about dodging their lines you'll find that boaters and anglers can quite happily co-exist.
You can put in at the road bridge in the town centre, parking in the car park to the south of the road bridge, but expect to find your car broken into when you return. Take care at the usual put in too (it is

Contributor:
Chris Wheeler

a quiet spot aside from anglers' cars) and hide away all valuables. White water intermediates looking for moving water experience may enjoy 'Swift Ditch', a backwater that rejoins the Thames downstream of Abingdon, providing a good 3-4 mile circuit. To get to it, put in above the weir and after about 500m look for a channel on the right, where there is a sudden 1.5m drop. There is an alternative entry channel slightly further upstream, which features a small weir part way along it. The ditch is narrow and tree strewn and does tend to gradually get overgrown over the summer, but is a quiet haven where you can experience moving water, tight moves and breakouts.

Sutton Courtenay Weirs, River Thames

Playspot

OS sheet **161**

Location   Sutton Courtenay weirs are located between the villages of Culham and Sutton Courtenay, 12 miles south of Oxford, and 2 miles south of the town of Abingdon (505944).

Characteristics   There is usually a stopper and wave train which varies from very easy to moderate (depending on water levels) and can be enjoyed by most levels of paddler. At high water levels a second weir (Weir 3) produces a big surf wave / stopper and wave train for the more adventurous.

Introduction   At Sutton Courtenay there are 4 separate weirs, which we have numbered 1-4, paddling upstream from Culham. The weirs bypass Culham Weir.
This venue is well frequented by local clubs as the most user-friendly weir (Weir 2) is open in most water levels.

Water level   Weir 2 is open during most normal water levels. It shuts during low summer levels and is washed out at flood levels. Weir 3 is only opened when the Thames is high.

Access   Take the A415 out of Abingdon and turn right at the traffic lights at the Wagon and Horses pub into Culham Village. Turn right into the large car park next to Culham Lock, immediately before the traffic lights and bridges over the Thames.
Carry your boat across the road and over the stile next to the traffic lights. The easiest place to get in is at the far end of the landing

stage. Paddle away from the lock to the end of the small island and turn right, back on yourself and paddle upstream under the bridge. Paddle upstream until you reach Sutton Courtenay pools. The first pool opens up on your left and has a double radial weir, which is only open in high flows. Continue a little further upstream until the river widens out into the main pool, which has 3 weirs.

There is a footpath from Culham Lock, upstream to Sutton Courtenay from which all the weirs can be viewed (5-10 min walk) but which does flood over when the river is very high.

Description   There are a total of 4 weirs at Sutton Courtenay pools:

Weir 1 - is in a pool by itself. It is a double radial, which is only open in very high water levels. There are a lot of boulders beneath this weir and a nasty stopper can form, so is best avoided.

Weir 2 - is situated in the main pool and is very user-friendly. This weir has two large radials in the middle that are only opened at high flows (when this weir is washed out), with two double smaller radials at each side. One or more of these small radials is usually open in all but the driest summer conditions and makes an excellent playspot for novice and intermediate paddlers, or anyone wanting to practise moving water and stopper skills. At times, slalom poles are hung across the river here (after gaining permission from the landowner) and local slalom paddlers practise on these waves.

Weir 3 - is a large, double radial and only opens during high winter levels when a large surf wave/hole forms (depending on the flow) followed by a good wave train with strong swirling eddies. Not recommended for novice paddlers, but good fun if you like big water.

Weir 4 - is the widest and consists of 3 very big radials. The flow from this weir forms a river-wide stopper between concrete sidewalls and has an anti-scour lip (horrible!). A lot of water comes over this and it should be avoided at all costs. I have watched many trees recirculating in this weir!

Contributor:
Louise Royle

Other important points   Although the weirs can be accessed by a footpath from the corner after the Fish pub, there is very limited parking in Sutton Courtenay so please use the Culham Lock car park for access.

Mapledurham Weir, River Thames

Playspot

OS sheet **175**

Location   Mapledurham is located 40 miles west of Central London, on the western edge of Reading. Mapledurham village, and the stately home of the same name, are situated on the northern side of the river, however the river bank is private and access to the weir is from the southern side of the river via Purley village (668767).

Characteristics   A wide, shallow, open chute in the middle of the weir complex that generates a small, friendly 6.1m wide and 0.6m high wave, part green, part stopper.

Introduction   When the Thames is in spate and the usual venues are washed out, Mapledurham is usually the final refuge for the playboating addict. This is a rare event, but when it happens the weir produces a sweet wave that is small but perfectly formed.

Water level   If flooding is making it onto the 6 O'Clock News and ruining lives, it's time to check out Mapledurham. For there to be any chance of Mapledurham working, Hurley will be on a big scary 4 gates and 'in the stanchions' and Shepperton will be washed out, (although even these conditions are no guarantee). The chances are that the river will be breaching its banks in places. It takes a lot of water to keep the Thames at this level and the river can drop off within 24 hours.

Gauge   There is a (tail) gauge at the downstream end of the lock that is readily visible from the southern bank. The wave is usually at its retentive best when the weir pool level is between 11ft 9" and 13ft 0". The optimum level is probably about 12ft 6". Between 11ft and 11ft 9" the wave gradually starts to get more retentive; above 13ft the wave becomes more and more flushy as it starts to wash out. Check out thamesweirproject.co.uk.

Access   From Reading town centre, head west from the Inner Distribution Road (IDR) following signs for the A329 and Pangbourne. Keep going for 3 miles, and shortly after the 4th roundabout, where the A329 heads right, take a right turn signposted 'Purley Village'. The road takes you down to and over a small humpback railway bridge. Immediately afterwards the road turns to the right, turn left and park up. Straight ahead at the junction, heading north-east, is a footpath along the edge of the village behind gardens. Carry your boat down this track and across a field and after 700m you will arrive at the river, just downstream of the lock, and opposite the gauge. An alternative is to access the river at Riverside Drive. To get there, follow the road to the right instead of parking up, take the first left and then turn right at the end of the road. After 300m, park up in the car park on the left in front of the local community centre. Carry your boat further down the road (marked Private Road) and put on to the river straight ahead. Head upstream; the weir is 500m away.

Description   Sitting in the weir pool below the weir, and looking upstream, from left to right, you will see the lock, followed by concrete shelving, radial gates, more concrete shelving, two more walled-in radials, the playboating wave and then more shelving, combined with small sluice gates. Stick to the wave; other parts of the weir complex can be dangerous. The wave can be accessed from both sides but less energy is required via the right-hand eddy. The eddy is user-friendly, sizeable and calm. The wave is generated by a 6m wide open sluice with a shallow concrete ramp under the water. The weir is set at an angle to the river, and as a result, flow from above bends to the right as it enters the weir, creating an asymmetric wave. Looking upstream, when the gauge reaches 12ft, the right-hand side of the wave consists of a gentle stopper and the left-hand side, a green wave. The upstream ramp of green water is almost horizontal. The result is a very user-friendly venue, excellent for playboating beginners and good for new school moves such as wheels and blunts, although this is not a big powerful wave, and good technique and a 2m boat are required to get genuine 'air time'.

Contributor:
Chris Wheeler

County Weir, River Kennet

Location   Located 35 miles west of Central London, in the centre of Reading, in the heart of the Thames Valley (714730).

Playspot
OS sheet **175**

Characteristics   A small, wide, open ledge on the River Kennet that creates a small, river-wide play feature, ranging from a stopper to a small green wave at different water levels.

Introduction   Many people's first sight of County Weir comes whilst driving at high speed along Reading's IDR (Inner Distribu-

tion Road). This is real 'urban boating'. County Weir generates a small wave and its real value is as an excellent venue for beginners.

Water level   County Weir is usually at its best when Hurley is on around 3 gates, creating a small green wave. At lower levels, the weir creates a small stopper and at higher levels the weir washes out.

Access   Reading has the most complicated one-way system in the world - fact. Good luck! To get to the weir, head in to Reading town centre and onto the IDR. Follow the signs for the Oracle Shopping Centre, which will take you to a roundabout under the IDR where it meets Bridge Street, which is on the southern side of the town centre. It's usually possible to park up on the north-western side of the roundabout from where the weir is visible 50m away, but there is only room for a couple of cars.

Description   Looking upstream from the weir pool, looking from left to right, there is a small lock and then a 13m wide, 0.6m high, open ledge drop. There is a clean eddy on surfer's left, whereas the far side is walled in. The weir produces a small, steep, little green wave at the right levels, or a small stopper at lower levels. The eddy line is well defined and useful for squirt boating but beware, this is supermarket trolley territory.

Other important points   Along the Kennet towpath check out upstream and downstream of County Weir. Doing so, you will find other small weirs that produce small shoots of water that are perfectly suitable for moving water training.

Contributor:
Chris Wheeler

In Reading town centre, 1 mile upstream of the confluence of the Kennet and Thames, is Reading Weir. Sadly, the weir itself is dangerous, although it has potential. Downstream on river left, Reading Canoe Club have set up a slalom training course, with poles set up over moving water on the edge of the weir pool.

Blakes Weir, River Kennet

Playspot

OS sheet **175**

Location   Located 35 miles west of Central London, just to the east of Reading, just before the Kennet joins the Thames (725735).

Characteristics   A small weir on the River Kennet that produces a small chute of water with a sharp eddy line.

Introduction   Blakes Weir has been a popular training ground for local paddlers, including members of Reading University Canoe Club and local scouts.

Water level   Blakes produces moving water at most water levels, although is usually closed in the middle of summer.

Access   From the M4 turn off at Junction 10 following the signs for Reading and the A329(M). Stay on the A329(M), following the signs for Thames Valley Park; don't turn off for Reading. After 3 miles you descend from an overpass to arrive at a roundabout. Go round the roundabout to head right then take the first left. You will arrive at the new boathouse that is the home of Woking-ham CC (amongst others). You will see the River Thames straight ahead of you, paddle upstream, turning left after 600 yds into the Kennet. Blakes Weir is 800 yds further upstream on the right.

Description   Looking upstream, to the left, there is Blakes Lock, then an island, followed by the weir. The chute of water is to the right, immediately next to a wall, which creates a sharp eddy line, which is good for tail squirts and eddy line cartwheels.

Other important points   The new boathouse is an excellent facil-ity and the clubs based there come highly recommended - this is a great place to get started in the sport. There is also a hardcore of serious sprint and marathon paddlers based at the Centre. The Centre is also the home of Marsport, the canoe shop. Marsport specialises in sprint and marathon boats but also stocks a full range of white water equipment.

Contributor:
Chris Wheeler

Hambleden Weir, River Thames

Location   Located 30 miles west of Central London, between Henley and Marlow. The weir is situated at Mill End (south of Hambleden Village) and is the next weir upstream of Hurley. Both these villages are north of the river although the usual access point for visiting paddlers is on the south side of the river (783851).

Playspot
OS sheet **175**

Characteristics   The main weir consists of 4 large radial gates that can, when the weir pool level is low and/or the underwater ramps are raised, generate a large green, partly breaking, wave with big

boily eddy lines. A useful, less crowded, alternative to Hurley.

Introduction   Hambleden was a major white water and slalom venue from the 1940s until, in 1996 the Environment Agency rebuilt the main weir. The new weir was far too efficient resulting in a flushy wave instead of the old classic surf wave and wave train. Following pressure from the local club, Chalfont Park, and the BCU, work was carried out to create underwater ramps that can be raised and lowered using air filled cushions that are pumped up using a cylinder of compressed air. As English White Water goes to press, attempts were being made to solve one problem that had become evident, namely that the ramps could only be kept open for short periods due to the need to maintain a flow of compressed air into the air cushions. As a result, the ramps have been down at their base level most of the time. The good news is that, when the weir pool is low enough, even without the ramps raised, a green, partly breaking, retentive wave does form.

Water level   Normal winter levels, typically when Hurley is on 2 to 4 gates. However, when Hurley is on a high 4 gates and Shepperton has started to work, the chances are that Hambleden will be washed out.

Gauge   The Hambleden wave is not easy to predict, so check the latest news on www.thamesweirproject.co.uk before travelling.

Access   The weir can be inspected from the northern side of the river, where Chalfont Park Canoe Club are based. However, car parking is limited and if you are not a club member then the nearest car park is 500 yds away on the road to Hambleden Village. Visiting paddlers usually access the weir from the southern side of the river. Directions are similar to those for Hurley, Hambleden is the next weir upstream of Hurley, 2 miles further west, heading towards Henley. 3 miles after the Hurley turn off, at a dip in the road at Remenham Hill, turn right following the signs for Aston. Fork right at the Flower Pot pub and carry on until the road ends, at the river, where there is a small car park. From the car park, paddle upstream 500 yds and you will reach the weir.

Description   Looking upstream from the weir pool, from left to right, there is the lock, followed by a small island, 2 small radials,

Hurley in high water

Hurley on two gates

Hurley up close

The Top Wave, Boulters

Installing the Temporary Flume, 2002, Boulters

Cartwheeling in the Canoe Flume, Boulters

Going for it at Hurley

The Blunt

a long tiered concrete shelf, the 4 radial gates of the main weir, another long tiered concrete shelf, 2 further radial gates, further shelving and a further, triple, radial. The weir structure zigzags from one end to the other, at an angle to the river, and as a result the main weir and radials nearest the lock are both tucked into corners with limited access from one side.

The main weir consists of 4 large radial gates which, looking upstream from the weir pool, can be numbered 1-4 looking from left to right. When the weir pool level is low enough and/or the underwater ramps are raised and at least 1 gate is open, the weir generates a wave train which is good for slalom training. Playboaters will want to see at least 2 gates open because this is needed to produce the new Hambleden wave. The top wave can be up to 9m wide and 1.2m high. When the weir pool is relatively low and/or the ramps are raised, the wave can be largely green, at other times the wave can be breaking and very retentive. It is suitable for the basic moves, front and back surfing and flat spins and ends, and new school moves such as blunts are achievable. Though not as good as Shepperton at its best, it is a useful, less crowded and more user-friendly alternative to Hurley.

The other smaller radials are dangerous most of the time, producing retentive stoppers between the stanchions. However, they do provide useful moving water downstream for training and coaching.

Other important points   Beware! At certain levels, typically when the weir pool level is relatively low, the top wave can turn into a very retentive stopper. Check carefully! It should be obvious from the eddy what you are about to let yourself in for.

Contributor:
Chris Wheeler

Hurley Weir, River Thames

Location   Hurley is located 25 miles west of Central London, between Henley and Marlow. The village is situated on the southern side of the river (821842).

Playspot
OS sheet **175**

Characteristics   The main weir consists of 4 radial gates that generate a series of steep, retentive, breaking playwaves/holes.

Introduction   Hurley is arguably the UK's premier playboating venue. Its attractions include its convenient location, the power and consistency of the Hurley wave and the fact that the weir is freely available 7 days a week for up to 9 months a year.

Water level   Normal winter water levels will usually produce 2-4 gates from October/November through to May/June. The Thames is an intensively managed river and levels usually only vary by 0.3-1m even though the total volume of water flowing through all the weirs at Hurley can range from little more than 10 cumecs in summer to 200 cumecs in winter flood.

Gauge   Paddlers either rely on a visual inspection to see how many gates are open or check which gates are open via the Internet. Information is available at www.thamesweirproject.co.uk, www.kayakojacko.com and www.playboating.com. The message board at the former is particularly recommended; this is where you will find the latest up to the minute news and gossip.

Access   From the M4 exit at Junction 8/9 and head north on the A404 (M), following the signs for High Wycombe. Turn off after 4 miles, onto the A423, following the signs for Henley and Hurley. After another mile, turn right into the village of Hurley. Continue to the end of the road, where you will find a car park to the left. From the M40, exit at Junction 4 and head south on the A404, following the signs for Maidenhead. Turn off after 5 miles, following the signs for Henley, heading west on the A423 for 1 mile until you turn into Hurley Village. From the car park, carry your boat northwards on the path to the river for 100m and put in either side of the footbridge. Then paddle upstream (left) until the main (furthest upstream) weir comes into view, below you. See the description and all will become clear!
Please note you are *not* allowed to shoot the radial gates; most paddlers shoot the concrete shelving before they reach the main weir.

Description   There are 3 weirs at Hurley, which link islands immediately north of the lock and lock cut. The downstream weir, the 'buck gates' nearest to the lock, consists of radial gates but this should not be confused with the main weir. Whilst rodeo competitions have been held here, the weir can be extremely dangerous. This is because the weir pool is heavily eroded, causing a retentive stopper to form between the concrete stanchions between the gates. The next (middle) weir upstream consists of vertical sluices, which are not usually of interest.

The main attraction is the furthest, most upstream weir. This consists of 4 radial style gates, situated between concrete shelving. Flow over the northern most shelving is controlled by a row of small radials and the gate nearest to the radials is usually left shut to protect the eddy. The southern shelving extends downstream of the gates by about 3m, boxing in the weir at one end. The river level drops by just under 1.2m at Hurley (one of the smallest drops of any Thames weir). However, with a shallow weir pool, the result is a shallow angled flow of water that produces a wave with a smooth, green trough and white, breaking peak, about 1m high. The gates, with concrete stanchions in between, create a unique series of waves / holes.

More gates are opened as the river rises (looking upstream at the weir, gate 1 is the gate furthest right, running through to gate 4 which is the furthest left, the corner gate).

1 gate - Usually, the lock-keeper will leave open the left hand / corner gate (the fourth gate). This produces a small, breaking wave immediately next to the concrete. 1 gate is generally considered to be suitable for beginners and paddlers new to playboating; forward and backward surfing are possible and there is a good clean eddy line for bow and tail squirts. It is possible to pull flat spins and smears / splats up and onto the concrete shelf.

2 gates - The lock-keeper will usually leave the left-hand gates open, next to the concrete shelf. Gate 3 produces a good cartwheel hole, next to the eddy. Gate 4, in the corner, is more green, with a nice shoulder to the right which is excellent for blunts and blunt / wheel combinations.

If two other adjacent gates are left open instead, you will find that the gates are less retentive. However, in the latest boats, long rides featuring cartwheel and blunts are possible, especially in the left-hand gate.

3 gates - Classic Hurley… everyone loves 3 gates. The right-hand 3 gates are usually left open, producing a symmetrical feature, with eddies either side, which eases eddy congestion. The side gates provide excellent cartwheel holes and the middle gate a flatter, greener wave with shoulders that is excellent for blunts (carved or bounced) and blunt / wheel combinations.

If the left-hand 3 gates are opened instead, at higher water levels the weir can start to behave like 4 gates… more retentive and not

for the faint-hearted. Occasionally, the middle gate produces a perfect 1.6m high green wave. This is rare and happens when the river is rising, and the water level above the weir is relatively high. **4 gates -** Some paddlers prefer the adrenaline rush of 4 gates, with up to 100 cumecs racing through the 4 gates at approaching 10 mph, but it's not for the faint-hearted at higher water levels. Whilst gate 1 can still provide a friendly cartwheel hole at lower levels, the other gates ('The Dark Side') tend to form fast, powerful stoppers. Expect therefore, an adrenaline fuelled cartwheel / full loop tumbling session, very different to the 3 gate chilled blunt experience.

At very high levels, when the river comes close to breaching or breaches the banks, upstream of the weir, the wave forms a heavy stopper. This tends to move upstream until it forms between the concrete stanchions between the gates. At these levels, you can be dragged onto the stanchions and find yourself doing numerous 'unintendos'. Usually, however, at these levels, Shepperton or even Mapledurham will be working.

Other important points   Hurley is very popular and can get very busy at peak times, especially during one weekend in March each year, traditionally the 3rd weekend, when the annual rodeo is held. Please change discretely and quietly, to help maintain good relations with the villagers. Theft from cars in the car park is a regular occurrence. Between Easter and September, you can park in the field next to the weir, which is accessed via the farm; turn left 100m before you reach the car park in the village. Great for BBQs. However, you will pay for the privilege and in theory you are supposed to leave before 6pm.

Contributor:
Chris Wheeler

Marlow Weir, River Thames

Playspot

OS sheet **175**

Location   Marlow is located 25 miles west of Central London (853861).

Characteristics   Sloping concrete ramps situated either side of double radial gates, which can produce various shallow, green waves and stoppers when the river is at the right level.

Introduction   Marlow Weir is a useful option when the Thames is high and the main Thames weirs are not at their best.

Water level   High levels but not too high, Marlow can wash out. Marlow tends to work when Hurley is on a high 4 gates and Shepperton is too high but Mapledurham is not high enough. An alternative worth considering at these levels is Boulters.

Gauge   Check out www.thamesweirproject.co.uk for the latest news of water levels, which may occasionally contain news on Marlow on the message board. The weir and the main wave can be seen clearly, albeit from 100m away, from the suspension bridge in the town centre.

Access   From the M4, turn off at Junction 8/9 and head north on the A404(M) and then the A404. From the M40, turn off at Junction 4 and head south on the A404. Follow the signs for Marlow and the town centre. The High Street, north of the Thames, heads down to a suspension bridge over the Thames. The weir is 100m downstream of the bridge. There is a slipway just downstream of the bridge and upstream of the weir, north of the river. To get to the slipway, head north from the bridge, and take the first right and first right again. Unload, change discretely and then park up as near as you can, preferably not in the nearby pub car park or the 'residents only' spaces!
Alternatively, head southwards across the bridge, then left at the next junction and head for the Longridge Centre, (a Scout outdoor pursuits centre), and ask a member of staff nicely. From here paddle upstream to the weir, staying river left at the lock island.

Description   Looking upstream from the weir pool, you will see the Compleat Angler Hotel on the left. Immediately next to the Hotel is a steep, open concrete ramp that creates a stopper at lower levels and small, green wave at higher levels. At the right level, usually lower levels, the stopper can be friendly and suitable for side surfing and steep forward and reverse blasts. Sometimes, it is best avoided.
Next, further to the right, in the corner there is an open chute. This can be shot from above. At the foot of the chute a nice little green wave can form where flat spins to the left and right are possible. Moving further to the (surfer's) right, there is a long row of small gates above a long, shallow, two-tiered concrete ramp, followed by two dangerous radial gates, followed by a further similar ramp. At the right level, waves form either side of the central two radi-

als, with a shallower wave on the right-hand side and deeper wave on the left-hand side, the latter getting deeper as you get nearer to the radials. Depending on the level, the ramps can generate shallow, green ramps of water leading into stoppers. Flat spins and shallow blunts are possible. The best, deepest spot is usually just to the (surfer's) left of the main radials. Paddlers may find that in higher water the easiest way of getting to the waves (left of the radials) is to work their way across from the eddy next to the hotel. It should be noted however, that the stopper next to the hotel is best avoided at certain levels, and it may be necessary to skirt it with care.

Contributor:
Chris Wheeler

Other important points   It is possible to check out the weir close up by walking round the back of the Complete Angler Hotel, via their car park. The staff at the hotel are friendly but whilst it is possible to get back upstream of the weir via their terrace next to the weir, it is better to carry boats around the hotel, (as we would like them to remain friendly).

Boulters Weir, River Thames

Playspot

OS sheet **175**

Location   20 miles west of London, on the eastern edge of Maidenhead, north of where the A4 and M4 cross the Thames (904827).

Characteristics   During the summer months, Boulters provides a small pour-over, suitable for cartwheels and steep blasts, that provides an alternative summer playboating venue to Chertsey. During the winter months, typically when the Thames is high (and Shepperton on 10 gates and therefore too high to be at its best), the main weir at Boulters can provide two, and sometimes three, consecutive fast-breaking, surging waves.

Introduction   The big Boulters wave used to be the stuff of legends, attracting paddlers from miles around whenever the Thames was high. Sadly, in 1999 the wave was lost when the Environment Agency replaced the old weir with a new 4 gate structure, situated about 3m further upstream. The new gates are too efficient for their own good, pushing water through so fast that the wave has been flattened, and whilst at certain levels waves can form, they are not in the same league as the big, old wave. However, local paddlers working with the BCU have now created a small pour-over facility to one side of the main weir, which provides a useful summer facility, albeit not for the faint-hearted.

Water level   Summer levels - when Hurley is down to 0 or 1 gate. Winter levels - high, when Shepperton is typically on 10 gates and slightly too high but Mapledurham not quite high enough (Boulters can wash out if the Thames is too high).

At the time of writing, local paddlers were busy assessing the optimum head and tail gauge levels during the winter months (these gauges being readily visible at the lock). The provisional results suggest that the optimal level is 23.6/22.2 and that at least one retentive wave should be present between around 23.5/22.0 and 23.8/22.3. This is assuming that, at the time, the 4 main weir gates are open and unobstructed.

Gauge   Information is available at www.thamesweirproject.co.uk and www.kayakojacko.com.

Access   Head for Maidenhead town centre. From there, follow the signs for Slough and the A4, this will take you eastwards. Just before the bridge over the Thames, turn left immediately after the petrol filling station, into Ray Mead Road (A4094). Drive along the road for about 500m (with the river on your right) until you reach the lock. Turn into the car park on your left, which is signposted. From here, carry your boat across the road, launch and paddle upstream. Turn right at the upstream end of the island and you will find the weir straight ahead of you. Paddle downstream, aiming for the right-hand end of the weir and portage down to the weir pool.

Description   Looking upstream from the weir pool, the pour-over is situated towards the left-hand (river right) end of the weir, between boards, towards one end of a long, concrete tiered shelf. To the right, further away, is the main weir, consisting of 4 large gates. The pour-over has been created by adding a structure to channel a chute of water over the concrete, producing a powerful flume of water entering the weir pool at a steep angle. The result is a very retentive feature that is good for ends and steep blasts but not for the faint-heated. This is not the ideal venue for beginners or solo-paddling. It may be that in the future permanent changes will be effected to make the pour-over more user-friendly.

Turning to the main weir, during the winter, when the Thames is high and all the main weir gates are opened, up to three waves can form. Firstly, a retentive top wave sometimes appears, that is good for flat spins and blunts. A second wave, and sometimes a third wave, can also form downstream, next to the surfer's right eddy, that are powerful and surging, like natural, high volume river waves. These waves are hard to master, but once mastered most of the new school hole and wave moves are possible, particularly on the second wave, which appears to work most frequently of the three. However, the weir is unpredictable and it is worth checking out the websites before travelling.

Other important points   The corner of the weir complex, between the main weir and side weirs parallel to the flow, is very dangerous. Do not access the top wave from the surfer's left side (river right) of the main weir unless the small radials in the corner are closed and even then, be very careful, the weir has killed in the past.
The Kayakojacko Freestyle event at Boulters has become an established event in the Freestyle calendar, held every September. Intended as a more relaxed, fun event, in 2002 there were temporary design modifications that made the feature more user-friendly.

Contributor:
Chris Wheeler

Jubilee River, River Thames

Playspot

OS sheet **175**

Location   A new 11km long flood relief channel that leaves the Thames immediately upstream of Boulters Weir and re-joins the Thames 1.5km downstream of Windsor and Eton.

Characteristics   A large man-made channel (as big as the Thames) that has been designed to look like a natural river, meandering its way along between shallow reed beds. Along the river there are 5 weirs. The main weir of interest, Slough Weir, consists of an open concrete ramp that can create a suitable pour-over feature in very high water.

Introduction   The Jubilee River, which was completed in 2002, was built to alleviate the flood risk to Maidenhead, Bray and Windsor.

Water level   When the Thames is bursting its banks, the channel has the capacity to cope with high flows, and at these times, when the usual playboating venues are all washed out (even Mapledur-ham), the channel can be worth checking out.

Gauge   The Jubilee River is only worth considering when all the talk on the www.thamesweirproject.co.uk message board is of weirs being too high and washing out.

Access   Of the 5 weirs on the Jubilee River, the one weir of interest is the fourth weir, running downstream, called 'Slough Weir', which is the one that is clearly visible from the M4. It is on the Slough to Eton road. Exit the M4 at Junction 6 and follow the signs for Eton. This will take you north and eventually south back under the M4. At the next roundabout, park in the car park next to the roundabout. This overlooks the weir.
The final fifth weir has potential and is close to Slough Weir. It can be found north of the Thames, at Black Potts Viaduct, just off the B3026 between Eton and Datchet. From Slough Weir, head south towards Eton and take the first turn left following the signs for Datchet. The road crosses the channel just to the east of Eton School's sports centre and playing fields. Take either towpath southwards/downstream.

Description   Weir 1 - Situated under the road at the start. This a lethal looking walled-in double radial.
Weir 2 - 1 mile downstream, this is another fairly unpleasant looking walled-in radial weir, situated just before a road bridge.
Weir 3- An open concrete ramp with fish pass, that creates a small stopper at the bottom. Similar to Slough Weir, but not next to a road.
Weir 4 - A concrete ramp, this is the one that you can see from the M4, by looking southbound, heading westbound, just before Junction 6. When the Thames is high, this creates a small pour-over that is OK for blasts and spins but little else because the weir pool is shallow. The stopper can also be very retentive so take a throw line and a friend. At very high levels, when even Mapledurham is washed out, the weir pool can become deep enough for vertical moves, and at the same time the stopper can become more friend-ly. Not the best playboating venue in the Thames Valley perhaps, but better than nothing when everything else is washed out.
Weir 5 - Another concrete ramp immediately downstream of where the Windsor to Staines railway bridge goes over the chan-nel, shortly before the channel re-joins the Thames. This has a

Contributor:
Chris Wheeler

smaller drop than Slough Weir and would appear to wash out flat when the Thames is very high. It might produce a pour-over feature at the right level but at the time of writing this was unproven.

Old Windsor Weir, River Thames

Playspot

OS sheet **175**

Location   Old Windsor Weir is located 20 miles west of Central London between Windsor and Staines, just to the east of Old Windsor Village (989754).

Characteristics   The main weir consists of an 'L' shaped weir. The upstream part of the weir (running at right angles to the flow) features a row of 8 radial gates creating a series of narrow, surfable waves.

Introduction   A few years ago Old Windsor Weir was a regular venue for slalom competitions and a popular playspot. With the decline in slalom and the rise of new school playboating, the weir is now little used and generally considered unsuitable for the latest playboat moves. It does offer a good introduction to powerful boily water and has some, albeit limited, interest for the modern playboater.

Gauge   Paddlers rely on a visual inspection to see how many gates are open. One radial gate equates to 1-2 gates at Hurley.

Access   From Windsor head out on the A308 towards Staines. When you get to a roundabout with the B3102 to Datchet, keep going on the A308 for 100m and turn left into Church Road. After another 500m and a left-hand bend, turn left again into Ham Lane. When you get to the iron bridge over the lock cut, park. Paddle 500m up the cut (to the left) and you will find yourself upstream of the weir.
From Staines exit at Junction 13 on the M25. Follow the signs for the A308 (Runnymede Road) towards Windsor. Drive through Runnymede (open grassland next to the Thames) and over a mini-roundabout. Continue past the roundabout for a further half mile and turn right down Church Road. Directions continue as above.

Description   The weir features a row of 8 radial gates, with two groups of smaller gates on either side. It is best to wait until there is at least one radial gate open before bothering, for which the Thames needs a reasonable flow, (there must be at least one gate open at Hurley Weir). Each radial creates a long, fast and narrow wave, where one can front surf, loop and (just about) flat spin. The weir is at its best when just one radial gate is open, in which case the wave is at its biggest and the eddies are more manageable. As more radial gates open, the weir pool level rises and the features become smaller and eventually flatten out.

When the Thames is at lower flows, the surfer's right (river left) set of small gates sometimes produces a useable stopper. It is good for practising side surfing skills and not much else. There is some dubious subsurface ironwork, responsible for a few broken paddles and ripped dry cags over the years. At certain levels the stopper can be very sticky and closed in. This is an option for the keen (or desperate).

Contributor:
Andy Levick

Other important points   Theft from cars parked by the lock used to be common… so be careful.

Chertsey Weir, River Thames

Location   15 miles south-west of Central London, 2 miles to the south-east of the M25/M3 interchange (054670).

Playspot
OS sheet **176**

Characteristics   A small, friendly pour-over that provides a popular summer playboating venue. During the winter months when the Thames is high, waves can form at Chertsey either side of the summer pour-over, with a very retentive stopper forming to the far left and a shallow surf wave forming to the right.

Introduction   For several years now, Chertsey has been a popular summer playboating venue for Thames Valley boaters starved of their usual Hurley fix. The pour-over provides a steep, narrow chute of water that is suitable for beginners and more experienced paddlers who want to stay paddling fit.

Water level   Summer levels - Hurley will be on 0 or 1 gate. Winter levels - Hurley will be on a very high 4 gates.

Gauge   Check out the websites at www.thamesweirproject.co.uk and www.kayakojacko.com for news.

Access   From the M25 turn off at Junction 11 and head in the direction of Central London on the A320. Follow the signs for Chertsey and then Shepperton. These will take you left at the first roundabout, right at a 'T' junction and then over Chertsey Bridge (over the Thames). Immediately after the bridge, turn left. Park where you can within the first few hundred metres and hide all valuables. Put in upstream of the lock, head river right and portage.

Description   The pour-over is located in the middle of the weir complex, between concrete walls. During the summer, when Hurley is down to 0 or 1 gate, Chertsey produces a friendly, steep flume of water. The wave is small, but powerful and steep enough for cranking end after end and for steep blasts. Some wave moves are possible, but Chertsey couldn't exactly be described as a green wave venue. There are clean eddies either side of the flume. In high water, waves can start to form at the base of the concrete ramps either side of the pour-over. A very retentive stopper can form to the far surfer's left and to the right of the pour-over, a shallow, green wave that is less retentive. Chertsey can therefore be worth checking out when Shepperton is too high.

Contributor:
Chris Wheeler

Shepperton Weir, River Thames

Playspot
OS sheet **176**

Location   15 miles south-west of Central London, on the edge of Greater London, close to the M3 and M25. Shepperton village and weir are located on the northern side of the river (073658).

Characteristics   One of the biggest weirs on the Thames, the main Shepperton Weir consists of 10 vertical sluices in a row, which, when the conditions are right, produce a large, powerful, challenging, bowl-shaped, green wave.

Introduction   The legendary Shepperton wave is generally reckoned to be one of the best playwaves in Europe, and with good reason. When the conditions are right, with approaching 100 cumecs dropping 2.5m through the middle 8 gates, the weir generates an awesome 12m wide, 1.6m high, bowl-shaped wave with breaking central pile and well defined green shoulders. If you can handle it, this is the perfect venue for pulling all the latest new school, green wave moves.

Water level   The downside of Shepperton has always been that that perfect wave is so illusive. Not only do you need high water levels (when Hurley is typically on a high 4 gates) but the relative difference in levels between water above and below the weir needs to be right… and this can change by the hour. Shepperton might work at any time between November and April, but only for a total of 2-3 weeks in an average year.

Gauge   Check out the latest news on www.thamesweirproject.co.uk or www.kayakojacko.com.

Access   From the M25 turn off at Junction 11 and head in the direction of Central London on the A320. Follow signs for Chertsey and then Shepperton. These will take you left at the first roundabout, right at a 'T' junction and then over Chertsey Bridge (where you can catch a glimpse of Chertsey Weir to your left). After the bridge, go straight over one roundabout and right at the next roundabout and then take the next right. As you arrive in the village, take a right-hand turn signposted 'Ferry Lane'. Follow this road down to the river, follow the road round to the right and then park up in the spaces either side of the road. The lock is immediately to your left. Carry your boat over the right-hand/ upstream lock gate and follow the path for 100m until you reach the weir.
From Central London head to Shepperton village. At a small roundabout, head south through the old village, soon after which you will see Ferry Lane on your left.

Description   Shepperton consists of a lock on the northern side of the Thames, with 2 weirs, which are linked together by an island. The main weir is the nearest weir to the lock. The 2nd weir is also a sluice weir that can produce a wave in high water. The main weir is one of the largest weirs on the Thames. The weir consists of 10 vertical sluice gates in a row, either side of which are concrete shelves, followed by 10 ft high concrete walls. The side stoppers are best avoided. However, these also serve to protect the side eddies and enable paddlers to get onto the main wave. The sluices generate a variety of conditions depending on levels.
1-4 gates - Whilst you will get a green wave, usually, the wave is not sufficiently retentive for playboating, although it does provide useful moving water for the local slalom paddlers.

5-8 gates - This is where the wave gets interesting. Generally, 7 or better still, 8 gates produce the big classic wave described in the introduction. Perfect for all the new school moves (air blunts, the lot), the wave is fast, powerful and violent. The gates create a ribbed wave, causing bounce that, once mastered, can be used to get lift for those air moves. Paddling up the eddies (most people use the near side, right-hand eddy) can be hard work, but it's worth it. As the level drops and the gates are closed down to 7,6 and 5 gates, the wave narrows down but is still worth checking out. Bear in mind that on a high 8 gates the weir can be hard work, with a tough battle to get up the ever-shrinking eddy line only to get a good work out on a fairly surging, violent, breaking wave.

9-10 gates - This is where the wave can get scary. On a low 10 gates expect a very 'grippy' stopper, where you can get ends but in practice it can turn into a survival exercise, which some of the more masochistic locals revel in. Plan your exit from the stopper and get a run up from the pile, heading down into the trough and outwards towards the right-hand eddy. Get out before you're too tired! You won't always succeed, in which case the wave will drag you back into the middle of the stopper!

High 10 gates - At this level the weir can flatten out so that the water only drops 0.3-0.6m. At these levels the weir gets friendlier. Whilst you won't get the classic green wave, flat spinning and blasting are easy and catch the right sweet spots and clean ends are there to be done. Any more water and the weir washes out.

Other important points   Solo paddling is not recommended at Shepperton. After paddling up the eddy, you paddle up onto a cushion before paddling hard, at a diagonal angle onto the wave. A lapse of concentration and you can easily slip off the wrong side of the cushion into the side stoppers, which can hold you at certain levels.

If the car park is full there are places where you can park on the road but please park considerately and change discretely.

There is a pub 100m upstream of the lock, on the same side of the river, which has a garden overlooking the river. Two miles to the east, at Shepperton Marina, on the same side of the river is a good shop (White Water the Canoe Centre). Other facilities at the lock include public coin operated WCs and a tea shop.

Shepperton Slalom Canoe Club is based at the weir. The club holds slalom competitions on the weir, typically in March and June.

Contributor:
Chris Wheeler

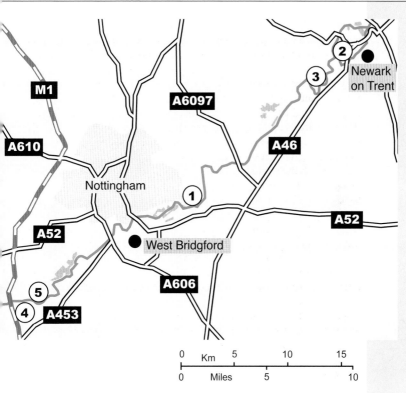

Trent Valley

Introduction

Many paddlers don't realise the playboating potential of the Trent Valley; everyone knows about the slalom course at Holme Pierrepont, but not so many people know that there are some incredible playwaves in the area. The weirs tend to work at higher water levels, often when the slalom course has been closed because of poor water quality. A lot of paddlers have been taken down by stomach upsets (the 'Trent trots') after paddling the weirs, so take sensible precautions: wash as soon as you get off the water, wear a nose clip and earplugs and try not to swallow any water.

The water levels are taken from an electronic gauge downstream of Nottingham. If you're in the area and levels are high, then either drop into the slalom control office or Desperate Measures, ask what the Trent's flowing at and then get out there and get amongst it. Alternatively check out the levels on the website www.hppslalomcourse.co.uk *before travelling*.

Holme Pierrepont, River Trent

Artificial WW Course

OS sheet **129**

Location   Located in the East Midlands, on the south-east edge of Nottingham, on the south side of the River Trent.

Characteristics   An artificial white water course approximately 800m long, with a drop of 7m, that consists of a series of drops and pools. Whilst the course was originally designed with slalom in mind, it is suitable for slalom, playboating, rafting and squirt boating, as well as an excellent venue for coaching and practising river running skills.

Introduction   The course was opened in 1987 as part of the National White Water Centre, primarily as a slalom training facility. Subsequently, the British Canoe Union moved its headquarters from London and they are now based in buildings at the start of the course. The centre also features a regatta course that is used for rowing and kayak/canoe sprint and marathon racing. The course itself consists of a concrete channel that bypasses the nearby Colwick Sluices on the river.

Water level   A full release typically consists of 28 cumecs. Lower flows may be set in summer, although this does not normally

have a significantly detrimental effect on the course. Lack of water
is very rare. However, during the winter, when the Trent is too
high, the course can start to wash out from the downstream end
of the course upwards, submerging the usual river features.

Gauge   Signs at the start of the course, outside the office and
changing rooms, state the flow for the day. In winter it is worth
checking the levels by phoning 0115-982-4717 or visiting the website: www.hppslalomcourse.co.uk.

Access   From the south and M1, turn off at Junction 24, following
the signs for Nottingham South (A453), heading east. After 8 or 9
miles, join the A52 heading south and follow the signs from there
to the National Water Sports Centre, it is well signposted. As you
arrive at the Centre, follow the signs to the left for the white water
course and keep going until the end of the road.
From the north and M1, turn off at Junction 26 and follow the signs
for the City Centre and then the National Water Sports Centre.

Description   The course is an excellent, safe, white water facility,
providing slalom paddlers and playboaters with a short, artificial
white water 'river' consisting of a series of pools and small drops,
interspersed with islands. Highlights are as follows:
The top wave - The pool upstream of the course narrows under a
bridge, under which there is a 4m wide, small wave/stopper between high concrete walls with no eddies. The wave is small but
retentive and in the latest playboats, blunts and ends are possible.
The first pool - This has recirculating eddies either side of a small
wave. A good quiet spot for playboaters to do eddy line cartwheels and for squirt boaters to mystery move.
River left hole - There are two waves immediately below the first
pool on river left. The first wave is green but shallow, the second
features a hole that is good for ends, that can be entered with a
wave wheel. Immediately downstream is a small concrete island
that is good for splats and smears.
A series of shallow green waves - These are good for carving and
wave wheels; flat spins are possible, but not easy.
The pyramid rock and wave - These are immediately downstream
of the waves, just before the next pool. The rock is on river right
and the wave on river left/middle. Surf across the wave from
the river left eddy and sit in the small eddy above the pyramid,

where you can pull splat wheels.

The pool below - This features a clean eddy on river left and a boily, surging eddy on river right, which is challenging in squirt and slalom boats. Leaving the pool, and passing under a foot-bridge, there are two successive small holes on river left.

'The Looping Pool' - Named after the old school loops generated by re-entering the main wave from the river left eddy. The wave has also proved to be an excellent mystery move venue for squirt boaters, the better paddlers travelling the full length of the pool underwater. Recent changes have created a narrower, pour-over type drop that is retentive and good for vertical hole moves.

'The Muncher' - Leaving the Looping Pool, there are two small holes before the water drops into The Muncher. Enter direct or break out on river left and join the queue. The stopper is on river right/middle, and turns green towards the river left eddy. River right provides a release point but a minimal eddy. All hole moves are possible. On washing off the wave, break out as quickly as you can on river left and either paddle back up round the river left side of the island or climb over the island.

Bottom Stopper - The main flow heads river right of another island, passing another small concrete island that is good for splats. The course then veers right, with the river right flow dropping into a retentive stopper, which is hard work and not for the faint-hearted.

Final pool - There is a nice, small, green wave at the upstream end of the pool. Break out on river left and walk back up to the top of the course.

Other important points   *The course can be modified and the above details may change. Paddlers should inspect the course before paddling.*
On arrival you must go to the course office to register and pay a fee. Paddlers are required to prove that they are Grade 3 standard, (see www.hppslalomcourse.co.uk for details).

The River Trent is not the cleanest river in the UK. Read the advice posted at the Centre and take all the usual precautions.

Sadly, the car park is no safer than any other. Hide all valuables, better still, use the lockers provided in the changing rooms.

Check out in advance if the course is open to the public. The course's main 'raison d'etre' is to provide a venue for elite slalom training, so many weekends are booked for competitions and squad training. The course is floodlit in the evenings.

Contributor:
Chris Wheeler and
Rob Yates

Newark Weir, River Trent

Location   Just outside the town centre of Newark-on-Trent.

Playspot
OS sheet **121**

Characteristics   It forms a clean green wave (or at least as clean and green as a flooded Trent wave can be) on either side of the concrete steps in the centre. There is good eddy access and a clean run-out.

Introduction   Newark Weir is *the* spot to head for if the river's flowing that bit higher than normal, an ideal introduction to the murky brown world of Trent weir boating.

Water level   If the level's just a bit too high for the HPP slalom course to be running, take a half hour drive to Newark. The wave generally works between about 2.1 and 2.4 on the gauge, though it has been known to work anywhere between 1.8 and 2.6, depending on the relative flows above and below the weir (the only way to be certain is to go and look). When the level is too high, the weir closes out and becomes desperate and dangerous, the waves becoming uniform stoppers with boxed in ends. Apparently a play hole forms in the middle at massive flood levels, but with that much water about you can probably find something better to do...

Access   Follow the B6166 into town and turn left immediately after the marina. Follow the road until you see Mill Lane on your left, then cross the humpback bridge to a small car park by the river (792537).

Description   When it's working, there are two separate waves, both with good eddy access. They're formed by water shooting over a concrete kicker ramp, so they're only a couple of inches deep. If you do catch an edge it's too shallow to capsize, so you just wash off the back of the wave into deeper water.
As for the moves, it may be a bit shallow to do much work on your donkey flips, but you can spin and blunt to your heart's content. The surfer's right face is faster and smoother, an ideal spot to sort out your clean spins. The surfer's left side is a bit steeper and has a more pronounced shoulder to play with for the big blunts.

Contributor:
Pete Cornes

Other important points   The usual caveats apply: *please* change discreetly, park sensibly and try not to upset anyone, especially

anyone local. Don't be tempted to get on if the level's too high; the stopper is dangerous and you can't pull any moves in it anyway. Be aware that Newark can get really busy, especially at weekends, and that was before anyone stuck it in a guidebook!

Farndon Weir, River Trent

Playspot

OS sheet **121**

Location   Just outside the village of Farndon on the A46, about ten minutes outside of Newark, heading towards Nottingham.

Characteristics   It's best described as a bigger version of the plughole (the stopper above the Muncher on the slalom course), even down to not having an eddy.

Introduction   If Newark's just that bit too high and you're absolutely bursting to go paddling, that's the time to get out to Farndon. The lack of an eddy means that you'll very seldom meet other paddlers there.

Water level   Farndon tends to go at those levels where you drive to Newark fully expecting the wave to be going and arrive to find that it's stoppered out. This tends to be about 2.4 on the gauge.

Access   Turn off the A46 in Farndon village and find the river-side car park in Farndon (768521). You'll need to paddle down-stream about a kilometre to see if the wave's working; if it isn't, at least you've had some exercise!

Contributor:

Pete Cornes

Description   The playspot's on the far river-left side of the river; the rest of the weir is a sloping affair with a thin film of water cascading over. It's got a big smooth shoulder for carvey right-hand blunts and a smooth stopper for left-hand blunts... and no eddy. If you wash out, you're walking back up!

Sawley Weir, River Trent

Location   Just outside Sawley, about 10 miles west of Nottingham.

Playspot
OS sheet **129**

Characteristics   A big, green, difficult to attain wave with good eddy access.

Introduction   The Trent's flagship weir, made famous by Peak's ID10T video, is urban boating defined: muddy brown water full of sewage, a concrete landscape and within sight of the M1…and a wave good enough to make you forget where you are.

Water level   The Trent needs to be high, over 3m on the gauge.

Access   To get there, find the B6540 as it passes under the M1 and then over the Trent. The pub at Sawley Marina don't object to you parking there if you go in for a drink or a meal (and a chance to wash off the river water), but they ask paddlers not to get changed in the car park. When you're ready, carry your boat back to the road bridge over the lock (471309) and then along the cut to the river proper.

Description   At normal high flows (above 3m on the gauge) the legendary green monster wave forms on river left. The face must be about five feet high and offering one of the smoothest surfs in the country. Bounced blunts are a no brainer and it's a common error to clean spin by accident. It is though, quite difficult to establish a surf. You need a reasonably long boat and a bit of perseverance, it's not just a case of paddle hard and hope for the best. Watch the locals, figure out what they're doing and brace yourself for some confused water on the run out, big waves and a strong, squirrely eddy line. The stoppery feature on river right can be quite good fun, but there are allegedly spikes in there, it's very shallow and there are no eddies. In very, very high flood, the wave disappears and a massive, legendary broken wave forms on river right. You'll need a strong stomach, though!

Contributor:
Pete Cornes

Other important points   At the height of the 2001 floods, a group of paddlers were ordered off the wave by police helicopter… the traffic on the M1 was slowing down to watch, and causing massive tailbacks!

Trentlock, River Trent

Playspot

OS sheet **129**

Location   About ten minutes away from Sawley weir.

Characteristics   Various features at various levels. The main play feature is a reasonably small wave which forms on river right.

Introduction   If you've driven all the way over to Sawley and it's not going, then it's worth taking a look at Trentlock. There is reasonably easy eddy access to the wave.

Water level   The wave seems to form most cleanly when Sawley is not quite high enough, usually just under 3m on the gauge.

Access   From Sawley, carry on driving north along the B6540 and take the first right, signposted to Trentlock. There's a large car park at the end of the road (489312). You'll need to put on the river and paddle down to just above the main weir (about a kilometre) and then bank inspect to see whether it's working or not. Afterwards, you'll need to paddle back upstream.

Contributor:
Pete Cornes

Description   A small wave forms on river right which allows for spins and roundhouses. The eddy line below is generally quite turbulent. There's also a nice wave on river left, but it kicks out into a concrete wall, so you really don't want to be capsizing in there!

Other important points   If the wave's not working there are two different pubs at the put-in, so you can console yourself with a ham sandwich and a pint of mild.

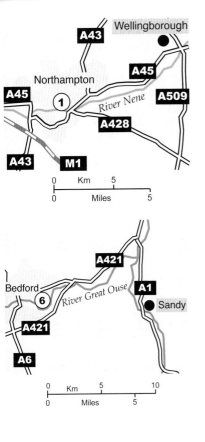

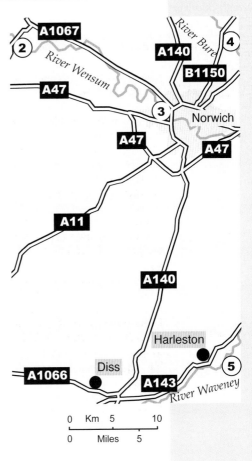

Eastern Counties

Nene White Water Centre, River Nene

Artificial
WW Course
OS sheet **152**

Location   Located 70 miles north-west of Central London, close to the M1, on the south side of Northampton.

Characteristics   Holme Pierrepont's little brother, a small volume, shallow, grade 2, 'U' shaped artificial white water course featuring a variety of small waves, drops, holes and eddy lines.

Introduction   The Nene White Water Centre is the most recent addition to the growing number of artificial white water courses in the UK. It provides a convenient venue for paddlers in the South East that is best suited to beginners and intermediates, although the local expert playboaters are pulling impressive sequences of moves in the best playholes.

Water level   Flows of up to 5 cumecs are possible, much less than Holme Pierrepont (28) and the Tryweryn (11). You will want at least 2, (but preferably all), of the 3 pumps to be running, otherwise the upper part of the course can get very shallow.

Gauge   For daily information on levels, call the information line on 01604-634040.

Access   From the M1, turn off at Junction 15A and join the A45 following the signs for Wellingborough. After 3 miles, turn off the A45 following the signposts for the City Centre and Bedford. Follow the signs for Bedford (A428). You will go over the River Nene and see the 'Eighth Earl Spencer Centre for Young People' building on the right, however, there is no right turn here. Continue for 500m until the next roundabout. Go right round the roundabout and head back down the same road. Just before you reach the bridge over the river again, turn off to the left, and then immediately afterwards, turn right. The Nene White Water Centre is round the corner of the building, fronting the river.

Description   The course is a 200m long, 'U' shaped course next to the River Nene. A channel from the river leads to 3 pumps at the start of the course. The course then runs parallel to the river before turning back on itself and returning to the start. At the halfway mark, there is another, smaller feed from the river. The course starts with a series of 3 progressively larger stoppers, each small and friendly enough for hand paddling (each drop is no more than 1.5m high). The flow then drops down a 1.8m high ramp of water into the first pool. Boulders have been added to create a good hole that, when paddling boats under 2.5m in length, is deep enough for vertical moves. The pool marks the halfway mark, where there is a small extra feed from the river. From here, the course doubles back on itself past boulders on either side where you can make breakouts and work your way back upstream. You then arrive at the second pool, which is good for eddy line cartwheels.

After the pool, there is another (0.6m) drop into a small stopper, with eddies either side, that is good for flat spins.

Next is the third pool. Water entering the pool is squeezed through a narrow channel in the centre of the river creating another pour-over feature, which is good for blasts, cartwheels and old school enders.

Downstream, there is the final drop, where the water drops 1m to create a small, green wave, followed downstream by the 'Splat Rock'. From the final pool, it's a short portage back to the start.

Other important points   The entry fee is currently £6 for those with a Nene users card and £7 for those without. Paddlers must prove that they are sufficiently competent to paddle the course by either presenting a BCU 3 Star certificate (or higher) or passing an in-house test. The Centre provides a car park, changing facilities and a café. Expect rafts and private parties before 1pm then kayakers only.

Contributors:

Chris Wheeler and Rob Yates

Slalom and freestyle events are held at the course.

Swanton Morley, River Wensum

Location   About 10 miles north-west of Norwich on the River Wensum. The last weir is underneath the road bridge (021185). Walk 100m up the footpath (river left) to reach the fast moving section.

Playspot
OS sheet **133**

Characteristics   A fast flowing section of the River Wensum with two weirs. One produces a broken pour-over type hole, the other is a long ramp which produces small stoppers and small surfable waves at higher levels.

Introduction   For a number of years, an annual Div 3/4 slalom

has been held on this stretch of water. This is a good place for clubs to run an introduction to moving water session, but not worth a long journey.

Water level   The fast flowing section and the weirs are paddleable at all levels other than summer lows, but as a general rule the higher the water, the better it gets.

Access   Follow the Fakenham road (A1067) out of Norwich. About a third of a mile after the first Bawdeswell turn off, turn left onto the B1147 towards Swanton Morley. Follow this road for 2½ miles through Bylaugh wood and you'll meet the river as it runs alongside the road on your right for 200m before going under the road bridge. There is ample off-road parking hereabouts. There is a large muddy lay-by on the right just before the bridge and another on the right just after the bridge, however the latter is the entrance to a property so please maintain access. There is a footpath on river left upstream from the road bridge; walking 100m or so up this path you reach suitable launch sites on the fast moving water section.

Description   This is a grass-banked section of river with long sweeping bends about 1m deep. There are two offshoots splitting left from the main channel, both of which have impassable shoots or weirs and are not worth exploring.
The main channel consists of a fast flowing left-hand bend at the end of which is the first weir. This is a broken affair which creates quite a sticky hole about 6m wide with a shootable tongue about 3m wide on river left. In particularly high water this can be quite a mean beast with a large tow back and retentive hole. This said, it remains fairly shallow in all conditions.
After this there is around 30m before the second weir in the series. The second weir under the triple arched road bridge is a long sloping ramp. At low to medium water this is just a drop with three small stoppers. In high water it usually forms three small waves under the three bridge arches. These are surfable, but are shallow and there is an upstand of steel piles at the lip of the ramp.

Contributor:
Jasmine Waters

Other important points   In the most extreme of conditions, at the highest water levels, this drop is *rumoured* to produce an exceptional surf wave.

Hellesdon Mill, River Wensum

Location   Four miles north-west of Norwich's city centre on the River Wensum. The mill is on Hellesdon Mill Lane, a small lane off the by-road, which joins New Costessey and Hellesdon (198104).

Playspot
OS sheet **134**

Characteristics   Hellesdon Mill is a disused mill with four sluiced arches. Usually only the middle two sluices are open. Looking upstream to the mill, the left of these produces a moderately retentive hole, ideal for most new school hole moves. The smaller right arch forms a simple jet.

Introduction   Though Hellesdon Mill has hosted a Div. 5 slalom event it is more suited to playboating and under most conditions is the best playspot in Norfolk. There is a Rodeo event held here, over two days each summer (see BCU freestyle website for details). If you want to meet other Norfolk paddlers, then this is the place to go. It is very easily accessible and safe with no nasty sting in the tail.

Water level   To work, these hydraulics need medium to low water levels. They will wash out very quickly as the river rises above medium levels. The larger of the shoots is usually best when the water level is dropping and when the smaller river left sluice is shut.

Gauge   You can see the mill from the bank, but as a guide there is a large old millstone on the first 'beach' area below the mill pool. If the mill stone is showing above the water, the mill should be working, if it's mostly or completely out of the water it should be at a very good level. If the millstone is not there the hole is probably going to be washed out. There is a ledge running around the mill wall; if this is just exposed, the mill will be working at it's best. The BCU river advisor is happy to give more info or check levels for you if you're planning on travelling from any distance (phone Tony Carter on 01603 453503).

Access   From the roundabout on the Norwich ring road at the junction of the A140 and the A1074 (west of Norwich), follow the ring road north (A140). Follow the main road up the hill, immediately after the big industrial plant on your left are the first set of traffic lights, turn left here down Hellesdon Hall Road. Follow this road down the hill to the crossroads and go straight over

down a very narrow lane. As this lane bends very sharply left at the bottom of the hill, the mill is immediately ahead of you. Follow round this left-hand bend and the river is on your right. There is ample (though often muddy) parking on the road on your right, alternatively about 50m on is the public car park on your right.

Description   Looking upstream at the mill there are 4 arches, each with a sluice at its upper end. The far left and right arches rarely flow.

The shoot left of centre produces a retentive hole, fairly consistent through spring, summer and autumn. The hole is created by a lip/ledge protruding from the wall, and it works best when this ledge is above water. The shoot is approximately 3m wide and drops into the large, deep mill pool below. The Environment Agency very helpfully adjust the sluices from time to time, providing optimum conditions for playboating here.

When it is in condition the hole is very smooth and allows for endless sequences of cartwheels and split wheels to be performed. Most modern hole moves are possible, loops, tricky 'wus' and matrixes have all been pulled here. It is an equally excellent spot for first time hole bunnies! It is retentive yet not overly difficult to get out of in most conditions. If you go over or swim it'll blow you out fairly swiftly at all water levels. Swimmers soon find they've landed on their feet at the shallow outer reaches of the mill pool and so they can self-rescue and get back to it again in no time. The shoot right of centre, when there's a reasonable flow, produces a good jet of water with clean eddy line. There is ample flow and space here suitable for moving water novices to practise breaking in and out, ferry gliding and other basic moving water stuff. In rare conditions it can also provide a small hole, which will just about hold a boat.

Contributor:
Steve Childs

Other important points   Please watch out for broken glass, it is best to wear footwear at all times.

Local fishermen are usually amenable enough. If you ask them which side of their 'swim' they'd prefer you to pass on, then keep out of the way of their lines (which are usually at the bottom end of the pool so not in your way), there are rarely problems.

There have been numerous cars broken into whilst paddlers are on the water only 100m from the car park. Please remember to lock up and stash valuables out of view.

Horstead Mill, River Bure

Location   About 6 miles north of Norwich off the B1150 and 2 miles west of Wroxham, Horstead Mill (270192) is a few hundred yards upstream of the start of the right of navigation on the Norfolk Broads.

Playspot
OS sheet **134**

Introduction   The site is more suitable as an introduction to moving water techniques than playboating. One shoot provides a small surfing wave and the other forms a jet.

Water level   Medium levels are best for the surfing wave, but it's pretty hit and miss. Low and high levels will still provide moving water and eddies for novice introductions but no more than this.

Access   Head north from the Norwich ring road on the B1150, signposted for Coltishall and North Walsham. After about 6 miles you come into Horstead. Go past one right hand turning (Green Lane) with a car sales garage on the corner. At the next turning, a crossroads with another car sales garage on one corner and the Recruiting Sergeant pub on another, take the right hand turning. After 200m there is a public car park on the left with a derelict building, the mill. There is ample parking here for 10 or so cars.

Description   This disused mill has a series of EA controlled sluices, which control the flow of water under three old brick arches of varying size. The main shoot is a sloping concrete affair with a lip at the end about 3m wide. This shoot is usually paddleable even for novices, provided they can line up to hit a 3m channel. In medium water levels this main shoot forms a small surfable wave suitable for novices. In high water this washes out to form a wide jet really only suitable for practising basic moving water manoeuvres or maybe pulling an 'endo' or two on the eddy lines. Under the middle arch is a weir dropping about 1m in most levels into a narrow, high walled channel. *Do not* paddle this drop or play in the weir as there is usually a substantial tow back with no exit! The last is a very small, low arch about one metre across, but has a powerful jet forming obvious eddy lines.

Contributor:
Jasmine Waters

Other important points   In the summer local youths will jump off the mill to try to catch a ride and fishermen are in abundance. However, the slightest bit of bad weather seems to frighten them off. The area is riddled with footpaths, so there are no access issues.

Mendham Weir, River Waveney

Playspot

OS sheet **156**

Location   On the River Waveney (269832), approximately 15 miles east of Diss, half a mile east of the Harleston bypass (A143).

Characteristics   A shallow concrete ramp split centrally by a tiny island produces a small stopper and a small surf wave.

Introduction   As this weir is not visible from any roads, fairly few paddlers make use of what it has to offer. However, those who find it seem to return on a regular basis.

Water level   The higher the better but anything from medium levels upwards will make it worth a visit. Below medium levels and it will be nothing more than a small trickle. Flood warnings need to be in operation for this weir to be at its best.

Gauge   If the river is far off bank full at Mendham Bridge, it's probably not worth it.

Access   From the A140 Norwich to Ipswich trunk road, take the A143 east towards Harleston. After the roundabout at Harleston, take the second turning right (a small turning but should be sign posted to Mendham). Go down the narrow lane to the bottom of the hill and straight over at the crossroads at the bottom. About 200m further on is Mendham Bridge, access the river from the downstream side of the bridge on river right. The landowner, who lives in the adjacent bungalow, doesn't mind canoeists using the field for access but please keep noise to a minimum. You can stop to drop boats off here if you're quick, there is a small pull in, but parking is in the village. Follow the road a little further and turn right into a reasonably sized public car park.
Not directly accessible from the road, the weir is a short paddle downstream from Mendham Bridge. If you don't want to paddle any further, you can get out immediately beneath the weir on river left and put in again above to paddle back to Mendham Bridge. Although there are no known access issues, please be discrete.

Description   The Waveney is a fairly slow, meandering river but its banks are adorned with many disused mills, hence it boasts numerous weirs along its length. It is in fact worth paddling a few miles of these upper sections of the river if dropping weirs is your thing. Mendham Mill is one of the river's many mills, but is one of the few with a weir considered worth playing in.

As you paddle round a right-hand bend and the mill buildings come into view about 50m ahead, there is a shoot off on river left which drops over Mendham Weir. The weir is of a sloping concrete construction, is quite shallow and is split into two channels by a weir block/island in the middle. At the bottom of the river left channel, a small stopper is produced which is good for spinning but not much else.

The river right channel creates a nice surf wave in anything above medium levels. The wave is great for learning spins and blunts as it is not very forgiving! You will only get them if your technique is smooth, but if it's not you can still surf this wave all day.

Other important points   Just downstream of the weir, around a few sharp bends, the offshoot on which you're paddling rejoins the main river just below a mill pool into which a further two weirs are fed. These are of no interest to playboating and the mill house owners have been hostile to paddlers in the past, so please keep clear to avoid jeopardising continued use of the playable weir.

Contributor:
Jasmine Waters

Cardington Artificial Slalom Course (CASC), River Great Ouse

Artificial WW Course
OS sheet **153**

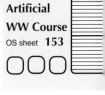

Location   About 4 miles outside of Bedford in Priory Country Park (072488) on the River Great Ouse.

Characteristics   A concrete flood relief channel that wasn't intended for use as a kayaking facility. It is approximately 9m wide by some 120m long. Water is controlled by the sluice gate at the top of the channel.

Introduction   For a number of years an annual Div 3/4 slalom has been held on this stretch of water. The course is not made accessible for individual paddlers, being only available for group bookings. Despite its quite restricted offerings it does make for an ideal introduction to moving water. One of the course rules is that there must be minimum of a Level 3 Coach supervising the use of the course at all times.

Water level   Water levels are controlled entirely by the event organisers via the sluice-gate, although there are restrictions in place

as to how long the gate can be left open at full flow (dependent on water levels above the sluice). For bookings contact: CASC Bookings Secretary, Graham Missing, 84 Priory Street, Newport Pagnell, MK16 9BP, telephone: 01908 611187.

Access   From the A1 take the A421 towards Bedford. Before you get into Bedford proper (still on the A421) you come to a roundabout. Turn left at the roundabout continuing on the A421. Take the first slip road left (signposted Priory Country Park). At the roundabout, ignore signs for Cardington village and turn right into Priory Country / Business Park (it appears you're going into an industrial estate). At the next roundabout go straight on, then take the first turn left. The road ahead splits, fork round to the right and park in the car park on the left.
To find the course, walk over the road across the sluice and follow a track over the lock. Follow the track, keeping the river immediately on your left (don't follow canoe slalom signs!).

Description   Absolutely ideal for clubs or groups to take youngsters or adults with little or no moving water experience. The course is surrounded on both sides by grassy banks, which form part of the Country Park. Most groups who book the site tend to camp beside the river, no more than 100m from the course. The course itself can be designed to suit the individual needs by the addition of fibreglass 'hippos', plastic pipe and wooden boards to divert the flow and form features. As the water rarely gets more than knee depth, the course has serious limitations but with careful use of the features a suitably challenging course for novices can be constructed. Time must therefore be allowed to construct and dismantle the course, as all obstacles must be removed and stowed in the site garage before you leave. Boats can be stored here overnight and it also boasts an electricity point (so take a kettle!)

Other important points   There is a definite security problem at the site. Great care must be taken to lock up all kit and empty cars before leaving them in the car park. As a result of vandalism there are no longer any toilets at the site, the nearest toilets are at Tesco's supermarket (20 min walk or 10 min drive) or take your own facilities. For people stopping overnight it has been possible in the past to arrange overnight parking in the Tesco car park to reduce risk to vehicles. Please seek permission.

Contributor:
Mark Wilkinson

Hambleden

Surfing the wave, Hambleden

Marlow

Hambleden

Surfing the wave, Marlow

No paddle, Hurley

Shepperton

Farndon, River Trent

The North-East

Contents

Cheviot

North Tyne

South Tyne

Tyne and Wear

Tees and Swale

Ure and Wharfe

North York Moors

Introduction

The north-east section covers the watersheds which lie north of the River Humber and east of the Yorkshire Dales and the Pennines right up to the Scottish border. Lying on the eastern side of England, they appear to be in the rain shadow of the western hills. However, in reality, the predominantly wet westerlies still have plenty of hydro ammunition with which to pound the Pennine chain. Consequently, many battlegrounds exist for the white water warrior. The bulk of white water runs lie in game fishing areas, which means that the majority of paddling is only viable in the 'closed game fishing season' of November to March (check specifically for each river with the BCU River Adviser). Fortunately this is also when the most consistent wet weather occurs.

Access varies, but is generally good due to 'Northern warmth and hospitality'. It is essential that paddlers visiting this area show common sense, consideration and politeness. The way you drive your car through remote villages, your pleasant manner with all you meet, these things go a long way to avoiding access problems generally, but nowhere is this more true than in North-East England.

Rainfall can be very high at times. Over the past decade or so it would seem that higher flood levels have been achieved on all north-eastern rivers. It is certainly the case that 'alpine volumes' are at least briefly present on rivers. As a result of more intense rainfall and drainage work by farmers, run-off can be more rapid and the flows achieved higher. In the Tyne valley for example, local newspapers have reported 'a 1m wall of water coming down a beck and washing away a car in a ford', Fire and Rescue crew reports bear these facts out. So it is advisable to check out the river level very carefully. The region also benefits from snowmelt to swell the rivers. In good winters, snowfall can be substantial and, depending on the rate and amount of thaw, the rivers can be brought into condition quite nicely. It is possible for snowmelt to keep the rivers up for days at a time.

Rob Cunnington
North-East Regional Coordinator for the Guidebook

Great efforts in conservation are now paying off with an abundance of wild life. Otters have made a successful comeback in parts, salmon and trout numbers are high, sea trout run some rivers in autumn. Kingfishers always give a dazzling dash of colour to drab banks and red kites have successfully been reintroduced to locations; buzzards are more frequently sighted, as are black grouse on the higher ground. The north-eastern rivers offer a great deal to the holistic paddler.

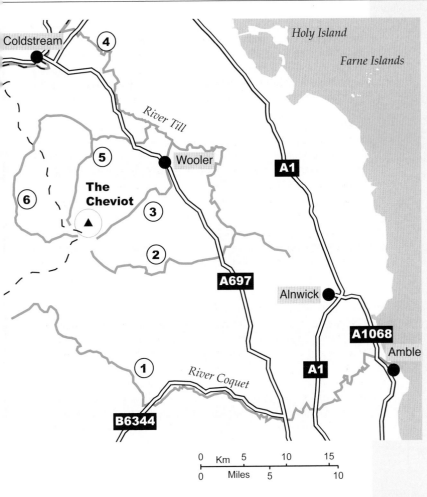

Coldstream

4

River Till

5

Wooler

The Cheviot

▲

6

3

2

A697

Alnwick

Holy Island

Farne Islands

A1

A1068

Amble

1

River Coquet

A1

B6344

0	Km	5	10	15
0	Miles	5		10

Cheviot

Coquet (Upper - Blindburn to Low Alwinton)

Grade   **3/4**

Length **17km**

OS sheet   **80**

Introduction   The upper section of the Coquet is tightly hemmed in by the Cheviot hills. It is exposed and very bleak in windy weather, frequently with snow on surrounding hills in winter and remote from civilisation… a superb place to be. In high water the paddling is heavy and alpine in feel.

Water level   This section of the upper Coquet requires very high rainfall to paddle it, and even then it drops off extremely quickly, it is an 'in the rain river'. I have seen it drop within the hour (immediately after heavy rainfall has stopped). It does benefit from snow melt, which will also bring it into condition. If you paddle it and it isn't 3/4 then you have missed the level and will find it a disappointing bump and scrape. In exceptional rainfall this section can rise to a solid, heavy grade 4.

Access   Anywhere along the minor road that runs alongside this section of river. Possible put-ins include: Blindburn (830108) in extremely high water, Carshope (845115), Barrow Burn (867108) and Linbriggs (892065).
Egress for this section at Low Alwinton (923056), or use it as an access point for the following section.

Description   In extremely high water the fall at Blindburn provides good sport. Most paddlers will start further down at Carshope or Barrow Burn. Swiftly moving water leads down to the bridge at Bygate Hall; a 'V' shaped weir lies upstream of the bridge and a smaller weir underneath the bridge itself. Between here and Shillmoor the gradient increases with continuous grade 2 rapids and falls of grade 3 to 4. Below Shillmoor the gradient continues with several falls (Gd 2/3) and a short gorge section (Gd 2). At Linbriggs the river twists down through a constricted rock band. It begins with a two-tier rapid above the bridge, with a possible sump (bottom right) at grade 3+ to 4 followed by the river dropping over a 2m rock sill (known as corkscrew) below the bridge. This fall, also 3+ to 4, depending on level, needs inspecting to pick the line; this rapid can look intimidating! Grade 2 rapids lead down to Low Alwinton.

Contributor:
Rob Cunnington

Coquet (Middle - Low Alwinton to Rothbury)

Introduction   At this stage the Coquet is just beginning to leave the tight confines of the upper Coquet valley. Its gradient has eased somewhat, but it still flows purposefully through beautiful countryside.

Grade   **2**
Length   **23km**
OS sh.   **80/81**

Water level   High to medium levels are required, following heavy rain. Prolonged rain will produce higher levels, but this section will still drop fairly quickly after the rain has stopped. Snow melt will also bring this section into condition. The river is quite shallow in parts so make sure you have enough water before you start. It is important to remember that once the rain has stopped the water will drop fairly quickly… whilst you are paddling it!

Access   Put in at Low Alwinton (923056, OS sheet 80). Egress at Rothbury (058015, OS sheet 81). Take out on river right upstream of the bridge.

Description   From Low Alwinton, occasional rocky rapids lead down to Harbottle Castle; here there are several small falls before a 0.75m horseshoe shaped fall at grade 2. After Sharperton Bridge the character of the river changes and shingle rapids predominate at grade 1/2. The river can be blocked totally with trees in this section, making a portage necessary. Further on the river weaves through encroaching alder trees, and some old meanders can provide blind alleys hereabouts. Below Hepple Bridge, the meanders increase in size and shape with lots of shingle rapids and 'V' jets. At Caistron an old drainpipe bridge needs portaging. Grade 1/2 rapids lead down into Rothbury.

Contributor:
Rob Cunnington

Coquet (Lower - Rothbury to Weldon Mill)

Introduction   The Coquet, now swollen with numerous side streams, is a bigger river but still shallow in parts.

Grade   **2/3**
Length   **12km**
OS sheet   **81**

Water level   High to medium levels are required. Snow melt will also bring the river into condition.

Access   Put in for this section at Rothbury (058015). Egress at Weldon Mill (138984). Take out 50m downstream of the

weir on river right, just before the bridge.

Description   Within 1km of the start the first notable rapid appears, Thrum Mill falls (Gd 3). This is an exciting 50m section of rapids with two big stoppers and a narrow constriction to finish. Fast, bouncy, grade 1/ 2 with numerous trees and boulders lead down to Pauperhaugh Bridge; below this lies a weir. Occasional small rapids lead down to Brinkburn Priory; here there is a 1m fall, grade 2/3, with standing waves below (enough to swamp an open boat on a crash and burn line!). Immediately below this lies a 100m section of grade 1/2. Fast, flat water continues down to Weldon Mill weir.

Contributor:
Rob Cunnington

Rivers and Burns of the Northern Cheviots

The rivers and burns of the Northern Cheviots are situated in the remote and often desolate countryside of the borderland with Scotland.

Contributor:
Rob Cunnington

After very heavy rainfall the rivers and burns come into condition. They also benefit from snow melt off the Cheviot hills. The steeper burns are shallow and all require very high water to float a boat.

Breamish

Grade	**2/3**
Length	**9km**
OS sheet	**81**

Introduction   Needs very high water.

Access   Put in at Linhope Bridge (964163), egress at 'C' class road below Ingram (033168).

Harthope Burn

Grade	**2+**
Length	**7km**
OS sheet	**75**

Introduction   Needs very high water.

Access   Put in at Langleeford (949220), take out at footbridge and ford (001261).

Till

Grade **2**

Length **16km**

OS sht. **75/74**

Access   Put in at Etal (925395 OS sheet 75), take out at Norham bridge (890473 OS sheet 74).

College Burn

Grade **2**

Length **2.5km**

OS sheet **74**

Introduction   Needs very high water.

Access   Put in at Hethpool bridge (walk!) (895280), take out at Westnewton (907304).

Bowmont Water

Grade **2**

Length **10km**

OS sht. **75/74**

Introduction   We've been a bit cheeky here in that this burn is just over the Scottish border, although it does run in to England.

Water levels   Needs very high water.

Access   Paddleable from Belford (814208) or Attonburn (815225).

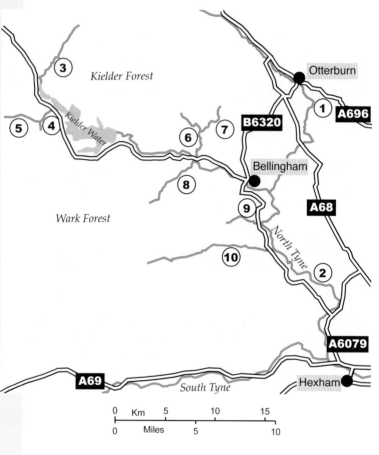

North Tyne

Rede

Grade **2**

Length **5.5km**

OS sheet **80**

Introduction   The River Rede flows from Catcleugh reservoir to its confluence with the North Tyne at Redesmouth, but it is only the section between Otterburn and West Woodburn that is of interest to the white water paddler. This trip starts on bleak moorland and descends to slightly more sheltered lowland.

Water level   High water levels are required to paddle this section and it gets very few descents.

Access   Put in at Otterburn (888926), or drive along a 'C' class moorland road to (904903) and walk across the moor. It is also possible to get in or out at a stone bridge (901876).
Egress on river right, some 300m below the A68 road bridge in West Woodburn (888867).

Description   The first 3km from Otterburn are slow and tedious; a better start is to walk over the moorland from the 'C' class road (904903). The gradient of the river now increases, the valley sides become steeper and minor rapids appear. At Yearhaugh Farm (situated on river left), there is a sharp bend to the left and the river becomes rocky. Soon after this is a fall of approximately 1m. The bed of the river changes to rock slabs with rapids falling over them in steps, down to a stone bridge, which carries a track. Over the next half kilometre there are four to five rapids with a fall of 0.5m or so. The river bends right and West Woodburn village comes into view, this is a rocky stretch, good in high water. This section is grade 2, but can become grade 2/3 in very high water.

Contributor:
Rob Cunnington

North Tyne (Upper - Bellingham to Chollerford)

Grade **2(3/4)**

Length **25km**

OS sht. **80/87**

Introduction   At Bellingham the North Tyne valley is wide and mature, the river is somewhat meandering , but with sufficient gradient and with some bedrock outcrops to produce a couple of significant rapids in high water. In autumn, the tree-lined banks provide a colourful backdrop to a river that appears to be remote.

Water level   The headwaters of the North Tyne are controlled by the massive Kielder Dam. However, big flows are not infrequent as the dam releases on a regular basis. Many feeder streams enter the river below the dam and these also serve to bring water levels up.

Access   Access points at Bellingham Bridge, downstream river right (835834, OS sheet 80), Wark (Gold Island) (873777, OS sheet 87), and Barrasford (921733, OS sheet 87). Egress at Chollerford Bridge, upstream river left (921705, OS sheet 87).
Details from river adviser, www.bcu.org.uk/access/riverinfonortheast.

Description   Starting from Bellingham, the river is fast flowing and the rapids become more pronounced. After some 7km there is a small fall, a little further down is Lee Hall Island. This has a good rapid down the right, which is fast with several drops (Gd 3 in high water), occasional rapids lead down to Wark. Fast flowing water continues down from here to the sharp bend in the river by Chipchase Castle; here there is a fall in the river, which is usually shot left of centre as this is where most water flows (arbitrary in high water). Soon the gradient picks up a notch and rapids become a little more frequent down to Barrasford. As Barrasford comes into sight, with Houghton Castle high on the right bank, the gradient increases further. Here are two rapids, the first of which is formed by the river breaking through rock slabs set at an angle to the river. A short distance downstream of here is the second, larger rapid. The middle and river right channels are rocky in low water and contain heavy water in high levels. The channel on river left breaks directly onto boulders. This second rapid is grade 3 (4 in flood). Just below here is an old broken weir and small weir, which may be covered, depending on water level. Soon, Chollerford bridge comes into sight.

Contributor:
Rob Cunnington

Other important points   Watch out for otters, which have made a comeback in recent times. They can swim better than the average paddler! In high water conditions the white water paddling at Barrasford, although brief, can be heavy.

North Tyne (Lower - Chollerford to Hexham)

Grade	**3/4**
Length	**8km**
OS sheet	**87**

Introduction   By this stage the North Tyne is in its mature lowlands, somewhat contradictory then that this is where its most significant rapids are to be found.

Water level   Medium and high levels are best, although this section is possible at lower winter levels. The headwaters of the North Tyne are controlled by the massive Kielder Dam. This does not mean that big flows are infrequent as the dam releases on a regular basis. As this section is well down the North Tyne valley it also benefits from all the feeder streams that enter the river below the dam and these also serve to bring water levels up.

Access   Access at Chollerford Bridge, upstream river left (921705). Egress at Tyne Green, Hexham, river right, upstream of the weir (938646).
There is an access agreement, so check for details with the river adviser, www.bcu.org.uk/access/riverinfonortheast.

Description   Start upstream of Chollerford Bridge on flat water. Immediately downstream of the bridge is Chollerford Weir. Depending on water levels this can be shot in a variety of places, however in high water conditions the back tow is significant and it becomes a portage. The river continues downstream with frequent small rapids. At Walwick Grange ('big house' on river right) there is a small grade 2 rapid on river left. This has a nice play wave at medium levels. From here the river's gradient increases a little and at the Mill Race, just downstream of the village of Wall, is a continuous grade 2/3 rapid on a bend. The rapid first swings right and then left before ending. The river becomes wider at this point, with a large pool on river left. After a short, flat stretch, small rapids lead down to a river-wide reef. This can be shot on river left or right, (in the centre in *some* conditions). The river right route carries a more constricted flow and is usually more interesting, although in very high conditions the river left route may be more appealing. This section can be grade 2/3. Just downstream of here is Warden Gorge; this consists of approximately 100m of rapids which flow over bedrock, boulders and slabs. It is rocky in low water, but at medium and high levels is bouncy and contains some powerful stoppers. In high water an awesome river-wide stopper forms at the very bottom of the rapid. Grade 3 in medium levels and grade 4 in flood, this section definitely becomes more powerful with every extra cumec that flows down it. In the very high flood conditions of the winter of 1974-75 (pre Kielder Dam), grade 5 was reported for this section in the old 'Guide to Northumberland Rivers'. The river continues through small rapids to the confluence of the South Tyne. The paddler continues on down the River Tyne, with the odd grade 1/2 rapid, taking out at Tyne Green on river right, upstream of the weir and stone-arched road bridge.

Contributor:
Rob Cunnington

Other important points   Water releases from Kielder Dam and high rainfall can produce big volume water on this section. There is an SSSI at Warden Gorge on river left.

The Kielder Burns

Kielder forest area contains many small, narrow burns (The Kielder Burns), which come into condition only after very heavy rain. Access is often very difficult, and trees across the burns are a common and often continuous hazard, as are low bridges and fences. Kielder is a wild and remote forest area and paddlers need to be very self-contained as a result. All the burns flow with consistent gradient and occasional rapids. The famous Kielder midge is always present!

After very heavy and prolonged rainfall the burns come into condition and then only very briefly. By briefly, I mean usually in the order of a matter of a few hours. All have been paddled at some time, but only a handful of runs are done in any one year, due to the aforementioned reasons, so view all information cautiously. It is not worth coming to paddle any of the Kielder burns speculatively, you need a very wet spell indeed in the Kielder catchment area to warrant the effort of driving up the North Tyne valley.

Contributor:
Rob Cunnington

Kielder Burn

Grade	**2**
Length	**5km**
OS sheet	**80**

Access   Access at East Kielder bridge (653958), egress at car park (633927).

Other important points   Includes several weirs.

Lewis Burn

Grade	**2**
Length	**3.5km**
OS sheet	**80**

Access   Access at Long Low house (ruin) (626877), egress at picnic area (643904).

Akenshaw Burn

Grade	2/3
Length	2km
OS sheet	80

Access   Access at bridge (611897), Lewis burn confluence is 2 km downstream (continue downstream on the Lewis burn and take out as for Lewis burn).

Tarset Burn

Grade	2
Length	6km
OS sheet	80

Access   Access at Sidwood picnic place (776891), egress from River North Tyne (783853).

Tarret Burn

Grade	2/3
Length	2km
OS sheet	80

Introduction   This is a tributary of the Tarset Burn, entering the Tarset Burn at Burnmouth. There are two falls (at the grade) on this section.

Access   Approach the burn by using the footpath (795884), walk along the footpath for 300m, then turn in a south-easterly direction and walk across the moor to the burn. This way you do not have to cross any walls or fences and upset any farmers. You have been advised!
Egress as for Tarset Burn.

Chirdon Burn

Grade	2+
Length	3-7km
OS sheet	80

Access   3km upstream from its confluence with the North Tyne there is an easy starting point at the footpath bridge at Cadger ford, (762832). This is a practical start for those contemplating the Chirdon Burn.
4.5km upstream from its confluence with the North Tyne, at the cattle grid, (750829) the Chirdon Burn is very difficult to access, with a long walk over rough, steep ground.
Another 3km further upstream of this point is Jerry's Linn, a

4m fall; just below the fall is 100m of boulder rapids. With even greater difficulty of access and right at the top of the Chirdon Burn is another section of falls know as the 'Seven Linns'.

Houxty Burn

Grade **2**

Length **4km**

OS sheet **87**

Introduction   Includes a 1.5m fall near Esp Mill. Fences are a problem.

Access   Access at 'C' class road bridge (823796), Egress is problematic so continue down the North Tyne for 1.5km and egress at Gold Island (873777).

Warks Burn

Grade **2/3**

Length **8km**

OS sheet **87**

Introduction   In the area of Roses Bower Farm is a fall of 2m. Fences are a problem.

Access   Put in at Stonehaugh picnic area (790763), egress at the B6320 (863765).

Other important points   There has been a landslide just upstream of Ramshaws Mill, (842766). The burn is clear to paddle, but debris exists. At Ramshaws Mill there has been a rock-fall, which blocks the burn in lower flows though it can still be paddled when the water is very high. However, it also acts as a gathering point for trees and thus can form a full, river-wide strainer; add the fact that from 50m upstream of Ramshaw Mill there is *no way* of portaging and this section could become extremely serious.

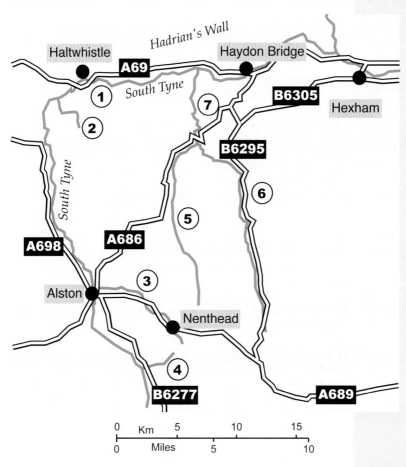

South Tyne

South Tyne (Upper - West Ashgill to Alston)

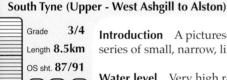

Grade   **3/4**

Length **8.5km**

OS sht. **87/91**

Introduction   A picturesque run, high up in the hills, through a series of small, narrow, limestone gorges.

Water level   Very high rainfall is needed to bring the run into condition and it drops off very quickly indeed. This is an 'in the rain river'. Rapidly thawing snow combined with a warm, wet westerly will also bring this section into condition.

Gauge   If the bedrock in the gorge upstream of Garrigill road bridge is well covered, then it is worth putting on. Remember that you are quite close to the source here, so plenty of water is needed to do the run this high up the catchment.

Access   Put in at West Ashgill, (OS sheet 91, 758394) and egress at Alston, (OS sheet 87, 716462). Considerate parking is required at both access and egress points.

Description   This river run starts after a short carry down the footpath at West Ashgill. The section down to just below Garrigill has a good gradient, so is a fast run in high water. There are many small falls and reefs, caused by the river flowing over limestone bedrock and for short distances the river is hemmed into small limestone gorges. The fall immediately below Windshaw Bridge is the most significant fall, a narrow twisting slot, with great back-loop potential! The ford at Gatehead needs caution as the river is channelled under the road of the ford in a series of culverts, and at higher levels the river flows over and under the ford simultane-ously! Below here a beautiful little gorge continues to Garrigill. A short distance below here is a natural limestone weir, which can be interesting in a good flow. The gradient has eased by now and the river continues down into Alston, flowing fast and encounter-ing many small reefs and rapids.

Other important points   Some 2.5km upstream of Alston, the Black Burn enters from river left, this is paddleable for some distance upstream of here (depending on the amount of water in the burn). The paddling is of grade 2 standard. Very heavy rainfall or a large quantity of rapidly thawing snow on the northern side of Cross Fell is required to bring the Black Burn into condition. Access is difficult and long, over the moor via a bridleway track, which leads south from the A686, (676422).

Contributor:
Rob Cunnington

South Tyne (Middle- Alston to Haltwhistle)

Grade	**2/3**
Length	**24km**
OS sheet	**87**

Introduction   Still tucked away in the hills and being fed by many side burns, the South Tyne has the gradient to provide a challenging run at higher levels, immediately after heavy rain.

Water level   From Alston to Bridge End high water is required, otherwise it is a bump and a scrape. From Bridge End to Haltwhistle medium water is required. Run-off is quick on this section and the South Tyne will drop quickly, although slow and prolonged snowmelt will extend this.

Access   Access and egress can be made at the following points:
Alston bridge, upstream river left (716462).
Slaggyford bridge, downstream river (681519).
Knowe Head (682553).
Lambley bridge, upstream river left (676596).
Bridge End, upstream river right (676618).
Haltwhistle bridge 'C' class road, downstream river right (700634).

Description   The run from Alston to Lambley is a fast grade 2/3 run in high water, with many rapids, some of grade 3 in spate conditions; these can be sustained and powerful. At very high levels it can resemble an alpine run with a surprising volume of water being discharged out of the upper South Tyne catchment. Just below the Alston road bridge is a small man-made weir, which is washed out in high water. The River Nent joins the South Tyne from river right, on the south side of Alston. Below Slaggyford the river tends to become more open in character, but still with many fast rapids. Immediately below Lambley Viaduct there is a good section of continuous and powerful grade 3. Downstream of Lambley road bridge there are grade 1/2 rapids. There is a weir at Featherstone Castle which is split into two sections: the right-hand section is boxed in, and is best avoided; in high water the left-hand section may not be a better option and is best portaged at such levels. From here to the next road bridge (Bridge End) is a good section of grade 2, which is a very useable site at lower levels and benefits from good roadside access. From Bridge End to Haltwhistle the river is more paddleable at medium levels, with sections of grade 2, (access can be made at the next road bridge downstream of the A69 road bridge). Park Burn enters from river right, some 3km upstream of Haltwhistle bridge.

Contributor:
Rob Cunnington

Other important points   In periods of high rainfall on the Pennines around Cross Fell, with rapidly melting snow, the South Tyne can become a very powerful and voluminous river.

South Tyne (Lower - Haltwhistle to Hexham)

Grade   **1/2**

Length **30km**

OS sheet   **87**

Introduction   The South Tyne by now is a wider, more mature and meandering river in pleasant countryside, yet still has enough gradient to interest the white water paddler.

Water level   Best in high water, but medium levels produce good quality paddling. This section, particularly below Haydon Bridge can be paddled at lower levels.

Access   Access and egress can be made at the following points:
Haltwhistle bridge, 'C' class road, downstream on river right (700634).
Haydon Bridge, downstream of A69 bridge, on river right (845644).
Warden bridge (910660).
Tyne Green, Hexham, river right, upstream of weir (938646).
There is no access or egress at the North Tyne/South Tyne confluence due to problems in the past with parked vehicles and access to the quarry road.

Description   Between Haltwhistle and Haydon Bridge the river is grade 1/2, which becomes a bouncy run in parts at medium to high levels; in lower levels the rapids tend to be shallow. Beneath Haltwhistle Viaduct is a sizeable weir with a fish shoot in the centre; it is rocky and needs inspection. Just before Haydon Bridge the River Allen enters from river right, and under the next bridge, which is a railway bridge, some good surfing waves form at specific medium to high water levels (between the river left bridge piers). In Haydon Bridge under the old bridge itself, there is a weir; inspection is necessary, especially at medium and higher levels. From here begins a very popular touring section down to Tyne Green, with plenty of grade 1/2 rapids. The most continuous of these is at Allerwash (marked as a spa well on OS sheet 87, 858647). Immediately upstream of here is a small gauging weir, which offers play potential at lower levels. Before the A69 road bridge the river North Tyne joins with the South Tyne from river right, and the volume of water is doubled. Take out in Hexham at Tyne Green.

Contributor:
Rob Cunnington

Park Burn

Grade	**3/4**
Length	**4km**
OS sheet	**87**

Introduction   With its catchment on Whitfield Moor, this short run, which flows through several small gorges, is fast and furious in high water.

Water level   Very high rainfall is needed to paddle this section. It drops off very quickly indeed. This section is only possible a handful of times each year.

Access   Access from a track at (698600). Walk down the track and across the moor to the obvious footbridge. Another alternative is to put in at the 'C' class road bridge (689610), downstream on the river right.
Egress at Haltwhistle bridge ('C' class road) (700634). Take-out downstream on the river right bank.

Description   From the put-in the burn is fast flowing. After approximately a kilometre is a 2m+ fall, best shot on river right down the angled ramp of water as opposed to the more vertical left-hand side. The burn soon enters a small picturesque gorge, fast flowing rapids lead down to the 'C' class road bridge. In very high water there are few eddies here and lots of tree debris can block the river, so be alert for strainers. Further on, the burn passes under the old railway and enters a second picturesque gorge by Park Village. Just before the next road bridge is a weir, then immediately after passing under the road bridge there is a 3m fall with a very shallow plunge pool. This is best inspected before putting on, even though inspection is difficult. Rapids lead down into the South Tyne; continue on to Haltwhistle.

Contributor:
Rob Cunnington

Other important points   Limited eddies in high water, lots of tree debris and barbed wire fences. You will need to be bold when you are on this burn!

Nent

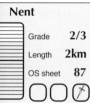

Grade **2/3**

Length **2km**

OS sheet **87**

Introduction   A tributary of the South Tyne, with its source above Nenthead, (a remote, ancient, lead mining village). This section is bounded by desolate hills and quickly runs down into the market town of Alston. All of the major rapids on the Nent are the result of the river flowing over outcropping limestone.

Water level   Very high rainfall is needed to bring the run into condition and it drops off very quickly indeed. This is an 'in the rain river'. Rapidly thawing snow combined with a warm, wet westerly will also bring this section into condition.

Access   Put in at a 'C' class road bridge (739469), egress on a track on the western side of Alston (721467).

Description   Floating fairly sedately through pastureland, you might wonder why you are here! Within some 700m of the put-in is a 3m vertical limestone fall (Gd3) into a plunge pool, (inspect from river left). From here the gradient increases and in the vicinity of Gossipgate bridge there is a limestone reef with a fall of 2m, (Gd 2/3). More rapids lead down for another 100m to the take-out, and a short walk out along the track into Alston.
 The Nent does continue from here through a limestone channel with a small concrete weir in it (which may be washed out) and then plunges over a 6m fall (which can be vertically blocked with trees!). From here 2 rapids lead down to the confluence with the South Tyne. The problem with this section, apart from the possibly blocked and thus impassable 6m fall, is that below the fall a great deal of industrial debris has been dumped into the river over the years.

Contributor:
Rob Cunnington

Other important points   In exceptional rainfall, the upper Nent is possible. In particular, the steep, bouldery rapid upstream of Nentsberry bridge (767449) has good gradient at grade 2+.

Ash Gill

Grade **4**

Length **500m**

OS sheet **87**

Introduction   Located in a gorge, which the Ash Gill waterfall has steadily created over many years, this is a spectacular and inspiring setting for a steep descent by kayak.

Water level   Very high rainfall is needed to paddle this section. It drops off very quickly indeed and is an 'in the rain river'. Rapidly thawing snow combined with a warm, wet westerly will also bring this section into condition. This section is only possible a handful of times each year.

Access   Access at Ash Gill bridge on the B6277 (758406). A steep walk on river left, down a footpath, leads down into the bottom of the gorge. Put in at the first footbridge, some 100m below Ash Gill waterfall.
To egress either continue down the South Tyne or take out and walk back up to your vehicle!

Description   From the Ash Gill Bridge, the first three falls to be encountered are each up to 2m in height and contain fairly shallow plunge pools in low water. The next fall is a two-tiered affair; the first tier consists of a 1m fall, which is immediately followed by a fall of 3m, with the water tending to flow close to the left hand wall. The river flows swiftly down to the next footbridge. Directly upstream of this is a wooden beam which spans the gill; it sits at water level or thereabouts and acts as a strainer (portage on river right). Put in below the footbridge. Within 20m is another 3m fall, best shot left of centre into the deep plunge pool (to avoid an undercut gully/pothole feature on the river right side). Small rapids lead down to the confluence of the South Tyne.

Contributor:
Rob Cunnington

Other important points   It is essential to inspect the whole run before you put in so as to determine the difficulty of the drops and the linking rapids. It is also a good idea to locate the breakout for the portage at the second footbridge.

West Allen

Grade	**3**
Length	**11km**
OS sheet	**87**

Introduction   Rising high up in the hills surrounding Coalcleugh Moor, this beck run, just like its sister the East Allen, is a tributary of the Allen.

Water level   Very high rainfall is needed to paddle the section from Limestone Brae to Ninebanks and high rainfall is needed to bring the river into condition below here. It drops off very quickly indeed. This river must be paddled whilst it is still raining. Rap-

idly thawing snow combined with a warm, wet westerly will also bring this section into condition.

Access   Access at Limestone Brae (802487), park on the hairpin bend; a short walk leads down a footpath to a footbridge and the river. A better place to start is Ninebanks road bridge (780541). Egress at Cupoila bridge (800592), upstream on river right or carry on down the Allen.

Description   It may be possible to begin with a fast start over a small reef leading immediately onto a 4m fall with rock-strewn debris below. The fall consists of multiple blocks at the base on river left. The base area on river right is flatter but still shallow, and at the time of writing there were three large trees sitting in the mini-gorge directly below the fall. This section, when free from debris, is only thinkable at extremely high water levels. Put in below these trees. The river continues with gradient assisted speed, and is fast and furious. This upper section is only feasible in very high water (only possible a handful of times each year, and the top 4m fall even less often).

From Ninebanks (a better put-in), the river is somewhat wider and benefits from the several side burns which by now serve to increase its volume. Just below Low Haber at Monk Cott is a 3m fall at grade 3 standard, which is best shot in the centre so as to avoid the back tow, which exists both left and right! Rapids up to grade 2/3 lead down to Whitfield Weir. This weir is in a steady state of decay and high water is not a good time to appreciate the extent of metal spikes that grow out of this weir (although they may well be covered)… check it out at low water. Downstream from here is the Elk's Head public house. The river goes under a road bridge here and there is a second weir, which is more easily shot. The next section of the river flows over occasional limestone bedrock reef formations, which produce several grade 2/3 rapids. Once the main Allen is reached, just upstream of Cupoila bridge the volume increases noticeably and spookily. In high water you are now on a big river!

Contributor:
Rob Cunnington

Other important points   Watch out for overhanging trees and strainers. Barbed wire fences also can cause problems on this river.

East Allen

Grade **2/3**

Length **11km**

OS sheet **87**

Introduction   A tributary of the River Allen, this beck run starts high up in the East Allen valley amongst the hills of Hexhamshire common and Allendale common.

Water level   Very high rainfall is needed to paddle the section from Sinderhope to Catton bridge and high rainfall is needed to bring the river into condition below here. This is an 'in the rain river'. Rapidly thawing snow combined with a warm, wet westerly will also bring this section into condition.

Access   Access at Sinderhope bridge (844523), or better still at Catton bridge (831566). Egress at Cupoila bridge (upstream on river right) (800592) or carry on down the Allen.

Description   This fast flowing beck run starts at Sinderhope bridge. Within 200m is Holmes Linn, a 3m fall (Gd 3/4) over a limestone outcrop. Plenty of water is needed here, as the bottom of the fall is shallow in parts, (only possible a few times each year). The East Allen continues with plenty of continuous grade 2 rapids and some at grade 2/3, all the way to its confluence with the Allen. At Catton bridge (a better put-in), is a good-sized sloping weir, which can have considerable backtow depending on water levels. The volume of the East Allen at Catton in high water makes it a good paddle from here into the Allen.

Contributor:
Rob Cunnington

Other important points   There are plenty of overhanging trees on this section, and in high water strainers are formed, which remain in the channel long after the water has dropped. Barbed wire fences also can cause problems on this river.

Allen

Grade **3/4**

Length **8km**

OS sheet **87**

Introduction   Swollen now at the confluence of the East and West Allen, the River Allen is born. Immediately it enters the deeply incised and wooded Staward gorge, where it flows through in a series of interlocking spurs and is very picturesque.

Water level   Medium and high levels are good; at very high levels the river becomes an excellent grade 4 run. Rapidly melting

snow will also bring the Allen into condition. Just like the South Tyne, if thaw is triggered by a warm, wet westerly, a big rise in water level is possible over a short period of time.

Access   Access upstream on river right of Cupoila bridge (800592), or alternately at Plankey Mill (795622), (a nominal parking charge is payable to the farmer). Egress at Allen Banks (798641).

Description   The Allen has excellent gradient, from Cupoila bridge to its confluence with the South Tyne (dropping some 85m over the 8km length of its journey). Once on the water, it feels like a big river and behaves like one too. Below Cupoila bridge is a natural slab weir, which may be shot anywhere, but in lower water is only possible on the extreme river right. Small stoppers lead to the first boulder garden, a technical piece of water. The route starts left, moves right and then exits left. Below this section are two excellent small play stoppers. From here a succession of rapids lead down to the second boulder garden, a little more technical than the first, but delightful to paddle. Stoppers and a third boulder garden culminate in a pool. Below here are two natural limestone weirs with a drop and backtow, the second one being slightly more powerful. Once again continuous rapids and a shale gorge lead down to Hagg Bank fall. This 45° angled slab across the whole width of the river acts as natural weir; the river loses some 4m of height here and carries a big stopper in high water. It needs inspection and may well be portaged at high levels. A voluminous, bouncy rapid leads to another angled slab hidden by a camouflaged 'horizon line'. This is smaller than its mother but does carry a good wave/stopper! Continuous rapids lead down from here through Plankey Mill to Allen Banks at grade 2 standard, and also to the South Tyne confluence.

Other important points   Strainers and trees moving down the river can present problems.

Contributor:
Rob Cunnington

Due to the increased drainage on the grouse moors of the East and West Allen catchments, the combined effect of this drainage and heavy bursts of rainfall mean that the Allen can rise extremely quickly; it can also drop quickly. This local factor also applies to the East and West Allen rivers.

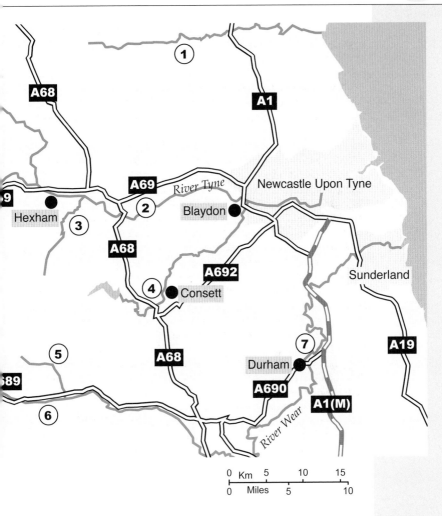

A68

A1

A69   *River Tyne*   Newcastle Upon Tyne

9

Hexham

2   Blaydon

3

A68

Sunderland

A692

4   Consett

5

A68

7

89

Durham

6

A690

A1(M)

River Wear

A19

0   Km   5   10   15
0   Miles   5   10

Tyne and Wear

Wansbeck

Grade **2**

Length **10km**

OS sheet **81**

Introduction   Rising up on the moors around Sweethope Lough in mid-Northumberland, the Wansbeck flows east for some 48km before entering the North Sea. It flows through pleasant country-side for most of the way.

Water level   Very high rainfall is required to bring the Wansbeck into paddleable condition.

Access   Access at Low Angerton bridge (093843) or Dyke Neuk bridge (120851). Egress at Mitford (174857), take out on river left before the weir.

Description   Low Angerton is a convenient starting point, the Hartburn soon joins from river left and swells the flow of the Wansbeck. Immediately downstream of the confluence is a footbridge and a short distance beyond this lies a small fall. Passing Meldon Hall on river left, the Wansbeck now flows through woodland with many small rapids down to Mitford. Around a bend a stone arch bridge appears, beneath this is a small weir. Below here are several small rock sills. Fontburn joins from river left; flat water leads to a concrete gauging weir, take out river left (before the weir).

Contributor:

Rob Cunnington

Other important points   From Mitford to Ashington, there are many weirs on the Wansbeck. These are more shootable than playable, at medium levels.

Tyne (Hexham to Wylam)

Grade **2**

Length **20km**

OS sht. **87/88**

Introduction   By this stage the rivers South and North Tyne have joined to form the mighty River Tyne. Flowing in a lowland valley the Tyne hides a secret, best explained in this quote from David Archer's book ,'Land of singing waters' (ISBN 187173276).

'The highest recorded flood flow on any river in England and Wales occurred on the river Tyne at Bywell gauging station. It exceeded the highest recorded flow at the furthest downstream measuring point on the Severn, Trent and Thames, with respectively two, three and four times the catchment area contributing to the river. The flow of 1586 cumecs is equivalent to nearly 1600 tonnes of water passing an observer on the bank each second'.

In simple terms, a tremendous amount of water can and does flow down this section. The Tyne is a noted salmon river and boasts a high number of fish returning to the river to spawn.

Water level   This section can be paddled at any level. Medium to high levels are best and grade 2 conditions are present on various sections at such levels. At very high levels almost everything is washed out, the river is very wide with few breakouts and the weirs at Hexham, Riding Mill pumping station and Wylam are lethal.

Access   Access and egress is possible at the following locations:
Tyne Green, Hexham, river right, upstream of weir (938646).
Corbridge, river right, upstream of bridge (988643).
Riding Mill, river right, upstream of Riding Mill pumping station, (018617). Bywell bridge, downstream river left, (053620).
Prudhoe Country Park, river right, (086634).
Wylam, upstream of bridge, river left (117645).
Access details from the river adviser, www.bcu.org.uk/access/riverinfonortheast.

Description   Starting at Hexham, put in at Tyne Green. If you intend to shoot the weir it is best inspected before putting on, as it lies some 50m downstream of the start, just under the large, stone road bridge. This large weir varies greatly with water level, so inspect and decide what you are doing. A further 200m or so downstream there is an old diagonal small weir, which at medium to low levels provides limited play opportunities. Occasional rapids lead down to Corbridge, with an interesting small rapid under Corbridge bridge 1.5km upstream of Corbridge, Devil's Water enters the Tyne from river right. The river continues in similar fashion, with occasional rapids leading down to Riding Mill pumping station, which can be portaged on river left. The river flows on down to Bywell, with a couple of more interesting rapids, which end at Bywell bridge. Once again, occasional rapids lead down towards Prudhoe. The rapids become more interesting upstream of Prudhoe bridge, these lead down to the bridge itself (this area is used for Slalom). Flatter water and occasional rapids appear on this section down to Wylam weir. This is the tidal limit of the Tyne and periodically a seal may be seen sitting on the rocky island below the weir. From the notices and water safety equipment placed around the weir, it is clear that the local council consider this weir to be dangerous to the public, and with good

reason. The weir does offer the experienced paddler opportunities at certain levels. It does, however, vary considerably with water level, and at higher levels backtow is extensive and serious. Immediately below the weir on river left is a short but continuous and voluminous rapid, grade 2/3 in higher levels and also at lower tide levels.

Contributor:
Rob Cunnington

Other important points   Care is needed at high and very high levels on the Tyne, and all three weirs mentioned become lethal.

Devil's Water

Grade	**3**
Length	**11km**
OS sheet	**87**

Introduction   This tributary of the Tyne has a small catchment area from the moors of Hexhamshire Common and Blanchland Moor. It is a narrow, fast run with good gradient, and gives an impression of running through remote countryside.

Water level   Very heavy localised rainfall falling in its catchment area is essential to bring it into condition. It rises and falls very quickly, but once up, prolonged rainfall will keep it up. It is possible for Devil's Water to be bone dry when the Tyne is in full spate and vice versa. It is very much a river that should be paddled while it is still raining.

Access   Access at 'C' class road bridge (944581) near the hamlet of Steel. Put in downstream of the bridge on river right. Alternately put in at the A695 road bridge, downstream of bridge, river right, (975636).
Egress at Corbridge, upstream of bridge, river right (988643).

Description   If you start from the 'C' class road bridge near the hamlet of Steel, immediately below the road bridge is a 2m fall, which is difficult to inspect and partially horseshoe shaped. Within 50m there is a mini-gorge; this starts with an angled rockslide, which loses some 2.5m in height. Below here is a tricky little drop, hemmed in by sandstone gorge walls. After a short distance, Rowley Burn enters from river left and the volume of Devil's Water increases noticeably. The river continues with good gradient and frequent rapids. Below the village of Ordley lies a significant fall over an angled limestone reef. The river drops steeply and continuously over the reef, for some 30m. There are numerous protruding rocks and some big stoppers in the centre, and in very high levels this can become grade 3/4. Just before Linnels Bridge is a concrete weir, which can have considerable back tow. A short but very narrow grade 2 section, with little chance of a breakout, leads down towards Linnels Bridge. On a left-hand bend, immediately upstream of Linnels Bridge, lies a grade 3 fall, usually taken centrally, but be aware that there is a block close to the surface here! The river continues with gradient and rapids and there is a picturesque sandstone gorge further downstream at Swallowship pool. Grade 1/2 rapids continue down to the Scout campsite at Dilston. At this point there is a 2m horseshoe-shaped weir with fish pass and ample backtow in high water! Next comes an ornate stone bridge, with a fall beneath it. A little further downstream the river swings left, then right, with rapids building. The river then swings left again to drop over a river-wide limestone reef. This obvious drop is impressive in high water, but is difficult to inspect at any paddling level. Take out below the road bridge, downstream river right, away from the houses and gardens, which lie upstream of the bridge. Alternatively, continue down to the confluence with the River Tyne and egress at Corbridge bridge, upstream river right.

Other important points   Trees and strainers are a real problem along with fences on this section.
In exceptional conditions Devil's Water can be paddled from the bridleway ford at (926542). There are sections of grade 2 and 2/3, along with fences, strainers, underwater culverts (at a ford), gates! and barbed wire; so be prepared to portage.
In very high conditions Rowley Burn can be paddled from Dye House bridge (936585). This 1.1km run contains a small weir/ford and a grade 2 rapid.

Contributor:
Rob Cunnington

Derwent

Grade	**2+**
Length	**14km**
OS sht.	**87/88**

Introduction   Flowing out of Derwent Reservoir , the River Derwent is a tributary of the River Tyne, which it joins at 'canny' Blaydon. In its upper section, above Shotley Bridge it has enough gradient to provide sections of grade 2. However, it is tree-ridden in parts and shallow at lower levels.

Water level   A good outflow from Derwent Reservoir is required to make it worthwhile.

Access   Put in at the bridge at (032512, OS sheet 87). Take out at Shotley Bridge (091528, OS sheet 88).

Contributor:
Rob Cunnington

Description   This pleasant river run offers sections of 2+, some small falls and a series of weirs. It culminates in a modest 1.5m fall at Shotley Bridge.

Rookhope Burn

Grade	**3/4**
Length	**3km**
OS sht.	**87/92**

Introduction   This little burn, a tributary of the river Wear, provides a spate run but has a fairly small catchment area.

Water level   Very high levels required. Possible after heavy continuous localised rainfall. Run-off is fairly quick, it is an 'in the rain run.'

Access   Put in at the wooden footbridge near the lay-by (944417).
Egress at Eastgate; paddlers have used the caravan site, *but* check at caravan site first.

Contributor:
Rob Cunnington

Description   This short run has a range of falls and rapids. It does have a 4m fall in one section, this has been turned into a gauging weir with the addition of a concrete construction! This drop needs careful consideration.

Upper Wear (Wearhead to Daddry Shield)

Grade	**2/3**
Length	**5.5km**
OS sheet	**92**

Introduction   It is rare to find this section at a good working level; if you are lucky enough take your time as you may not get another chance.

Water level   High, needs to have rained in area for many days.

Gauge   If at the put-in at Wearhead Bridge it is possible to paddle without a bump and scrape, "she's a goer".

Access   If the river is very high you can get on even higher up, however the best access and more frequently used due to water levels is at Wearhead (road bridge). On river right below the bridge is a path giving access to the river (857397). Cars are best

parked along the main street next to the shops.
Egress at Daddry Shield; there is a path on river right just before
the road bridge (896380).

Description   The River Wear is reliant on high water levels
for many days to support a descent and the grade could vary
massively depending on height. The river could be a bump and
scrape grade 2 or a stomach shrinking muddy grade 4. A limestone base forms several small drops throughout the trip. Deep
waves are rare for playing on unless ran in flood conditions. From
your put-in at Wearhead you negotiate bridge stanchions and
overhanging branches. Although the section does not contain any
serious holes or rocks, the water is fast with overgrown sides so
rescues can be painful and lengthy. A triple-arched bridge warns
you of West Blackdene Falls where an inspection from the path
on river left is advised. The next section with limestone shelves
creates the best of the play waves in high water until your first
possible egress at Daddry Shield bridge.

Contributor:
Lawrence 'Hoopla'
Harris

Other important points   Access is delicate and due to few paddlers using the section in years gone by locals and landowners
have been very tolerant. Keep numbers to a minimum, smile, if in
doubt ask a local.

Upper Wear (Daddry Shield to Stanhope Ford)

Introduction   It is rare to find this section at a good working level.

Water level   High, needs to have rained in area for many days.

Gauge   As for previous section.

Access   Put in at Daddry Shield road bridge where there is a
path upstream and river right of the bridge (896380).
Egress at Stanhope Ford (993392).

Description   After Daddry Shield the river widens and becomes
more of a grade 1/2 with the exception of Stanhope weir, which is
best shot river left. Exit at Stanhope Ford.

Other important points   See previous section.

Grade   **1/2**
Leng. **11.5km**
OS sheet   **92**

Contributor:
Lawrence 'Hoopla'
Harris

Wear (Durham to Finchale Priory)

Grade   **2**
Length **8.5km**
OS sheet   **92**

Introduction   From Durham down to Finchale Abbey the River Wear meanders, partly in a deeply wooded gorge and partly through farmland. In medium to high water it is swiftly flowing.

Water level   Can be paddled at low levels, but medium is probably the most entertaining as high levels tend to start to wash out river features.

Access   Access at Durham at Framwellgate (993392).
Egress at Finchale Priory (298473).
There is an access agreement, details from the river adviser, www.bcu.org.uk/access/riverinfonortheast.

Contributor:
Rob Cunnington

Description   Initial flat water soon gives way to fairly consistent gradient and flow, with numerous falls and occasional chutes. Pipebridge rapid, just upstream of Finchale Priory can be a chunky little number. From here flat water leads to the rocky reef which forms the final rapid at Finchale Priory.

Other important points   Higher up Weardale, immediately upstream of Wolsingham lies a short section of 2+ water.

Low Force, River Tees

Salmon Leap Falls, River Tees

Salmon Leap Falls

A.K.A. The Dog-leg

Devil's Water

Slenningford Mill, River Ure

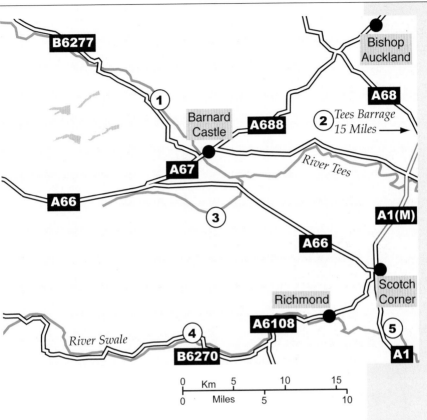

Tees and Swale

Tees (Upper - High Force to Scooberry Bridge, 'Low Force Section')

Grade **3/4(5)**

Length **2.5km**

OS sheet **92**

Introduction   This upper section lies with the backdrop of the northern Pennines clearly visible. This can be a serious and heavy run in high water. It does have good access from the river right bank throughout.

Water level   Can be run at most levels, inspection is vital at higher levels on some rapids.

Access   Put in at High Force Hotel (use the footpath downstream of the actual footpath to High Force, walk down steps to river (885285). Egress at Wynch bridge (905279), or Scooberry bridge (911274). A small charge is payable at the High Force Hotel to paddle this section.

Contributors:
Russ Smith and
Rob Cunnington

Description   There is an easy start, rocky in low levels. The rapids are pool drop and reef fall in nature. This run has several sections which require inspection and safety cover. The first notable fall is the 'Dog Leg'; this diagonal groove provides a short but sustained rapid. Low Force is an easy shoot in low to medium flows, but the small fall above carries a punch (it has even unseated the BCU Director of Coaching and one of his large and buoyant sidekicks!). Below Low Force there are a series of falls and reefs which end at Scooberry bridge. In high water this whole run becomes a very heavy section, with many powerful stoppers, which can take time to paddle! The grade can rise to 5 in parts.

Other important points   Below Scooberry bridge there are a few playspots of no more than grade 2 down to Middleton bridge.

Tees (Middleton Bridge to Cotherstone)

Grade **3/3+(4)**

Length **11km**

OS sheet **92**

Introduction   Starting from Middleton bridge the Tees meanders its way to Egglestone bridge, from here to Cotherstone is the classic white water racing section of the Tees… not to be missed.

Water level   Low levels are a rock bash. The best levels are when both sides of the Egglestone bridge are flowing. Some rapids wash out in flood conditions.

Access   Put in at Middleton bridge (947253). Egress at Cotherstone (014201). On white water racing weekends only, *and only then*, the bridge at Egglestone may be used.

Description Just downstream of Middleton there is a small gauging weir; a further kilometre downstream of here lies a reef drop which at certain medium levels produces a good surf wave. Below here the River Lune enters from river right. Further on, the Egglestone Beck enters from river left. Occasional rapids lead down to Egglestone bridge. From here good grade 3 rapids of a pool drop nature exist, with plenty of playwave opportunities. Opposite the River Tyne outflow tunnel (which brings pumped Tyne water from the Riding Mill pumping station) is a good playwave… in the right conditions. The two most notable rapids on this section are Little Woden Croft and Big Woden Croft, both are on bends in the river. At Cotherstone, the River Balder enters from river right.

Other important points   Below Cotherstone the Tees becomes easy grade 2 down to Barnard Castle. The big weir upstream of 'Barny' requires inspection… and can be portaged on river left! The River Lune is runnable in high water at 3/4 standard, but does contain a lot of tree and fence debris. For the access situation, check with the river adviser, www.bcu.org.uk/access/riverinfonortheast.html.

Contributor:
Russ Smith

The Egglestone Beck is also runnable at 3-4 standard, it requires very heavy rain and run-off is very quick indeed. For access situation, check with the river adviser.
The River Balder provides grade 3/4 paddling and is only runnable in high water, like the Lune it contains plenty of debris. For access, check with the river adviser.

River Tees (Barnard Castle to Winston)

Introduction   Running from Barnard Castle to Winston the river changes from small limestone gorges to a more open aspect.

Water level   Low levels are a rock bash, this section is better at medium to high levels. Flood levels are fast through the Abbey rapids section.

Access   Access in Barnard Castle at the 'Desmens' Field below

Grade **3/4**
Length **12km**
OS sheet **92**

the green bridge (052159). Access and egress are possible at Abbey bridge by Egglestone Abbey (063152), Whorlton bridge (107146) and Winston bridge (143163).

Description   Below Barnard Castle there is a river-wide reef by an old mill. At Abbey rapids there is a good grade 3 section, which also continues in the limestone gorge downstream of Abbey bridge. There are some good playspots here and further on down to Whorlton bridge. Downstream of Whorlton bridge is Whorlton falls, this is large river-wide reef which is undercut in parts, so be careful.

Contributor:
Russ Smith

Downstream of here are numerous rapids and reefs, which at the right level provide plenty of play opportunities.

Other important points   In high levels this whole section can become heavy and serious. At certain very high levels it provides tough alpine conditions! The grade on this section can rise to 4+.

Tees Barrage, River Tees

**Artificial
WW Course**

OS sheet **93**

Water level   Variable... The course runs around low tide, therefore contact centre for release times, Telephone 01642 678000.

Access   Via A66 near Stockton, follow the signs.

Contributor:
Russ Smith

Description   A man-made course 350m long and between 5-10m wide with adjustable bollards allowing the course to be changed. The course provides grade 2+ white water and is open all year.

Greta

Grade   **3/4**

Length   **11km**

OS sheet   **92**

Introduction   This 'narrow river' flows through a secluded wooded valley. It can carry a lot of water to provide a fast run.

Water level   Needs to be in spate for best conditions.

Access   Access and egress points are available at Bowes bridge (995133), Rutherford bridge (032123) and the A66 road bridge at (085133).

There is no egress at the confluence with River Tees, though it is easy to paddle down the Tees to egress at Whorlton Lido.

Always consult the river adviser for up-to-date information as access is challenged! www.bcu.org.uk/access/riverinfonortheast.html.

Description   A good continuous stretch of water with several testing sections and final rapids at Mortham Tower before the Tees confluence. These rapids need inspecting.

Contributor:
Russ Smith

Swale (Upper)

Grade	**4/5**
Length	**5km**
OS sht.	**92/98**

Introduction   This steep run is not for the faint hearted and the portages at times are more serious than the falls!

Water level   Needs to be middle to upper levels. The levels rise and fall quickly after rain.

Access   Put in at Hoggarts Bridge B6270 (871013, OS sheet 92). Egress at footbridge upstream of Muker (910986, OS sheet 98).

Description   A steep pool drop section. All drops need inspecting before running and safety cover is required.

Contributor:
Russ Smith

Swale (Reeth to Richmond)

Grade	**2(3)**
Length	**19km**
OS	**98/99/92**

Introduction   Nice scenic paddle. Easy rocky rapids.

Water level   Rock bash when low. Better with middle and upper levels.

Access   Put in at Reeth, actually on the the Arkle Beck (043992, OS sheet 98); within 500m it joins the Swale, alternately at Grinton (046985).
Take out at Richmond town centre.

Description   At Richmond town falls, shoot on far right for pool drop. Good rapids below in high water.

Contributor:
Russ Smith

Other important points   Easby Abbey has a good playspot in high water… although access is not ideal!
The Arkle Beck is paddleable at grade 2/3. Access is from Whaw bridge or Langthwaite. The water level needs to be high as the

levels drop quickly. It provides a quickly descending, narrow, rocky run down to Reeth where it joins the River Swale.

Catterick Playspot, River Swale

Playspot

OS sheet **99**

Location   Catterick Bridge.

Water level   The wave forms at medium levels and eventually washes out at higher levels.

Access   Access and egress at Catterick Bridge; upstream of the bridge (228995) on river right there is a car park that is used by the racecourse.

Description   The playspot is formed by the bridge. As the water falls off the lip of the bridge foundations it forms two waves, one under each arch. The two waves are quite different. The left-hand wave is formed by two small diagonal waves whilst the second is more linear. There are good feeder eddies formed by the bridge stanchions. The only downfall is that in lower water levels the river is quite shallow.

Contributor:

Rob Arrowsmith

Other important points   Bacon butties can be bought at the newsagent-cum-cafe in Catterick village. Sundays are busy as the racecourse hosts a Sunday market that is very popular so parking may be a problem.

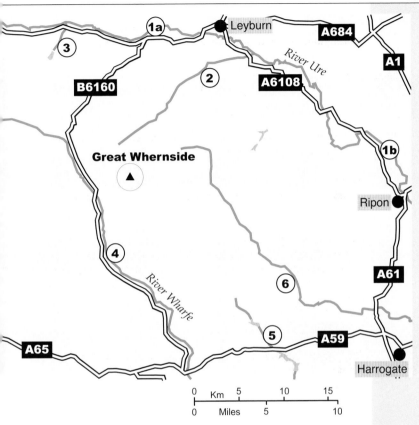

Ure and Wharfe

Ure (Upper - Apperset to Aysgarth Falls)

Grade **2**

Length **20km**

OS sheet **99**

Introduction   This is the highest section of the Ure and has very little in the way of rapids.

Water level   High water levels are required on the upper sections.

Access   Put in at the road bridge in Apperset (868906). The river is actually Widdal Beck, which is paddled for a short distance to the confluence.
Egress at either the metal bridge (995889) or directly above the falls (008885).

Description   The section contains a number of easy grade 2 rapids as it flows through the beautiful upper reaches of Wensleydale. After 19km a metal bridge is reached which is the usual egress for this section. The more adventurous will continue the short distance below and paddle Aysgarth Mill Rapids, (Gd 2/3). Make sure you get out before Aysgarth Falls!

Contributor:

Rob Arrowsmith

Other important points   Below here lies Aysgarth Falls, a three tier, serious waterfall, sections of which are reported to have been paddled at certain water levels.

Ure (Upper - Aysgarth Falls to Wensley Bridge)

Grade **3**

Length **11km**

OS sheet **99**

Introduction   The river at the start of this section is quite wide and falls over increasingly smaller shelves. As you run down to the take-out the river starts to lose some of its potency. This allows time for you to take in the scenery of this very open and scenic dale.

Water level   High water levels are required on the upper sections.

Access   The best access point is below the lower force of Aysgarth Falls (009885). Follow the NT footpath past the falls and continue on past the lower force. Just after this a path to the right leads down to the river. An alternate and less recommended start is to get on at the road below the High Force and portage the Middle and Lower Forces on the way down.
Egress at Wensley Bridge (092895).

Description   The first rapid is directly at the put-in. It consists of a long shelf that in low water can be difficult to get down, more through lack of water than difficulty. This ends in a small drop. Care should be taken, as the drop will not be shootable along its length in all water conditions.

After about 2 km trees flank the river, a further half kilometre brings you to Redmire Force. In spate conditions this force is graded 5, as the ledge will form an impressive stopper. However in lower water there are a number of options depending on the group. The fall has two sections to it and is best inspected.

The fall at Redmire is the last drop of this section and marks a change in the river. From here the rapids become more gentle (2/3 depending on water) as the river gradient decreases. This gives a relaxing run during which the scenery can be admired; both Bolton Castle and Bolton Hall can be seen from the river. A private bridge that is some 2km above Wensley Bridge serves the latter.

Contributor:
Rob Arrowsmith

Other important points   Cafés can be found at Aysgarth Falls, Leyburn and a popular bikers' café in Masham town centre.

Ure (Lower - Hack Falls to Slenningford Water Mill)

Introduction   This run is quite popular in the area and sees many descents. The site at the end of the run is open all year round and hosts various events including slaloms. Whilst it is not the hardest run on the Ure it must be treated with respect. Particular attention should be made to Tanfield Weir as this has seen some deaths in previous years.

Grade   **3**

Length **6.5km**

OS sheet   **99**

Water level   The lower sections of the Ure can be paddled in all but very low water levels.

Gauge   Situated by the small footbridge near the car park at Slenningford Water Mill, 37.9 is spate (see access agreement).

Access   If you are paddling Hack Falls use the public footpath (231776). If you are paddling from Mickley Weir the put-in is just out of Mickley village (251768). A small lay-by is available for parking so consideration must be given to the shuttle as other paddlers and walkers will be using this parking space.

Egress at Slenningford Water Mill (280784).

Please note that the BCU have negotiated the following access

agreement on this section of river. Full details can be found at Slenningford Water Mill or by contacting the river adviser www.bcu.org.uk/access/riverinfoeast.html. As of Jan 2003 the cost of using the facilities at Slenningford is £2.50.

1st April - 30th September access is allowed on the 2nd and 4th Sundays of the month. 1st Oct - 31st March open access.

In addition to these dates access is allowed each and every Thursday. Access is also allowed in spate conditions. This is when the gauge at Slenningford reads 37.9m or higher.

Description   Hack Falls is a 75m sloping rapid. The following Mickley Weir is easily shot in all but the highest water levels. At these it becomes an impressive river-wide stopper. A little way downstream from the weir is another smaller broken weir. Please take care here as there are some exposed bars that have formed part of its construction. From here the run is pleasant and provides plenty of opportunity to practise and sharpen your skill. The first place of note is Tanfield Weir. Here care must be taken as a deep recirculating stopper with plenty of tow-back can be formed on river left through to the centre. The best route down the weir is on river right; from here it is both easily viewed or portaged.

You are now at the start of Slenningford Water Mill Rapids. For the next 500m the rapids are formed by a series of rocks and ledges. Depending on the water level the rapid can provide a number of waves and holes for playing. It is also easily portaged back to the top for another run.

Contributor:
Rob Arrowsmith

Other important points   The site at Slenningford also provides a shop, camping and shower facilities. There is also a changing area for boaters.

Ure (Lower - Slenningford to Ripon)

Grade   **2**
Len. **10.5km**
OS sheet   **99**

Introduction   This run is seldom paddled, has a number of anglers in its lower reaches and has much to hold the interest of the novice paddler. Near the start is a Site of Special Scientific Interest (SSSI). The various anglers in its lower reaches will have you believe you are not allowed to paddle it for this reason. You can as long as you don't land on the bank.

Water level   Can be paddled in all but very low water levels.

Gauge   Situated by the small footbridge near the car park at Slenningford Water Mill, 37.9 is spate (see access agreement in preceding section).

Access   Put in at Slenningford Water Mill (280784). Egress at either Hewick Bridge (332702) or Ripon Marina (324704).

Description   A succession of small grade 2 rapids are formed on this section mainly by shingle banks. A number of standing waves can form just downstream of North Bridge and the A61 bridge in high water, and a small weir is to be found under Hewick bridge.

Contributor:
Rob Arrowsmith

Cover

Grade	2/3
Length	10km
OS sheet	99

Introduction   The River Cover is in a small, and at times deep, valley to the south of Wensleydale. and joins the river near Middleham.

Water level   The river has quite a large bed and needs some good rainfall to make it viable.

Access   Access at Nathwaite bridge (066837). To egress paddle down to River Ure and find a suitable take-out (use the River Ure guide sections to assist in this).

Description   The river has a fairly constant gradient and at times is flanked by deep valley sides. In its lower reaches, below Coverham bridge, the river enters a steeply wooded vale. In the trees can be seen a number of cliffs that the river has carved in its younger years, the main one being the long Cover Scar.

Contributor:
Rob Arrowsmith

Bain

Grade	3
Length	4km
OS sheet	99

Introduction   The Bain is reputedly the shortest river in England.

Water level   Medium to high levels are required.

Gauge   Look over the bridge at Bainbridge.

Access   Access at bridge over river at Semer Water (922877). To egress paddle down to River Ure and find a suitable take-out (use

River Ure guide sections to assist).

Description   A short run with the main rapid of interest being the falls at Bainbridge. These can be scouted from the road prior to getting on the river. Please be aware that they form powerful stoppers in high water and should be scouted with care, as it may not be possible to paddle them.

Contributor:
Rob Arrowsmith

Wharfe

Starting on Oughtershaw Moor in the Yorkshire Dales, the Wharfe offers a range of interesting trips with some exciting rapids. Its large catchment area means the river can rise quickly when some of the rapids in the middle section become a serious proposition. Access is problematic which is a pity as the river has much to offer: Conistone Falls, Ghastrills Strid, Linton Falls, Loup Scar, Appletreewick Falls, and The Strid (described as…. *'impossible and must be portaged'*, in the 1966 BCU 'Guide to the Waterways of the British Isles'). With a number of access points, the length and difficulty of trips can be geared to any level of paddler. Wharfedale is a particularly beautiful limestone valley with many interesting villages, quaint pubs, and walking potential.

Contributor:
Martin Burgoyne

Wharfe (Upper - High Bank to Hubberholme Bridge)

Grade **4**

Length **4km**

OS sheet **98**

Water level   Can be paddled in all but very low water levels.

Access   Put in at High Bank (877802), take out at Hubberholme bridge (926782).

Description   There are waterfalls above this put-in on the Wharfe and its tributary the Green Field Beck. The majority of this section can be viewed from the minor road which follows the river up the beautiful Langstrorpe dale. The main difficulties are in the first mile as the river flows over a number of interesting limestone steps. Take out river left just below the old humpback bridge at Hubberholme. Over the bridge is a convenient pub. The next ten miles or so are flat and meandering, though the valley continues to be scenic.

Wharfe (Middle - Kettlewell Bridge to Burnsall Bridge)

Water level   Can be paddled in all but very low water levels. Care must be taken in very high levels as some of the harder sections may not be paddleable.

Grade   **4(5)**
Length   **4km**
OS sheet   **98**

Access   Access is possible at Kettlewell bridge (968723). Alternative access is at Conistone bridge (979675), Grassington footbridge (001632), and Hebden footbridge (026624). As access is problematic along the whole river a start at Conistone bridge is preferred. Egress at Burnsall bridge (033611), the car park is on river right just below the bridge.

Description   Half a mile below Conistone bridge is Conistone Falls (Gd 4), a double-stepped drop over a limestone ledge probably best on the right. A flat section leads to a longer rapid Ghastrills Strid (Gd 4). Below Grassington road bridge are two weirs. The first (Gd 4) needs inspection but can be shot down the ramp on the right. The second, a diagonal grade 3, marks the lead in to the most serious rapid of the section, Linton Falls (Gd 5), an impressive double drop. This can be inspected and photographed from the footbridge directly over the top of the rapid. Portage river left if you don't like what you see. In low to medium water a twisting route from extreme right to the centre is possible. Below the falls there is a long quiet section to Hebden footbridge below which the river picks up speed and the left-hand bend against a limestone cliff marks Loup Scar (Gd 3). It is then flat to Burnsall bridge.

Wharfe (Lower - Burnsall Bridge to Bolton Bridge)

Water level   Can be paddled in all but very low water levels.

Grade   **3(4)**
Length   **4km**
OS sh.**98/104**

Access   Burnsall bridge (033611).
Take out on the right at Bolton Bridge (071528) on the A59 Harrogate to Skipton road.

Description   There is a shorter popular section down to Barden bridge (051574), the venue for a white water race. The main point of interest in this section comes after just over a mile where a stand of pine trees on the right bank mark Appletreewick Falls (Gd 4). This is best viewed from the right bank, and shot on the

right of the island. A short shallow gorge follows after which the river is flat down to Barden bridge and a possible take-out river left above the bridge.

Just below Barden bridge a more resistant band of gritstone is the cause of The Strid. It starts with a left-hand bend, Tankers Corner (Gd 3), which flows straight into the Little Strid (Gd 3). 300m below is The Strid (Gd 4), a very narrow, undercut slot, not the place for a swim! The Strid is easily inspected from either bank. The river opens out below the gorge and quietens down as it flows past Bolton Priory with its footbridge and stepping stones, a popular picnic site in summer. Take out on the right at Bolton Bridge.

Washburn

Grade   **3**
Length **3.5km**
OS sheet **104**

Contributor:
Martin Burgoyne

Introduction   A short yet reliable paddle governed by releases from Thruscross Reservoir. Canoeing competitions coincide with release days, which also provide access for river running.

Water level   Information on releases can be obtained from the BCU Yearbook in the Programme of Touring section or by using the Washburn Information Line on 07626-978654.

Access   Put in below Thruscross Reservoir by the car park on the right bank (155574). Take out river right below the A59 road bridge (168553).

Description   Put in below Thruscross Reservoir by the car park on the right bank. A enjoyable narrow run with every river feature on a small scale. On race days it is possible to get the shuttle back up to the start and repeat the experience over and over again.

Nidd

The Nidd is a small shallow river at its upper reaches due to a number of reservoirs restricting the flow of the river. It barely rises above grade 2 from initial access at Wath Bridge to its confluence with the River Ouse at Nun Monkton. The majority of the river is slow moving, with regular shingle rapids being a frequent characteristic. The main interest for most paddlers is provided by the numerous weirs, which inhabit the river at regular intervals.

It is worth noting that above Hampsthwaite paddlers are likely to be challenged by anglers or river officials.

Nidd (Wath to Darley)

Water level   Medium to high water levels are needed.

Grade	**1/2**
Length	**12km**

99/104/105

Access   Put in at Wath (144678) and egress at Darley (205598).

Description   A short paddle from the put-in at Wath Bridge brings you to a small weir, which is an easy slide. Pateley Bridge soon arrives, and with it another small weir under a footbridge at Castlesteads (5km). On the left of the river is Glasshouses Dam and after the girder bridge is Glasshouses Mill (home of Wildwater Equipment). The next 3km provides a pair of weirs. The first a 1.5 metre sloping drop, is easily shot. The second is a big weir with exposed reinforcement rods protruding from the base of the weir. Inspection is advised. The next weir at Summerbridge is easily shot on the left. Darley appears 3km downstream of Summerbridge.

Contributor:
Pete Breckon

Nidd (Darley to Ripley)

Water level   Medium to high water levels are needed.

Grade	**2/3**
Length	**11km**

99/104/105

Access   Put in at Darley (205598) and take out at Ripley (288597). Ross Bridge (230603) has an alternative access/egress point and a car park, which can avoid conflict with anglers.

Description   Birstwith weir is a 2.25 metre, 5-step drop with the main channel washing through to the left. Inspection needed. Hampsthwaite Church is 100m above the road bridge and easy water leads downstream to Ripley bridge. Egress can be made downstream on the left bank (288597) after a small broken weir shot on far right.

Other important points   Downstream of Ripley the river is now pretty easy, but very picturesque as it meanders through woodland and pastures. The stretch between the viaduct and Knaresborough presents several weirs with which to contend.

Contributor:

Pete Breckon

The Mill weir and the Footbridge weir can be both shot in the centre. Knaresborough town is reached some 27km from Wath; egress is possible on the left before the flat boat hire section. A steeply angled 3-metre drop weir is at the mill on river left, and inspection is needed. There is no surprise to discover that several more weirs and matching fishermen adorn the Nidd below Knaresborough, and Ship Bridge (60km below Wath) on the A59 (483560) can allow a final egress if required.

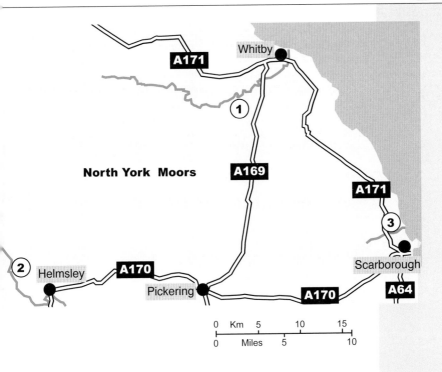

North York Moors

Esk (Crunkly Gill to Egton Bridge)

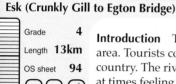

Grade **4**

Length **13km**

OS sheet **94**

Introduction   The Esk Valley is a remote and infrequently visited area. Tourists come as the area is best known as 'Heartbeat' country. The river changes a number of times along this section, at times feeling like an Alpine run albeit without the crystal blue waters.

Water level   Very high water levels are needed. A minimum of 1.5 on the gauge is required.

Gauge   Downstream of the road bridge at Egton Bridge (085052).

Access   There are a number of starts depending on the length of paddle you would like:
The bridge near Houlskye (734074). This access is 3km above Crunkly Gill.
A short walk from the road at (747076). This access is 750m above Crunkly Gill.
Lealholm, car park and toilets (762077). This access is 1km below Crunkly Gill.
Egress can be made river left at the bridge at Egton Bridge (085052) or river left as the river enters the village of Egton Bridge.

Description   Your reward for paddling the flat from Houlskye is Crunkley Gill. Here the river steepens and enters a wooded vale. The rapid is formed, much like others on this run, from a bouldery garden. This gives the paddler many route choices and decidedly more to interest them than the preceding few kilometres. There is nothing of great note in the rapid, just a kilometre of enjoyable boating.
After Lealholm the river becomes more sedate with some minor rapids. The most notable point on this section is the fallen trees, which at times form river-wide strainers. In low water care must be taken at these points and in high water extreme caution must be exercised. A mill house on river right signals the next rapid of note. Glaisdale Rapid (Grade 3) is again in the bottom of a wooded valley giving a different atmosphere from the previous few kilometres. The rapid itself is again bouldery offering many route choices and eddies on which to hone your skills. After this is a small weir which can be shot down the centre. After this a number of bridges are passed and the railway follows the course

of the river for a short section. A little way downstream the railway embankment comes very close to the river bank. This is the
start of the Arnecliffe rapids (Gd 4-).

The rapids here flow into one another in quick succession leaving
little or no time to recover from any mishaps. This means the interest and concentration of the paddler is kept for some considerable time. This section is most reminiscent of some rivers found in
the French Alps. At all water levels good scouting is necessary to
make the right route choice. Throughout its length the rapid offers
boulder-choked rapids, fallen trees and small drops that require a
long neck or to be scouted from the bank. The rapids eventually
fizzle out and some flat water leads you to the village of Egton
Bridge. If the run has been done in low water it may be worth
egressing at the upstream end of the village. Alternatively there
is a sloping weir that can be easily shot. This feeds you into a set
of stepping stones which, if showing are harder to navigate. The
egress is at the bridge on the river left.

Contributor:
Rob Arrowsmith

Esk (Egton Bridge to Whitby)

Introduction   The Esk Valley is best known as the location for
'Heartbeat'; whilst you are not likely to be featured on the TV
show the area can still be worth visiting. This section has the
unique distinction of being able to finish at Whitby harbour and a
paddle out to the sea.

Grade   **2**
Length **16km**
OS sheet   **94**

Water level   Very high water levels are needed. A minimum of
1.5 on the gauge is required.

Gauge   Egton Bridge.

Access   Put in at Egton Bridge (085052) and take out at Whitby
harbour.

Description   The main feature of this run is that you can paddle from the hills to the sea. Whilst not at the same standard of
the previous section of the Esk it can still be an enjoyable paddle.
There are a couple of grade 2 rapids within a kilometre of Egton
Bridge. Once these have been negotiated there are few other
rapids. After about 10km you arrive at Sleights Weir. This is a 2m
vertical drop which is usually shot far right. After a further 2km

Contributor:
Rob Arrowsmith

another weir, Ruswarp, is reached. This consists of a sloping drop of around 1.5m. Both these weirs should be treated as you find them on the day, with good judgement rather than this guide being used as an indication of whether you should paddle them.

Rye (Shaken Bridge to Rievaulx Bridge)

Grade   2
Length   **6km**
OS sheet   **100**

Introduction   The Rye is a secluded and rarely visited (by boaters) dale. In its lower reaches it is a good touring river but this is the only white water section. Around Helmsley it has various places of interest and heritage including Rievaulx Abbey (pronounced reevo). The run itself is good for beginners to moving water. It has nothing of great note but is a good day out. Whilst paddling this run recently we saw either 6 kingfishers or the same one 6 times. There is an abundance of wildlife on this stretch so it's worth keeping your eyes peeled.

Water level   Very high water levels are needed.

Access   Access can be made at Shaken Bridge (559884). Parking here is limited so please be considerate.
Egress at Rievaulx bridge (574843). Parking is a little better here but only just.

Description   The run contains a number of grade 2 rapids. The majority of these are formed by shingle banks and have the odd rock in them to avoid. There is also the occasional tree in the river so be on the lookout for strainers.

Other important points   If this run is of insufficient length then the River Seph can be paddled as well. It is of a similar grade and style to the Rye only a narrower river bed. As it is paddled once in a blue moon there are a few river-wide fallen trees, access can be made at Laskill Farm (562907).

Contributor:
Rob Arrowsmith

Scalby Beck

Grade	**3/4**
Length	**3km**
OS sheet	**101**

Introduction   A strange run that can take you from the wilds of the North York Moors, through the suburban sprawl of Scalby to the sea at the North Bay of Scarborough and where the majority of interest comes from shooting weirs. This run has been described as a grade 4 run. My personal opinion is that it is a grade 3 paddle that requires the skills and judgement of a more advanced paddler. Weirs are dangerous and do kill those who are unable to judge their severity. Some weirs can look very easy but are in fact killers. This run contains a wide variety of weirs and should be treated with the respect you would show a grade 4 river.

Water level   Very high water levels are needed. 38.6 on the guage is paddleable.

Gauge   Upstream of the road bridge at A171.

Access   Access upstream of the 'C' class road bridge at (014903). Egress just before you reach the sea (036908), a final weir stops you going any further and egress can be made on the right bank.

Description   Shortly after starting the run you come to the first set of weirs. The first is a multi-stepped at the top section with a large sloping part below it. The overall drop is quite impressive, about 8m. Slack water takes you to the next bridge and the next weir. This consists of a small vertical drop that falls onto a concrete shelf. Some minor rapids lead you to another bridge and weir. Here there are four steps dropping around 4m in all. There is some exposed ironwork at the bottom on the far left and right. The next weir follows quickly. It is a short drop with a concave slope below. A fish ladder can be found on the left and this is a natural draw for debris.

The next two weirs are again quite close by and are both potentially dangerous. The first has the larger drop of the two and both should be carefully scouted in high water. After these the river takes on a more natural feel and some old bridge stanchions signal the only natural rapid of note on the river. Here a rocky shelf can be shot left or right. The left is a small drop, the right a slope. The river continues in this vain, no more weirs, until it reaches the sea at North Bay. A final *dangerous* weir stops you going any further and egress can be made on the right bank.

Contributor:
Rob Arrowsmith

The North-West

Contents

Eden Catchment

Derwent Catchment

West Lakes

Windermere and SW

Kent and Lune Catchment

Introduction

Cumbria is very much an 'upland' county and most people either think of the 'Lakes' (Windermere, Ullswater, Wastwater) or the steep, central volcanic mountains. You may even think of the Lakeland artists and poets such as Wordsworth, Turner and Byron. However, for a white water paddler, it is the huge diversity of landscape and style of river that makes this area so attractive... steep boulder-strewn becks to large lake-fed rivers, and everything else in between. It is this superb variety that ensures interest to all types of paddler, be it the 'creek warrior' or the long distance 'white water cruiser'.

Steep becks we have aplenty, from those more akin to a 'canyoning' adventure such as Church Beck, to the less steep but equally taxing becks such as Mosedale and Langstrath. Access (in terms of private land and fishing interests) is rarely a problem here, apart from the physical problem of actually getting to them! They are not often paddleable and less often paddled.

The small lake-fed rivers such as the superb Crake and the gentler Derwent and a few of the larger rivers such as the Lune and Eden provide the main thrust of paddling in Cumbria. These are paddleable far more often than the becks, but access agreements need to be respected on all these rivers, to ensure that others can enjoy these Cumbrian jewels.

Of the rest, it is undoubtedly their variety that is so special... from the beautiful sandstone gorges on the Gelt to the open moorland of the upper Irthing, the deep limestone gorges of the lower Kent and upper Dee, or the superb conglomerate cliffs of the Rawthey.

Nigel Timmins

North-West Regional
Coordinator for the
Guidebook

This is a superb place to paddle, enjoy the white water, but occasionally lift your head and look at your surroundings. Observe the geology, the human occupation and history: Iron Age, Roman, as well as the present day hard-pressed mountain farmers and communities. Enjoy the flora and fauna; otters, herons, dippers and kingfishers are not unusual in this area and a quiet paddle down will often pay dividends to all concerned. Relax in that eddy, rest on your paddle awhile... enjoy all that these wild Cumbrian rivers have to offer.

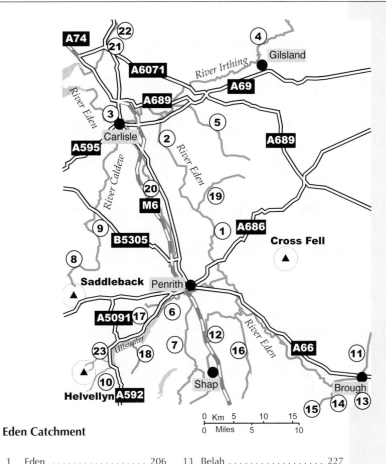

Eden Catchment

Eden (Middle - Lazonby to Armathwaite)

Grade	**2/3**
Length	**8km**
OS sheet	**86**

Introduction Perhaps the best known stretch of water in the Northern Lakes. The rapids are good, but it is the scenery that makes this a classic river trip. Run it in the autumn when the trees are turning 'golden' and it is one of the pleasantest trips you will ever do. The river is ideal for novices as most rapids have large collecting pools below to pick up the pieces!

Water level Can be run in quite low water, but obviously it is better when it is higher. It does however keep its water level for a considerable time, being partly fed by Ullswater, the second largest lake in the Lake District.

Gauge On the bridge at Lazonby is a marker on the left pillar (difficult to see from the road). Anything over 1ft on the gauge makes this river paddleable but it is better at 3ft or above.

Access This river has an access agreement so please contact the river adviser first, www.bcu.org.uk/access/riverinfocumbria.html or www.cumbriacanoeists.org.uk. Get on at Lazonby; just upstream of the bridge (551404) there is good car parking and steps down to the river. The egress is far more complex. The access agreement states you must get out just before Armathwaite weir on river left and carry round the mill house, over the stile and right along the fence and across the field to a track. Turn left and head up to the road. Parking by this track is not encouraged (and is dangerous) so you are asked to park up the hill by the railway viaduct. An absolute nightmare of a carry, but this access agreement has taken ages to agree and it is not worth jeopardizing. River take-out (503453), parking (501453).

Description After the little rapid under the bridge the current is swift but flat for a few hundred metres, till a right-hand bend where a very shallow rapid causes some interest, best line down the left. Then an island with a pleasant shoot and good break-outs either side. The river now bends to the right and you enter a superb section of rapids with a sharp left and then a long straight, and a hidden rock at the end. Another right with a nice playwave follows, before a quiet section where the Nunnery walk and Croglin beck can be found on the right. Immediately below is a good rapid with a magnetic rock in the main channel river left. Beware,

a number of open boats have been redesigned on this!
Another straight shoot with good eddies and then a pleasant
pool before the crux of the river appears around the next right-
hand bend. A superb, tall, sandstone cliff is on the left (Wirewalk
buttress) but the river enters a choked section, which you pick
through on river right before some huge waves are encountered
in high water. Good break-out, river left and then into another
complex rapid followed by some magnificent standing waves
down the left-hand bank. At the end of this is a large flat section
with some extremely 'boily' water to cross in high water. The
main sections of rapids are now over and you can relax and enjoy
the spectacular scenery. One or two rapids do exist however to
keep your interest up for the next 3km.

Watch out for a large cliff and sandy bay just above Armathwaite
weir, river right, as there are some superb rock carvings here
almost certainly the work of William Mounsey, scholar, traveller
and local gentleman of the 18th century.

Below can be heard the roar of Armathwaite weir. Get out on river
left just above it, by a tiny tributary stream. The shoot on river
left is straightforward and avoids the carry round the back of the
house, but is not technically allowed in the agreement. The main
shoot on river right is a very different proposition, particularly in
high water. If you are going to shoot this then it is best to inspect
from the right bank.

Other important points   Above Lazonby lies Eden Lacey falls, a
vertical fall of grade 3, that you can only access by paddling all
the way down from Langwathby - 5km of flat water. The falls lie
below the railway viaduct and can be shot river right.

Further upstream still, the river is easy and does not often have
enough water. If you are lucky, it is worth looking at the section
in Kirkby Stephen (see 14 Upper Eden). Beware though, as a huge
set of falls (unshootable) can be found just upstream of the town,
but directly below them lies a good but short section of grade 3
or 4. From the small packhorse bridge in Kirkby Stephen to one
of the small road bridges near Warcop gives a pleasant section of
grade 2 with one easy weir. Well worthwhile if there is enough
water.

Contributor:
Nigel Timmins

Eden (Lower - Armathwaite to Wetheral)

Grade   2
Length **11km**
OS sheet   **86**

Introduction   Perhaps the *least* known stretch of water in the Northern Lakes, as most people only know about the section above. The rapids are surprisingly good, if a little spaced and the scenery is still pleasant, though now more pastoral.

Water level   Can be run in quite low water, but obviously it is better when it is higher. It does however keep its water level for a considerable time.

Gauge   From the bridge in Armathwaite the whole river bed needs to covered. Some rocks appear on river left on the downstream side when the river starts to show signs of being too low to contemplate a run.

Access   The easiest start is from the bridge in Armathwaite via the public footpath on river right. This however is in full view of the village and a quieter, more discrete spot can be found downstream, still on river right, from a small lay-by next to a small stream and another public footpath (513465). Egress can be made about 500m below the railway viaduct in Wetheral where the road comes alongside the river and there is a convenient lay-by on river left (467554).

Description   There are a number of small gravel rapids with straightforward shoots. The only exception to this is about halfway down. Here a gravel rapid takes you over to the right but below lies a small rock ledge with the main shoot over on the left bank. Another series of rapids lies by the islands just above Corby Castle. After shooting under the railway viaduct, look for a small lane on river left and the take-out. Below lies a sloping weir but this is an Environment Agency fish counter and they ask that people do not paddle over it in low water.

A rarely paddled section that is well worthwhile, with some nice rapids, particularly round an island just before Wetheral. You can carry on all the way to the Sands Leisure Centre in Carlisle if you feel strong, but this is a long and tedious paddle!

Contributor:
Nigel Timmins

Wetheral Playspot, River Eden

Playspot
OS sheet **86**

Introduction   A fairly new weir put in by the Environment Agency to act as a fish counter and measuring device. It can when the river is in flood, produce a super-smooth, green wave… an absolute delight.

Water level   Needs to be in flood, brown and seething.

Access   Turn off the A69 at Warwick bridge and take the B6263 towards Wetheral. A short distance down it a large lay-by is found on your left (467554), launch here and the weir is some 50m below.

Description   A fairly small sloping weir divided into 3 sections. The central shoot is the obvious site with a super-smooth, green wave at high river levels. Beware though as below lie large anti-scour boulders, which would probably give you a good head bashing if you capsized. A site for experts only!

Contributor:
Nigel Timmins

Other important points   This weir is also a fish counter and the Environment Agency would like paddlers to refrain from paddling over it as it distorts their figures!

Carlisle Playspot, River Eden

Playspot
OS sheet **85**

Introduction   A simple, moving-water site with a pleasant shoot down a small broken weir, this is ideal for introducing novices to the delights of moving water or freestyle paddling.

Water level   Any, but is better when the river is medium to high as some pleasant, small waves can develop.

Access   The best access is next to the Sands Leisure Centre in the centre of Carlisle (403565). Turn left off the large roundabout signposted to the Sands. Do not turn into the leisure centre but continue into the next 'pay and display' car park. The river is just behind the car park. If you want a free parking site and don't mind a short paddle, access it from the other side of the river by taking the B6264 and then take the first right into Rickerby Park (406569).

Contributor:
Nigel Timmins

Description   The weir provides a straightforward shoot with nice eddies on either side. It is a great place to introduce novices to moving water.

Other important points   Access is available all year round as the site is on council land.

Irthing

Grade   **3(5)**
Length   **14km**
OS sheet   **86**

Introduction   A Northumberland gem, running in a wild and remote area to the north of the A69. This is a broad river with numerous rock ledges, unlike many of the Cumbrian rivers. A notable feature is the almost continuous rapids, making this river a delight!

Water level   Wet, needs lots of water but does hold its water for about a day. It is a difficult river to gauge in terms of how much rain will make it paddleable, since it needs rain from a north-westerly direction, unlike many of the Cumbrian rivers, which happily fill up with rain from the west to south-west. Persever-ance will pay dividends though, as this river should be reserved for that 'one day' with good water levels.

Gauge   Look at the river from the bridge just downstream of the picnic site and if it is paddleable without bumping and scraping it is OK. At Gilsland bridge if you look at the upstream true right hand side, there needs to be one and a half blocks showing or preferably less, before the arch proper begins.

Access   Take the A69 from Carlisle towards Newcastle. For the lower egress take a left turn after Brampton, down a small road to Low Row, and drop steeply down to the river and park at the picnic site where the road meets the river (571638). Egress from the river is just downstream of the picnic site via a small track. For the upper access, head back to the A69 and take the turn-off for Gilsland (632665). Either start here, for the lower section (park just over the river at a parking spot by the left-hand turn to roadhead), or continue past the Gilsland Spa Hotel and shortly after entering the forest, take the small right-hand turn. Do not go straight on, as you will be accosted by gun-slinging Services personnel at the barracks gate! The small road is marked as a dead end road, which it is, but the road can be driven on for some 7 miles deep into the Spadeadam Forest and live round ranges. Fortunately you soon come to a small track signposted to the waterfall just before you enter the range (638699). A shortish carry will bring you to the river and waterfall, or you can drive a little further and get on above the waterfall where the road meets the river just before Horseholme Farm (663710), provided the red flags aren't flying. You can put on much further up, but it looks flat apart from one set of falls marked on the map.

Description   For 2km above the waterfall the river is fairly flat, but wide with superb open scenery. A few simple rapids enliven things before you come to the first of many ledges across the river (very much a feature of this river). The ledge proves to be only a metre high and easily shootable. Beware though as you only go a few hundred metres before the world drops away before you. Take the portage track on river right just above the entrance rapids. This 8m fall has been run (Gd 5), but the fall itself, though spectacular, is not the problem, the lead-in rapid is. Anyway inspect carefully and either 'go for it' or more prudently, carry round. From here down to Gilsland is a superb section of grade 3 ledges, sloping falls and rapids, all in a deep spectacular gorge. Watch for the sulphurous smell coming from a small inlet on river right just downstream of the first footbridge. This is the outlet for the spa water that the hotel is built on. A few more falls before things ease and the road bridge in Gilsland comes into sight. You can finish here, or start here for a slightly easier section, but one that is still very worthwhile.

A short distance below the bridge you come to a 2m ledge which would be difficult to portage. Fortunately there is a small island in the middle on which you can land and inspect. Easy shoot just left of the island or more difficult shoots to left or right. Then take either channel round the island and on down easily to a sharp left-hand bend with a high mud cliff on the right. From here you run down a superb section of continuous grade 2 rapids with cliffs on one side or the other, making it feel very committing. You then come to yet another vertical fall, easily shootable, but this marks the start of the next grade 3 gorge. The most notable rapid here is a two-tier drop. The first is simple, taking a line on the right to a small eddy above the much bigger fall. Shoot the second, (the main fall) either on the left or bump down the staircase

to the right. After this, things quieten down and you are left with a short kilometre or so paddle to the finish just below the picnic spot.

Other important points   If the river was very high, the vertical fall below the bridge in Gilsland would have the landing spot on the island awash, making this a serious and difficult blind drop. If this is the case, a walk down the field from the bridge would be prudent.

Contributor:
Nigel Timmins

Gelt

Grade   **4(5)**
Length   **8km**
OS sheet   **86**

Introduction   I have not talked to anyone who has done this river, who has not had an epic on it! Steep, technical drops, lots of trees, and a catchment area that causes the river to rise or drop alarmingly, always seems to create problems. It is however unique, running through a beautiful area in the northern Pennines in interesting sandstone gorges.

Water level   Very wet as it takes some time to come up and needs to be at a good level, but when it is high it's serious.

Gauge   Look over the B6413 bridge just outside Castle Carrock, upstream side. If the river is coloured and the little sandstone gorge is just full, then it is ideal.

Access   You can start at a number of places, but the norm is to go back into Castle Carrock (having checked the level) and turn left signposted Geltsdale, and drive up the steep hill till you come to a sharp right turn. Park here (558556), as you are not allowed to take your car down the unmade road to the river. Or if the river is very high, continue along the tarmac road for 2km to its end and enter the river over some muddy fields. Egress is at Geltbridge just off the A69 some 3 miles after crossing the River Eden heading towards Newcastle (520593), good parking on river right just after crossing the *old* road bridge.

Description   Starting at the end of the tarmac road, the beck is fast and tree-ridden. There is nothing really serious however until you come to a 1m high diagonal fall, shootable middle left. On down till you meet the bridge at the end of the unmade road.

Upper Coquet

Warden Gorge, North Tyne

Barnard Castle, River Tees

Playing on the Dog-leg, River Tees

Wain Wath Force, River Swale

Middle Force, River Tees

Above the bridge is a small rapid which leads to a small weir, which in itself is directly above a difficult and extremely narrow series of falls. Below lies another fall, with a possible large stopper. It has an undercut left-hand bank. Things open up suddenly and you breathe a sigh of relief. A short way down, the river suddenly narrows and goes round a sharp right-hand bend with large trees piled up on the left-hand bank. Fortunately it presents no problems and you can cautiously but blindly head round it. Things ease for some way, with simple bouldery rapids, but the river soon cuts into the sandstone again, so be on your guard, as you will come to a small fall normally blocked by trees and requiring a portage. Another short easy section before more difficult and narrow falls, which lead to the B6413 road bridge. Be extremely careful here, as below lies the one grade 5 fall. A large rock blocks the channel, take the left shoot as the right is blocked with trees and has a nasty siphon, not the place to swim!
To access the river if you have portaged, or are starting the trip here is difficult, the easiest option being to enter the field on river left and then, using your throw line, lower boats and yourself down a muddy gully to the river some 10m below. Once again the river eases for a bit before another fall near Gelt mill. More small falls bring you to the railway viaduct and small road.
There is now a popular footpath on river right all the way to the finish, through Gelt woods. About halfway through is another vertical fall often blocked by trees, but normally shootable on river right. At the finish is a sharp right-hand bend with a difficult and narrow fall on it and another just upstream of the finish bridge. Somehow the grade does not adequately describe this river, as most people's nerves by this stage will be in tatters, but you can feel right proud of yourself.

Contributor:
Nigel Timmins

Other important points If the water is high enough to do the very top section then beware, as the lower bits are now in a very serious condition. Good fun if you can handle it!

Eamont

Introduction Running from Ullswater to the River Eden and then subsequently to the sea at Carlisle, this river (or rivers) can truly be called 'A Mountains to the Sea river'. It has for this reason been paddled on for years and a number of references occur

Grade **2**

Length **18km**

OS sht. **90/91**

in the earliest canoeing books. I have even paddled it in a wild
water racer from Ullswater to the sea in a raging flood, in a day!

Water level   The lake needs to be reasonably high to give a good
run. If it is low at the start, you are in for a lot of scraping! A considerable amount of rain is therefore required to get the lake up,
but once high it will stay like this for at least a week.

Gauge   At Pooley Bridge the river needs to be flowing right
across its width. It is shallow here, but if you can float down
through any of the three arches, then it is at a good level.

Access   This river has an access agreement so please contact the
river adviser first, www.bcu.org.uk/access/riverinfocumbria.html
or www.cumbriacanoeists.org.uk.There is no canoeing allowed at
all during the month of November due to the salmon spawning.
Start in Pooley Bridge at the riverside 'pay and display' car park
(469244) and finish or start in one of a number of places:
Eamont Bridge (523288), upstream of the River Lowther junction
at Brougham Castle (535293) or on the River Eden at Langwathby
bridge (565335).

Description   A gentle current leads you to a sloping weir about
20m from Pooley Bridge. The central shoot is always safe and
straightforward, though the side ones aren't when in flood! (You
can just paddle down to this and paddle back up afterwards, if
a play on the weir is all you want). On downstream, trees begin
to encroach and become an ever-present problem. A shallow
area, just before the A592 comes alongside the river, is best taken
hard on river left, though if the river is high there should be no
problem running it anywhere. A suspension footbridge and then
an island, which is run on river left, leads to a quiet area before
a natural but awkward fall, normally run river right. Dacre Beck
enters on the left and this can sometimes bring in a large quantity
of water. A beautiful stone bridge is passed under, before the real
battle with overhanging trees starts. A number of rapids keep
things interesting all the way down to the large railway viaduct.
A short distance on, the river doubles back on itself and a large
weir is now encountered. It is sloping but is best run left of centre
into some quite large waves. Then under the motorway and so
down to Eamont Bridge and the first reasonable take-out, just

below the bridge on river left. Just below this lies a very awkward weir (at least to shoot and portage). It is a vertical, one metre high, horseshoe-shaped weir, with a shallow plunge pool that can be fairly dangerous in high water. In low to medium water it can be shot in a number of places though the landing might well be rocky! Unfortunately the only real place to portage or inspect is from the right bank, but you first have to negotiate a barbed wire fence. Once through this however, it is easy to inspect the weir and re-launch just downstream. The left-hand side holds a now redundant mill shoot that is completely overgrown and impenetrable. Another couple of hundred metres brings you to yet another weir. This is far friendlier and is easily shot down the middle.

The A66 will be heard on your left as you pass down through open fields. The next take-out is on your left just before a building (the old swimming pool, now converted to a residential house) A public footpath leads across the field to a track and tunnel under the A66 accessed from the Brougham Castle access road. Below the old swimming pool house lies a broken weir, with an easy shoot down what appears to be just another rapid and you pass the River Lowther on your right in the midst of the fast water. Below is a road bridge and the start of the lower section. Unfortunately gaining access to the river from this bridge is not easy (locked gates) and it is far better to get out or start via the aforementioned footpath just before the old swimming pool.

This lower section is far more often paddled, as it is more open and not troubled by overhanging trees. Unfortunately the best rapids happen fairly early on and you are left with a rather flat 3km paddle down the River Eden to finish. A couple of kilometres downstream a gorgeous red sandstone cliff forms the right-hand bank, and an interesting left-hand bend and powerful eddy on the left makes for a pleasant playspot. A short distance down is the best grade 2 rapid on another left-hand bend. Just below is an island and is best taken down the left. Now keep your eye out for 'Honey Pot' cave, some way down on the left. This is about 20m above the river and is very hard to spot, but well worth knowing about as it provides a large dry bivvy spot, for those who wish to spend a night here. As the cliff recedes the river enters its last good rapid with a couple of large boulders at its start. A long flat straight before the Eden is met, at a very quiet and unassuming junction. You are almost unsure which way is downstream! Yet another broken weir is encountered but it presents no problems, being merely

a couple of concrete groins stretching out from the left bank. They again make for good eddy work practice. Simple rapids and flat stretches then remain, till Langwathby bridge comes into view and a good take-out and parking, just below it on river left.

Contributor:
Nigel Timmins

Other important points   The Eden can of course be continued down to Lazonby at a very easy grade, but watch out for Eden Lacey falls (Gd 3) just after the large railway viaduct, normally best shot on the right. Below here lie more caves on river right that could also be used as an emergency bivvi.

Lowther

Grade   **3**

Length **6.5km**

OS sheet   **90**

Introduction   A pleasant river that can be split into two major sections. The first is high up near Shap and requires a good flood level to make it paddleable and is therefore only given a brief mention at the end of this text. The second lower section has considerable interest and runs down to the junction with the Eamont close to Penrith.

Water level   Needs to be wet, as despite its large watershed, much of the water is held back by two major dams/reservoirs.

Gauge   Check the river out in Askham and if there is a route down the weir below the bridge then it is at a good level, or at the A6 road bridge and if the boulders in the river upstream of the bridge are covered then it is also at a good level.

Access   Get in at the minor road bridge south of Askham (517223) though parking is very limited, probably best to park near the gates 50m over the bridge. Egress can best be gained at the A6 road bridge, upstream side river right (525283). Park in the minor road opposite, or at a lay-by some 150m up the road. Alternatively you can take out a little further down on river left at some steps which lead into a residential street 'Lowther Glen' which is accessed next to the Beehive pub just in Eamont Bridge.

Description   Access the river by the footpath sign on river left and get in below or above the bridge dependant on a clear route being available through the large sheep fence. Easy water then leads you off downstream. The entry rapid to a limestone gorge is quite technical with medium-sized waves. In the gorge itself there is only one simple rapid. You float down to the road bridge in Askham and below lies the first weir. This is awkward and can normally be shot centre right. A long section of grade 3 water then ensues, passing a wood yard and on finally to a double bridge. Below the second bridge lies yet another weir. Small, but it often holds a very grabby stopper. No problems shooting it, but you are brave to go back and play in it! A little way on, a large caravan site is seen along the left bank. Watch out for a left-hand turn in the river after a long straight, with trees on the right bank. Below lies the most difficult rapid on the river with a shallow entry to a quite sizable fall. It is probably easier to run this first on the left and then down the middle of the fall. It certainly needs inspection if you are just a grade 3 paddler! It is fortunately, easily portaged or inspected on river left. Below the fall is another nice rapid before the river runs right and charges down another grade 3 section. No surprises here, just clean good fun, though somewhat technical in an open boat. After this the river reverts to grade 2 but keeps its interest with another fun rapid just above the railway viaduct. Under the motorway and a short distance below lies the A6 road bridge and exit on river right. Below this lies easy water to the junction of the Eamont.

Other important points   You can run the upper section of the Lowther in very high water from up above Shap. It is tree-strewn and has a number of fences, but is still a nice grade 2/3 run. Start at the bridge (560127) and exit at the bridge in Bampton (521180). The intervening section below is not worthwhile, being flat and uninteresting. If you want to run both sections, it is best to use your car to run you down to Askham.

Contributor:
Stephen Timmins

Upper Caldew

Grade	**4**
Length	**3km**
OS sheet	**90**

Introduction   A unique river in the Northern Lake District, in that it is a high mountain river, easily accessed by vehicle. No trees here to spoil your view or make undue difficulties! It flows off the back of Saddleback or Blencathra, in an easterly direction and provides a wild and often windswept paddle.

Water level   Very wet, lots of rain and probably only when it is still raining.

Gauge   At the bridge near Mosedale, it should be bank-full on the downstream side, just covering the gravel bank on the right.

Access   Turn off the A66 Penrith - Keswick road signposted to Mungrisdale, and follow the minor road northwards through it (good pub) to the tiny hamlet of Mosedale. Egress is at the bridge just before the village of Mosedale (356320). To reach the access, go into the hamlet and turn left up the wild and remote valley. As the road approaches the river, you can see the end of the exciting bit and can easily view the falls further up. You soon come to the end of the tarmac road; cross the beck (Grainsgill Beck) and park on the left (326327). You can continue further up the rough track for about a mile, but the river is only grade 2/3 and it will depend on how much respect you have for your car or how far you want to drag your boat!

Description   The short hard section consists basically of 3 falls. The first (3m high) is a large sloping slab with a difficult entry on the left, with a fast descent down the slab into a large but friendly stopper. The second is much smaller, but far harder, with a rocky entry on the right into a boat-gobbling cauldron. Then follows a short rocky section, before you reach a complex one metre drop. This can best be shot by boofing the drop on the left of the large rock. Next is a superb rock garden that provides 'no rest for the wicked'. As you leave the road, you approach a right-hand bend and rocky island. This rarely has a clear channel and some bumping is inevitable. The river then eases and allows you to enjoy the scenery before a short slalom through some bushes and a break-out below the first road bridge.

Contributor:
Nigel Timmins

Other important points   A barbed wire fence is sometimes in place on the lower section but fortunately it is on an easy part and can readily be seen and avoided, normally by 'limbo dancing' under it. A superb short paddle with no access problems... as yet!

Lower Caldew

Grade	2/3
Length	7km
OS sht.	85/90

Introduction   The lower section of the Caldew is an easy but fairly pleasant paddle, running through a remote and less well-known part of the Northern Lake District.

Water level   Wet, a fair bit of rain is required if you do not want to bump and scrape down, but it does hold its water better than the upper section.

Gauge   If you can obviously paddle the river at Sebergham it is OK.

Access   It is accessed via one of the minor roads running northwards towards Hesket Newmarket off the Penrith-Keswick section of the A66 or by following the B5305 (Junction 41 M6) towards Wigton. You could start at the end of the upper section, at the bridge near the hamlet of Mosedale. However the river is flat, fast and almost completely blocked by bushes. Not recommended! Better to start just downstream of the bridge at Haltcliff (368366), where the river goes round two sharp bends. On the second bend is a small farmhouse and easy access to the river. Only room for one or two cars, so please change and park discreetly and sensibly.
Finish the river at the bridge in Sebergham (358418) where there is a good lay-by and egress the river on river left. You can go all the way to Carlisle if you wish, but it is not that interesting.

Description   From the farm put-in, you quickly get swept round the left-hand bend (take the left-hand channel) into a small section of rapids, which fortunately are straightforward. The river is constantly on the move from here on, with blind bends, unclear channels and overhanging branches. You just need to keep an eye out for fallen trees, but on the whole it presents few major problems. Just over halfway down you pass the Caldbeck on your left, a major tributary and a warning that the crux, a small gorge, is just around the corner. The Caldbeck junction is unusual, in that it enters the Caldew in an upstream direction. The difficult water below proves to be short and exciting. You are then left with a pleasant paddle down a remote and isolated tree-lined gorge before arriving at the take-out.

Contributor:
Nigel Timmins

Other important points   This river really only gets a mention, as it has provided me with a pleasant paddle in the height of the fishing season, when most other rivers are out of bounds. It is tree-strewn and needs water (though not as much as the upper section does) and I have as yet never seen a fisherman on it. The grade would suggest this is a good open boat river. But

beware; far too many open boats have been redesigned on this section. Fine if you know it well or have checked it out recently, but it is not a river to take beginners on.

Grisedale Beck

Grade **4+**

Length **2km**

OS sheet **90**

Introduction   A superb steep beck easily accessed by car (though parking is a big problem). You need to be very careful as trees can often block this river!

Water level   Very wet, this is a spate river.

Gauge   Check the river as it flows under the A592 in Patterdale. It clearly needs to be in spate to even consider this beck.

Access   The beck can be accessed by an obvious footpath on the north side, at a bridge, via a gate on river left (382156).
Egress the river on Ullswater at the public jetty and steamer pier in Glenridding (390169).
Permission is required as it lies on private land, permission is gained through Patterdale Hall Estates, tel 017684 82308.

Description   After 300m of warm-up through boulders, a wooden platform, river left with a cable spanning the river (no hazard even in high water) marks the start of more technical rapids. 100m past the platform there is an "S" bend. This has a large tree and debris river left, and focused paddling is required to avoid the debris by keeping on river right. Boulder gardens continue downstream. Next is a three-tier boulder garden with trees partially blocking the most direct line. After negotiating the three trees the beck poses no real problems until the main falls are reached. Here there is an obvious constriction with two drops, giving a 20m section of rapid. The main drop is guarded by a shelf which drops into a pool. The pool becomes a cauldron in high water and a powerful stopper forms. Immediately after this is the narrow main fall, (2m). This washes through, however rolling can be awkward in the narrow pool. Downstream from the drop is fast; two large trees spanning the river may need the boater to semi-capsize. Downstream of the two trees the beck is straightforward. Once under a stone bridge the river is then a float down to the lake.

Contributor:
Dave Watkinson

Other important points   Many large trees can block the river or cause substantial risk of pinning.

Swindale Beck

Grade **3/4(5)**

Length   **7km**

OS sheet   **91**

Introduction   This small beck gives a very adventurous trip. You feel very isolated and the river is continuous and difficult, with many blind bends and drops.

Water level   Very wet. It probably needs to be raining and have done so for some hours beforehand.

Gauge   The take-out and weir/fall in Brough need to be inspected, so this is ideal to check the water level at the same time. If you can float down the river below the fall without scraping and the weir is shootable on the left, it is on!

Access   Egress the river just below the A66 road bridge in Brough. There is a small playing field accessible from a minor road or from the slip road to the A66, westbound (794143). Obviously it is not advised that you park on the slip road! Check out the weir/fall just upstream of the A66 road bridge. Access the river by driving up the B6276 Middleton in Teesdale road to a gate that leads down a track to the river (817182).

Description   The start is on fast but smooth water, but only about 100m downstream is the first of two difficult falls (Gd 5). Another kilometre or so brings you to the second, 4m fall, which though large is somewhat easier than the one above. Continuous rapids then ensue down a superb gorge. The gorge relents, the river eases and you can take your first real breather! A second gorge marks the start of yet more difficult water. An overhanging left wall with frequent rocky rapids make for an interesting time; watch out for the other bit of grade 5 on some horrid rocky falls. Things ease a bit, except trees now become a problem and an ever-vigilant eye needs to be kept. You soon sweep into the centre of Brough and you quickly face the 4m weir/fall, which hopefully you inspected on the way up. Immediately below lies the A66 and the take-out on river right. You could press on down to the next bridge or even the Eden but all is flat and uninteresting and, after the frantic but superb paddle upstream, it is not really worth it.

Contributor:
NIgel Timmins

Leith

Grade **3/4**

Length **5km**

OS sheet **90**

Introduction   A super little river, winding its way through farmland and forest. It lies to the south of Penrith close to the M6. One would call this 'an adventure river', you never know what problem you will encounter round the next bend!

Water level   Very wet, only worthwhile when it is very high.

Gauge   If you look over the bridge on the approach to Great Strickland the river needs to be brown and seething.

Access   Access is awkward, but can be gained by climbing over the fence on the approach to the bridge over the railway, on the minor road that leads to Thrimby (557203). Drop steeply down to the river on its left-hand side. The best take-out is by the ford in Melkinthorpe (556250).

Description   No sooner have you got on the river than it passes under the railway with a large sheep fence blocking the way. You can normally squeeze under this with a determined approach. Though if you get it wrong you will get capsized and might not be able to roll, as the fence itself will hold you under! All great fun for those watching!

It then runs down through a forest with some superb rapids of continuous grade 3. At the bridge near Great Strickland things begin to quieten down, but once again after the odd fence you come to a couple of exciting drops, the second of which is a long shoot, down a slab of rock. It is at least easy to inspect this from the left bank, unlike the forest section above.

Contributor:
Nigel Timmins

As you approach the next minor road bridge beware, as yet another large sheep fence bars the way. One final rush through another forest with some nice rapids brings you to Melkinthorpe and the egress. You can continue below Melkinthorpe but the river is now much easier and eventually joins up with the River Eden near Temple Sowerby.

Small Becks of the Eden Area

Contributor:
Nigel Timmins

The following are small becks in the Eden area that are not often paddled due to difficulties such as low water, access, trees and the like.

Belah

Grade **4/5**
Length **4km**
OS sheet **91**

Introduction   A remote river running off the Tan Hill / Kaber Fell area. It is small but runs down a steep boulder-strewn gorge with frequent ledges and drops. Trees inevitably are a problem and good scouting is necessary.

Access   Possibly the best access is to take the small 'no through road' up the true left bank of the river, past Heggerscales and on to its head at a track junction (837096). The tarmac road finishes, so it is best to walk in following the continuation of the road towards Wrenside. When on the open moor, drop down to your left and find a way down the steep gorge sides to access the river. Egress is much easier at the road bridge (823119).

Upper Eden (above Kirkby Stephen)

Grade **3/4**
Length **10km**
OS sht. **91/98**

Introduction   A wild and remote run that will only be 'on' in very high water. Not often done as it alternates between difficult drops and fairly easy water.

Access   Access and egress anywhere along the B6259 road. Do not on any account stray into the falls area just upstream of the Stenkfirth bridge (77307), they would be lethal as trees nearly always block them.

Scandale Beck

Grade **3/4**
Length **6km**
OS sheet **91**

Introduction   A tiny beck that can be interesting… watch out for frequent fences.

Access   Access at Ravenstonedale or the A685 main road bridge (720040) and egress in Soulby (749109).

Lyvennet

Grade **2**
Length **8km**
OS sheet **91**

Introduction   A small beck with the odd weir and small rapids running through pleasant pastures and wooded areas to the west of the Eden.

Access   The bridge in Crosby Ravensworth (623149) to road bridge north of Kings Meaburn (613233).

Dacre Beck

Grade **2**
Length **4km**
OS sheet **90**

Introduction   A small river with a number of sheep fences that make life difficult... still good fun anyway.

Access   Start at Sparket Mill (439265) and finish on the Eamont or at the road bridge just before the junction (477267).

Sandwick Beck

Grade **3**
Length **2km**
OS sheet **90**

Introduction   A short, small river that is pleasant and worth checking out if you are in the area... beware of the odd fence.

Access   Access at the minor road bridge (434190) and egress either on Ullswater or at the track/road bridge in Sandwick (423196).

Croglin Water

Grade **2(5)**
Length **6km**
OS sheet **86**

Introduction   A small beck with tree and fence problems. The final falls into the Eden are spectacular and it is unclear whether these have been 'done'.

Access   Access at the road bridge just south of Croglin (575470) and egress at the road bridge near the Nunnery House Hotel (538428). Below this lies the falls and if you do these you would either be forced into finishing much further down on the River Eden or you would have to walk back up the side of the River Croglin, which was once a famous walk. The walk way is now derelict.

Petteril

Grade **2**
Length **19km**
OS **85/86/90**

Introduction   A small rural river that has been paddled from as high up as Greystoke. A pleasant section runs past Southwaite services on the M6 down to the next junction just south of Carlisle.

Access   Numerous bridges give access and egress points but the best access is at a minor road bridge (498341) and egress at a picnic spot just off the minor road to Dalston next to Junction 42 on the M6 (434513).

Esk

Introduction   The best bit of the Esk is above here (Langholm to Canonbie grade 3) but is a Scottish river. This section runs in England and provides a pleasant but easy open boat trip.

Grade **1/2**
Length **9km**
OS sheet **85**

Access   Access the river in Canonbie on the downstream west side of the bridge (395764) and egress on river left near an island just upstream of the main road bridge in Longtown (379690).

Liddel Water

Introduction   A 'Jeckell and Hyde' river having a quite complex set of falls just downstream of the B6318 bridge (Gd 4), and then a massive long paddle out on very easy water.

Grade **2(4)**
Length **15km**
OS sheet **85**

Access   Access either at the B6318 road bridge or just slightly further up at Harelaw mill (444789) and egress in Longtown on the upstream east bank of the River Esk bridge next to a small island (379690).

Glenridding Beck

Introduction   Some very steep falls exist at the start of this beck which have been run. The rest is fun bouldery water with 2 sheep fences to beware of.

Grade **3(5)**
Length **2km**
OS sheet **90**

Access   Access the beck below the youth hostel (365174) and egress either just before the bridge in Glenridding or down by the lake at the steamer piers and car park (390169).

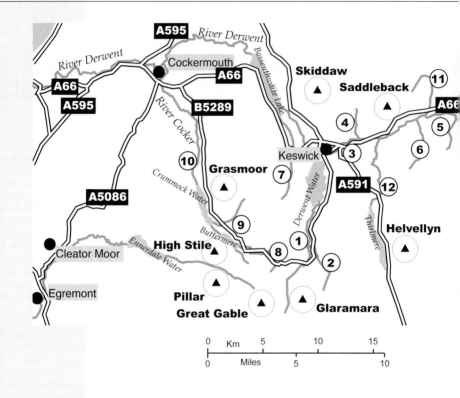

Derwent Catchment

Derwent

Grade	**2(3)**
Length	**8km**
OS sheet	**98**

Introduction   The Derwent is the longest and biggest river in the Northern Lakes and can be paddled from source to sea. It is very picturesque, but there is little on offer for the hardened white water enthusiast. The section described is high up on the river and naturally here it is a small fledgling river, beautifully clean. Lower down it is much bigger and has a number of easy sections that are worth paddling, and a playspot near Workington, all mentioned at the end of this text.

Water level   For this top section it needs to be wet… not an uncommon occurrence in the heart of the Lake District!

Gauge   If you can float down the section at the top of the river, it is at an ideal level.

Access   Start from the bridge over the upper Derwent at the head of Borrowdale, on the small road that leads to the one farm hamlet of Seathwaite (239128). Take out either at the bridge in Grange (254175) or Kettlewell car park on the east shore of Derwent Water (267195).

Description   From the road bridge at the start, the river is canalized but easy at only grade 1/2. As you approach the village of Seatoller, the river becomes more natural with pleasant grade 2 rapids, the major difficulty being trees or overhanging branches on the frequent sharp bends. The major rapid (Gd 3) is located next to the youth hostel just above Rosthwaite. A small stream enters from the right coming from Combe Gill and the river swings left. Land on the right and inspect, as the route is complex, winding through a series of large boulders. There are two rapids, the first you take on the right and the second middle left. After this things quieten down to pleasant grade 2 rapids and you soon pass the campsite above Grange. From here on the river is fairly flat and many people get out at the bridge in Grange. Parking is difficult however, and it is pleasant and easier to continue down into Derwent Lake and egress at Kettlewell car park. This is a National Trust car park though and you have to pay.

Other important points   Below Derwent Water, the river is much more reliable with regards to water level due to the influence

of the lake, and it can often be paddled when the upper section has almost completely dried up. From Derwent Water to Bassenthwaite it is easy, at only just grade 1. From Bassenthwaite to below Cockermouth it is pleasant but only occasionally reaches grade 2. The best section is from the road bridge leading to Great Broughton (082403) down to the outskirts of Workington, about 10km and 'just' grade 2. The main rapid is on the large bend that almost encircles Camerton church (035300) which can have very large waves on it in high water. The weir below is normally portaged on the left, and the next on the right (though this can be shot down a narrow shoot in the middle). The next sloping weir a few metres below, provides local paddlers with an excellent playspot, which is often used year round. Get out on river right below the weir next to a dirt road, accessed from the main A596 road bridge. This lower section is a very important fishing section and to paddle it during the fishing season is just going to invite problems. Beware of scraping down through the 'Reds' (spawning beds) in November, as water bailiffs have arrested at least one group. Make sure there is enough water to float your boat, damaging spawning beds is a *criminal* offence.

Contributor:
Nigel Timmins

Langstrath Beck

Grade **5**

Length **3km**

OS sheet **90**

Introduction   A unique paddle… mostly a pool drop river, but with some fantastic slabs to slide and bounce down. It is all easily inspected and portaged if you wish but, with the prospect of a long carry in, you really want to be sure you can paddle everything it throws at you.

Water level   Quite wet, this beck needs a surprising amount of water to make it a reasonable proposition.

Gauge   If you park at Stonethwaite, take the small track to your left down to the river. It is wide and pebbly here, but it must have a reasonable amount of water flowing over the whole width of the river to tempt you to shoulder your boat. If it is low, then at least walk up and dream!

Access   Drive up Borrowdale and turn left towards Stonethwaite (263138). Parking here is limited, but as it will need to be wet, i.e. raining or having just rained, it is unlikely many walkers and their cars will be around. Park by the old red telephone and letter-box (room for about 6 cars) and check out the level by the bridge on your left. You can either start walking from here or continue through the village along a very rough track into the campsite. You will have to pay, but it does save you nearly a kilometre of carrying. Egress at the bridge in Stonethwaite or continue on down to the Derwent.

Description   The river can easily be inspected on the walk up. Many people just paddle the first set of big rapids below the first footbridge, near where Greenup Gill enters (274129), about 1.5km from the village. However from the footbridge above the main falls, you can see Black Moss slabs twinkling in the distance and if you have not been put off so far, it is worth the extra 20 minute carry to include these excellent drops.

Black Moss Pot, which lies just above the slabs, is relatively straightforward, being a 1-1.5m drop into a very narrow slot, though the stopper can be large in a big flood. Below lie the slabs that consist of 3 falls. The first has a small, fairly easy straight drop that leads to the first set of slabs with two routes, left or right. The right is a little rocky but means you are nicely set up for the next slab. The left is much smoother and easier but leads you into a rock wall that is difficult not to hit. The next large slab is probably best run on the left, which leads you straight into a 2m drop and large plunge pool before a narrow chicane finishes the series. Easy water then leads for 1km down to the footbridge above the falls, passed on the way up. Grade 3 water leads to the top of the slabs from the footbridge but it is easy to stop before the river swings left and disappears from view. This huge set of slabs is guarded by a 2m drop, which makes things difficult. It is easy to run on the left but makes the entry onto the slabs difficult. To run it on the right is hard, both on you and the boat as the landing is straight onto a rock. It does however leave you with an easy entry down the slabs. These slabs are fantastic, being nearly 25m long and falling some 3 to 4m. A short boulder-strewn section then leads to two falls. The first this time is fairly easy but it is the second that will cause problems, with a rock right in the middle causing you to support or smear yourself down the left-hand wall. The river is now joined by Greenup Gill and increases in volume, though it does not feel like it at first, as it runs through a very bouldery rapid. When the river turns left, get out and

inspect, as in front lies a tight and difficult 1.5m slot. The plunge pool is not that deep either and some people have bottomed out in here. Beware! People have been pinned here.

A steep-sided canyon leads you over two small drops to the lip of a two-tier fall. The first is easy, but a boulder splits the second. Either shoot awkwardly on the left, or more easily on the right, or boof the flat-topped boulder in the middle. That's it… just easy water now remains for you to wind down on, as you drift down to the take-out in Stonethwaite.

Contributor:

Nigel Timmins

Other important points   As you walk past the Langstrath Country Inn in Stonethwaite, keep an eye out for the amusing little memorial stone near the door, "In memory of a sunny day in Borrowdale."

Greta

Grade   **3**

Length   **8km**

OS sheet   **90**

Introduction   Possibly the most paddled river in the Northern Lakes, and at its grade, one of the best. Easily accessed off the A66, between the M6 and Keswick. The Greta runs through a beautiful section of mostly boulder-strewn rapids but does have the odd bedrock fall to enliven things. Interestingly most of the best playspots are on these bedrock falls.

Water level   Wet! This river needs rain and unfortunately it does not last long. Can be paddled for a maximum of only 24 to 30 hours after the last rain.

Gauge   Local paddlers use the little steps in the wall bordering the park at the top end of Keswick. One step covered, it is just paddleable, 2 and it is at its optimum level, and if the wall is covered you are in for one hell of a ride! Though extremely continuous and serious, it does not really change its grade much in high water, possibly 4 because of the seriousness and likelihood of a long swim if you capsize and can't roll.

Access   Access the river from the 'old' A66 road bridge signposted Castle Rigg stone circle (314246), just past the turning to Thirlmere B5322. A small footpath leads down to the river, but please park carefully and do not block the entrance to the house opposite. Egress is best made from the Climbing Wall car park in

Keswick (264239) or more discreetly by the suspension footbridge just after the Greta has joined the Derwent (253238).

Description   The first 500m is on slow-moving water and you wonder what all the fuss is about. Don't worry, things will warm up in a minute! (You pass a small side stream, Naddle Beck, on your left, which can make an exciting alternative start in high water. Start this, just further down the old road by a little bridge, tree strewn grade 3 and then down through a dark tunnel under the A66.)

On down the Greta, the Glenderaterra Beck enters from the right and you pass under the old railway (yet again.) A complex rapid ensues with a small playwave/stopper in some levels on the left, and then the river runs rightward with a large boulder river right. Here lies the first grade 3, with a rock that is often just covered and lays in wait for the unwary below the main fall. From here on is pure heaven, with loads of rapids, breakouts and playwaves. You eventually come to a broken weir, best started on the right with a couple of huge waves near the bottom in high water. A little further down another weir is encountered, although it does not look it at first, being hidden behind an island. The island is guarded by large boulders, so sneak through on middle right, but keep moving right to take the hidden fall further down hard against the right bank. You soon pass under the A66 viaduct high above and just below is an old bridge, which has the best play-wave on the river. Whatever you do, do not miss this superb spot! Some people come just to paddle here.

Another couple of rapids and you find yourself in the middle of Keswick near the park with the measuring 'steps'. A tiny weir is encountered with a fun stopper and the climbing wall car park rapidly comes up on the left. If going on to the suspension footbridge, the river is much easier and you can easily float down, under a road bridge and down to the junction of the Derwent. Egress on the right just before the bridge, on a bend.

Contributor:
Nigel Timmins

Other important points   For those with only one car and a bike, or keen runners, the old railway line that follows the river has been turned into a good footpath/cycle way, making for a pleasant trip back up to the start of the river.

Glenderaterra Beck

Grade **4**
Length **2.5**
OS sheet **90**

Introduction   A very small beck running off the western side of Saddleback and Lonscale Fell. It would be a good intermediate creek run, for those wanting to move into this style of river running, except for the numerous trees and fences.

Water level   Very wet. This beck needs rain and lots of it! The run off is extremely fast so it needs to be done in the rain.

Gauge   Nip down the old railway/cycle path near Threlkeld (315248) to its junction with the Greta and if you can run this section just upstream of the junction, then it will be on.

Access   Park up by Blencathra Centre at the end of the road (304256) and then walk up the good track for about 1500m. Drop down to the beck by the small isolated coniferous plantation or the old mine workings slightly further up (296270). Finish down the River Greta (see that description).

Description   If there was ever a beck that would benefit from an 'adopt a beck' scheme, then this is it!
I paddled this many years ago, but walked up it recently to check it out. It had clearly not been paddled for a number of years as numerous trees, branches and two wire fences blocked the beck. However it is a pleasant run and not particularly hard – each section only being about grade 3, but because of the continuous nature, small breakouts, and numerous trees and fences it must get a grade 4.
Starting up by the mine, the beck drops quickly for a while before the gradient relents and you can settle into some wild, high mountain paddling. A fall next to the isolated coniferous plantation on river right is no real problem and about a kilometre of very pleasant paddling ensues. As you approach the much larger forest on river right beware, as 100m down by the reinforcing blocks on river left is a 'decapitating' fence… and it would be difficult to stop just before it. A little further down, the beck opens out and you encounter the first of a number of large trees blocking the river.
At a sharp left-hand bend is the second fence that blocks the beck. Below this is a footbridge with a small pleasant fall just above it. 50m below is an island with another tree blocking the river. 50m below this, in a little gorge are another two or three trees blocking

the river. *It would be prudent to portage the whole of this section.* You are near the end now, but just as you see the final bridge, a strange tree grows out horizontally from the left bank almost blocking the beck. Either paddle over it on river left or go for the small gap hard on river right. Under the final bridge and into the much larger Greta for what will be an exciting descent, as the Greta will be massive if the Glenderaterra Beck was at a good level.

Contributor:
Nigel Timmins

Other important points   It is possible to walk up the beck on river left (though lots of fences have to be crossed), but it would be worth it just to clear some of the trees.

Troutbeck (Upper Greta)

Introduction   A committing tree-strewn river, running parallel to the A66 Penrith - Keswick road. It is nonetheless well worthwhile as you are totally unaware of the proximity of the road and it has a bit of everything, from vertical falls to long complex rapids.

Grade	**4**
Length	**3km**
OS sheet	**90**

○ ○ ○

Water level   Very wet. It needs a lot of water to be worthwhile.

Gauge   From the lay–by on the A66 (384270) you can see the river. It should be brown and seething. Whilst you are here it is prudent to check out the main, vertical fall directly below the lay-by.

Access   Turn down the A5091 and almost immediately turn right onto a minor road (389269). Park here and launch 'discreetly' over the fence, just past a sheep fence in the river. Egress is further down the A66 taking a left turn (opposite the Mungrisdale turn) signposted to Wallthwaite. Drive about a kilometre to the small bridge over the river (358267).

Description   Easy water leads you back towards the A66 and you will probably have to portage a low beam in the river. Then down over a rocky fall of about a metre, and through the boulder-strewn rapid seen from the lay-by. Below lies the impressive yet easy 3m vertical fall. This is best shot on the right but can be done on the left... you just go a bit deeper! Pleasant water now leads you down through a little gorge and under the old railway bridge. From here on, it is frantic boulder-strewn rapids with

only small breakouts. Two large fallen trees spanning the river are fortunately easily spotted, on one of the few straight sections. Then a small footbridge, which provides the first reasonable eddy! Beware as below lie two strands of barbed wire. One of these is quite high and should not be a problem but the farmer often re-places the lower one. Another small footbridge is passed and the river begins to relent a little. Again beware of two low telegraph poles across the river, which often carry a strand of barbed wire below them. Fast easy water then takes you on down to the egress bridge and a footpath on river left.

Other important points   If this river is high enough to paddle, it will be an easy but fast descent down the next 5km to the start of the normal section on the Greta. The Greta will then be 'stonking'!

Contributor:
Nigel Timmins

Mosedale Beck

Grade   **5**

Length **3.5km**

OS sheet **90**

Introduction   This is a *wild expedition* that needs to be taken very seriously. It is remote and boulder-strewn, with virtually no break-outs. Its one redeeming feature is it is easy to inspect and portage. Full on paddling and absolutely superb if you can handle it.

Water level   Very wet, the river must be very high to stand any chance of getting down without bashing hell out of your boat.

Gauge   The best way to check whether this river is on is to check the Troutbeck (upper Greta) from the A5091. If that is 'humming' and it is still raining, then it is worth the long walk in. Or you can look at the river at Wallthwaite Farm but it is perhaps not wise to advertise your presence as the farmer is not happy about canoe-ists paddling the beck.

Access   Access the river from High Row (380219) and walk along the 'Old Coach Road' for 3.5km. Get in when you cross the river (350227). Egress is best made at Dobsons bridge (349265) where there is limited parking up the hill, or continue downstream to one of the other bridges, or the lower Greta put-in. Alternatively, if you want to get out early, climb onto the railway viaduct and walk westward and exit onto a minor road well to the left of a house next to the road (349258). This is not a public right of way.

Description   The river starts easily enough, though the weather will have to be wild, wet and probably windy to make this a possibility, so you will be glad to get in your boat to escape the worst of it. Fast grade 3 paddling, with the odd fence for the first kilometre or so, leads to a sharp left then right bend and fall. Here things change dramatically as the river drops quickly through a massive boulder field and continues for at least another 1.5km like this. Breakouts are non-existent, so your paddling buddies will need to be ready to catch you at vague eddies to be able to stand any chance of running this full-on section. Fortunately it is easy to inspect on river right and portage what you or your boat doesn't fancy. Further down, access is best from the left bank and a few more fences are encountered that need great care, as you cannot stop easily. The river is a little easier by the railway viaduct but becomes tree lined and could be lethal if blocked by a tree or branch, beware!

Contributor:
Nigel Timmins

A truly wild river and great expedition. Who needs to go to far off places when you have this sort of monster in the area?

Newlands Beck

Grade	**4**
Length	**2.5km**
OS sheet	**90**

Introduction   A good run of its type, continuous and fairly clear of trees.

Water level   Wet, only feasible on a handful of days a year.

Gauge   Check the level at Stair and at the put-in, where the small beck should be navigable across its width.

Access   Parking is available near Chapel bridge (232194)where access needs to be discreet. Egress below Stair bridge (238215). Parking (pay and display) at the village hall or a one-car pull-in 150m downstream (river right).

Description   After 500m of bush slalom the rapids start, well supplied with small breakouts, continuous grade 3, with 3 harder chutes. The river has been cleared of trees and was still in good condition with any new trees being at least navigable at the time of writing (spring 2003).

Contributor:
Peter Carter

Other important points   The run can be extended in very good

water levels by driving up towards Newlands Hause and putting in on Keskadale Beck, a bushy grade 4 run with tree problems.

Gatesgarthdale Beck (Honister)

Grade **3**

Length **1km**

OS sheet **90**

Introduction   Gatesgarthdale Beck is mostly straightforward and easily seen from the road.

Water level   Very wet, flood conditions.

Access   Descend down Honister Pass towards Buttermere and put in at the first road bridge (222138) or just above it. It is best to egress the river where it meets the first wall and sheep fence (198149).

Contributor:

Nigel Timmins

Description   Gatesgarthdale Beck is really a slightly harder alternative (Gd 3) to the upper Derwent. If you want something a bit more committing than the upper Derwent take the drive over Honister Pass. Get in at the first bridge for a fast but straightforward run down to the egress, or start as high as you like, though a difficult fall a short distance upstream is often the normal start point. Whether you run it or not will depend on water levels. This beck is open and has no tree problems.

Sail Beck (Buttermere)

Grade **4**

Length **2km**

OS sheet **90**

Introduction   Sail Beck is small, steep and tree-lined and was badly blocked by fallen trees when I went to do it. You basically just walk up and do what you want. Small, tight, technical paddling!

Water level   Very wet, flood conditions.

Access   Park in the car park (pay and display) right in the centre of the village next to the beck and follow the footpath up the true right bank from the road bridge (175169).

Contributor:

Nigel Timmins

Cocker

Grade	**2(3)**
Length	**11km**
OS sheet	**89**

Introduction   The Cocker is a lake-fed river draining Buttermere and Crummock Water. It flows northward towards and through Cockermouth to its junction with the River Derwent. It passes through some pleasant rural scenery, but apart from the start and finish the rest of the river is flat, as it has been canalized to help with flood prevention. Pleasant but not exciting.

Water level   The river holds its level well because it is fed by the lakes of Buttermere and Crummock Water, but it does require a fair bit of rain to bring it up in the first place.

Gauge   If you can easily paddle down the river without scraping at the start, then it is at a good level. It is not worth bothering with if it is low.

Access   It is difficult to access Crummock Water without having to cross the major part of the lake, so get in just downstream of the outflow where a minor road crosses it and there is a good car park on river right (149215). Egress is best in Cockermouth just after the Cocker joins the River Derwent. Park in the large 'pay and display' car park, next to the children's park which adjoins the river. Access this by crossing the Derwent on the A594 and turn immediately right.

Description   The river is small and swift at the start, with a series of quite technical but interesting rapids. There is no warm up here; you are straight into the main grade 3 crux of the river. After a series of bends things quieten down, as the river enters the canalized section. With plenty of water it is a swift ride down towards the A66, so lie back and enjoy the scenery. The river slowly reverts back to a more natural state and a small weir is eventually encountered, but presents no problems. You then pass under the A66 and some way below you will notice a large chunk of concrete creating an island on river right. This is a broken down weir and is the only other difficult bit on the river. Some large standing waves and a strong current take you round a sharp left bend where you have to avoid the right-hand bank. You pass on down through the centre of the town, with more small but fun rapids and under a number of footbridges before you burst out into the much wider Derwent. Cross the river and get out by the park and footbridge.

Contributor:
NIgel Timmins

Other important points   This is a popular fishing river and is not recommended during the fishing season.

Small Becks of the Derwent Area

Contributor:
Nigel Timmins

The following are small becks in the Derwent area that are not often paddled due to difficulties such as low water, access, trees and the like.

Glenderamackin

Grade   **4**
Length   **5km**
OS sheet **90**

Introduction   A small, fun beck, with the odd fence. The main difficulties (Gd 4) lie at the start, in the village of Mungrisdale.

Access   You could walk up the valley for several kilometres if you wish but most get on just upstream of the farm/car parking at (363304). Egress at a small bridge (354268) just downstream of the junction with the Troutbeck.

St John's Beck

Grade   **2**
Length   **6km**
OS sheet **90**

Introduction   This river has been ruined by Thirlmere reservoir and virtually never has water in it. However, occasionally as the reservoir overflows it puts enough water in the river to make it worthwhile. It has a superb sloping ramp to start but after that it is only worth it from a novelty point of view.

Access   Put in at the dam outflow (307188) and egress at the Greta put-in (314246).

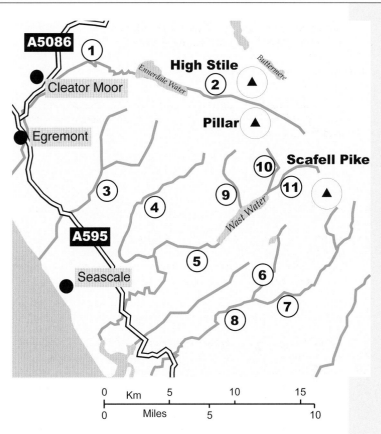

A5086

①

High Stile

Ennerdale Water

② ▲ Buttermere

Cleator Moor ●

Pillar ▲

Egremont ●

Scafell Pike

⑩

③

④

⑨ ⑪ ▲

Wast Water

A595

⑤

⑥

Seascale ●

⑦

⑧

0	Km	5		10		15
0	Miles		5			10

West Lakes

Ehen

Grade **2**

Length **7km**

OS sheet **89**

Introduction   This lake-fed river runs out of Ennerdale, the furthest west of the Lakes, and though normally accessed from the north side of the Lakes, is independent of any other area. It presents a small, easy stream for open boats or beginners. It is heavily fished and should only be done out of the fishing season.

Water level   Needs to be high but holds its level well.

Gauge   If you can easily paddle the river at Wath Brow bridge it is at a good level. It would be a slow, annoying 'scrape' at lower levels.

Access   Start at the large car park at Broadmoor Forest, just below the outflow of Ennerdale (086153). Finish either at Wath Brow bridge (030145) near Cleator Moor or at any number of bridges further down.

Description   Put in above the car park and just above 2 small weirs. Shoot these easily and then pass under the road bridge. A short distance down is another much larger weir. It is sloping and easily shot, down the centre or side shoots. The river now flows gently with no real rapids, but winds like a lost soul towards Ennerdale Bridge. Trees are a massive problem but fortunately, as the flow is gentle, you can easily inspect them, push through them or under them. It would be ideal territory to introduce beginners to the trials of beck paddling. Eventually you reach Ennerdale Bridge and open fields mean the tree problem is much reduced, though not removed completely. A short distance on you enter a very pleasant section of grade 2, paddling down a number of small rapids and tiny boulder-type weirs. As the river winds back on itself you get beautiful views back up the Ennerdale valley. Things ease a bit before a couple more easy rapids bring you to the picnic spot of Wath Brow bridge.

Other important points   You can continue further down if you wish at a similar grade, with numerous egress points at the bridges. This river is a prize fishing river; do not paddle it in the fishing season.

Contributor:
Nigel Timmins

Liza

Introduction   A super mountain stream, which is very difficult to access as the dirt road up Ennerdale is private.

Grade	**3**
Length	**3.5km**
OS sheet	**89**

Water level   High

Access   Access from the small bridge (165135) and egress either on the lake or at the bridge (133141).

Contributor:
Nigel Timmins

Calder

Introduction   A steep and scenic run with fairly continuous boulder rapids leading into pleasant mini-gorges. Very worthwhile, despite awkward access.

Grade	**3**
Length	**6.5km**
OS sheet	**89**

Water level   Wet, won't be easy to catch at the right level. It drains a small, steep catchment, only up a few days a year and not often paddled.

Gauge   Best place to gauge the character of the stream is at Stakes Bridge, halfway down.

Access   Located in the far western Lakes close to Sellafield. From Calder Bridge, drive up the little road past Stakes Bridge (057068). Continue over the moor and either park on the moor before the road descends (067087) or go down the hill to Thornholme Farm where the road abruptly ends, where you ask the (currently very friendly) farmer if you can turn round in his yard and leave a car (067088). A 200m carry along the bridleway leads to the confluence. Please maintain a low impact, this place is unsuited to large groups.

The take-out is even more sensitive! The BNFL complex has high security, so you can't just park anywhere. To drive to the take-out, go in on the BNFL road past the visitor centre. Turn in here (closest hassle free parking?) and look for a phone box on the left and 50m later the footpath sign. You can drive along here to the sewage works (035049) and pick up your boat (*or risk leaving a car here, anglers have a 2 car agreement, but paddlers don't*).

If that's all too much hassle, park near the pub and take out on the right below the second bridge in Calder Bridge (039058), (Pelham House, again don't park here; BNFL property).

Description   From the confluence, steep continuous boulder rapids lead after 300m to 'Charlie's Pleasure' (Gd 3), a more meaty drop followed by a sharp right bend. Now the beck eases to continuous grade 2 passing under Stakes Bridge after 3km. The Abbey ruins come into sight and on a left bend is a nice grade 3. The paddling becomes more interesting as the pretty Calder Bridge Gorge is entered and some tight bends just about warrant a grade 3. 300m below is the second bridge and a possible egress at the end of the village before the gorge peters out. The gorge restarts after the river leaves the road and again some tight bends near Pelham House just about warrant grade 3. The river leaves the woods and an 'S' bend is passed soon leading to a pipe bridge marking the footpath leading to the egress point.

It is possible to continue for 800m on swift water past a small weir with a little surf wave, round a horseshoe bend to the BNFL concrete bridge with fence, and then walk back on the fishermen's path on river right.

Contributor:
Peter Carter

Other important points   This river can be started much higher up at (075129) by walking in from the sharp left bend in the road on Scaly Moss (066129). It of course needs high water levels, and this upper section is definitely grade 4.

Bleng

Grade   **3(5)**
Length   **4km**
OS sheet   **89**

Introduction   A super little beck, which has a short hard section at the start and then eases to pleasant paddling in a beautiful wood. Worthwhile if in the area and it is wet, but not worth driving a long way to.

Water level   Very high water is needed to enable a descent of this river.

Gauge   If you can paddle down without scraping at the finish it is at a good level.

Access   Access is possible by car up the forestry roads above the village of Wellington. Drive up alongside the river ignoring the 'access only' sign, up and beyond a car parking area used by many 'dog walkers' etc. Cross the river at the first bridge and ascend the hill, till a turning left takes you back down to the river and the start (097072). Egress at the bridge in the village (079040) or at the parking spot higher up (083053).

Description   No sooner have you started than you come to a series of difficult falls, the last of which is quite badly blocked by trees, scouting this short section would be prudent! As the river bends to the right things begin to ease considerably and you are left with a super run down grade 3 water. A footbridge is passed (this would make a nice short section for those who do not want too testing a time) and then on down to the bridge you crossed on the way up. A number of overhanging trees do however make the descent somewhat difficult and a vigilant eye is needed upon rounding each bend. Wild, dramatic and accessible by car, just what the doctor ordered!

Contributor:
Nigel Timmins

Irt

Grade   **2**

Length **6.5km**

OS sheet   **89**

Introduction   A very easy river that is kept at a reasonable level by Wast Water.

Water level   If the river looks runnable at any of the bridges downstream of Wast Water then it is worth doing.

Access   Start from Wast Water itself at any number of lay-bys on the way up the lake. Finish at the minor road bridge at Santon Bridge, downstream left-hand side (110016).

Description   Despite the mountainous and austere landscape around Wast Water this is very much a flat water / easy river as it wends its way lazily to the sea. There is nothing of note on the river apart from numerous overhanging trees.

Other important points   Like many of the rivers in the Lakes, it is a prime fishing river. Only consider this trip during the closed fishing season.

Contributor:
Nigel Timmins

Whillan Beck

Grade	**4/5**
Length	**1km**
OS sheet	**96**

Introduction   This beck consists of large falls, one after another, with many jammed trees. Nonetheless it's a fun run when water levels are too low for most other becks.

Water level   Low to medium.

Gauge   Inspect from the bridge in Boot, it does not want to be high.

Access   Drive up the Esk valley to the small village of Boot where a bridge crosses the river (176012). A path leads alongside the river but very soon you take to the river bank for the carry to your chosen put-in. It is possible to inspect all the falls on the way up. Egress is back at the bridge in Boot.

Contributor:
Josh Litten

Description   There are too many falls to describe individually, but the run starts at the farm where there is a large fall. From here the river enters a gorge with many large falls, *every fall must be inspected for trees*. The beck emerges again for the last 500m, where there are excellent rock slides and a series of grade 5 falls.

Upper Esk

Grade	**5(5/6)**
Length	**3.5km**
OS sheet	**89**

Introduction   Even if you aren't considering the waterfalls at the start of this run, the river below is well worth the long drive and the walk in if the river is at the right level. The walk in allows inspection of the various falls on the way up. It is possible to portage all the difficult sections but if you don't like the look of the first drop you see on the way up it is unlikely you will like the rest of the river! The significant drops and rapids are all fairly obvious from the water.

Water level   Quite wet, heavy rainfall the night before will normally mean the beck is worthwhile. If you approach by driving over Hardknott and Wrynose Pass you should see numerous smaller streams flowing off the hills indicating that the river should be up.

Gauge   At the parking spot you will be able to see the river running over shallow shingle beds, these will need to be covered (paddleable) to make it worthwhile. As you walk up you are able

Mill Force, River Leven

The Brickshoot Weir, River Leven

250

Armathwaite Weir, River Eden

Armathwaite Weir, River Eden

'Old School' on the River Brathay

Fun and Games on the Eden

Surfing on the Nith

to see the river at various points, which will give you a better idea of whether it is worth paddling. If not, the nearby Whillan Beck can be done at a lower level.

Access   Park at the small farm turn-off near the public payphone at the western bottom of Hardknott Pass (212012). From here it is necessary to carry up the side of the river along a well defined path. Continue for about 2.5 km to just below the confluence of the Esk and Lingcove Beck (227915) for the start of the river run or continue up the Esk to look at the seven waterfalls.

Description   The seven waterfalls have all been paddled. However several of the falls flow together (Gd 5/6) with some precise lines being required, meaning that most will want to 'leave them for another day!' Low water is preferred for several of the falls but at this level the section below would be quite a scrape. The last waterfall is probably the hardest and has been known to pin boats.

The section below the confluence provides an exciting boulder run with 3 distinct rapid sections linked with some interesting white water.

The first rapid consists of a slightly angled ledge drop, with a fairly obvious line to avoid rocks, then continuous water leading to another small ledge normally taken river left.

The river eases for a while before the approach of the next rapid is signalled by a sweeping left-hand bend and an obvious restriction. The rapid consists of a very narrow chute with rocky sides. There are two innocuous looking small drops in this section, the first of which has a nasty habit of backlooping with the distinct possibility of broaching upside down afterwards.

The next and final significant rapid consists of a broken lead in to a rounded drop over a large boulder. This can unseat paddlers because the river flows towards an inconveniently placed rock above the fall on river right.

Contributor:
Ian Wilson

From here the river gradually eases with some more drops before giving way to grade 2/3 water until the take-out.

Other important points   Unfortunately the valley is a target for car thieves and care should be taken to avoid leaving valuables in vehicles if possible. The nature of the trip also means that there are good photo opportunities.

Esk

Grade   **2/3**

Length **8.5km**

OS sheet   **89**

Introduction   A very scenic paddle, and very fast flowing in high water. This is a classic run with no major difficulties but the river rises and falls quickly making it difficult to catch at a good level.

Water level   Needs plenty of water from recent rains.

Gauge   Water should be flowing over a good portion of the shingle bank below Forge bridge at the finish.

Access   Drive to the top of the Esk valley and park near the entrance to Brotherilkeld farm (212 012), which is just before the Hardknott Pass. Carry along the footpath toward Scafell and access the river just past the footbridge. Egress is at Forge bridge (148 995).

Description   The river is fast flowing for the first 3.5km but with no major difficulties apart from the speed of this section which will catch out the unwary. Doctor's Bridge is the first proper rapid where a rocky step forces the river to the right. This is the normal route apart from in very high levels when left is preferable to avoid the hole that forms on the right. The river continues to Boot where a narrow, deep gorge is encountered. This is impressive but not particularly difficult except in very high water when a 'folding' wave forms in the gorge.

Contributors:

Dave Shawcross and
Tony Phizacklea

A very picturesque section follows as the river now flows through stepping-stones and on to the next bridge near Stanley Ghyll. Waves and boulders make confused water immediately below the bridge and the river then runs on fast but easier to a large bend in the river. Here the river drops over a ramp with a large boulder towards the left. The easiest route is on the right, or you can take the route through the playhole on the left. Easy water leads to the finish.

Small Becks of the Wasdale Area

Contributor:

Nigel Timmins

It is strange that Wasdale, in the heart of the mountains, offers so little to the paddler. There are, however, numerous small becks which, when they have water in are worth a look, but on the whole there is not a lot to interest the white water addict who is visiting from afar.

Nether Beck

Grade **5**

Length **1km**

OS sheet **89**

Introduction   A boulder run... you walk up and do what you fancy!

Access   Park next to the bridge over the beck at (62066) and walk up as much as you feel you can manage.

Mosedale Beck

Grade **4/5**

Length **1.5km**

OS sheet **89**

Introduction   A wild little beck. Ritson's Force has not been done yet so put in below this.

Access   From Wasdale Head (187088) walk up the valley to the 'force' and egress either back at Wasdale Head or at the road.

Lingmell Beck

Grade **3/4**

Length **2.5km**

OS sheet **89**

Introduction   Out of the heart of the Lakes runs this beck, which can carry huge amounts of water. Though not too hard it is fast and committing, and does require some walking to get to the start.

Access   Leave Wasdale Head (187088) and follow the track up Sty Head and put on when the river and track come close (198092). Egress at the track/bridge (182076).

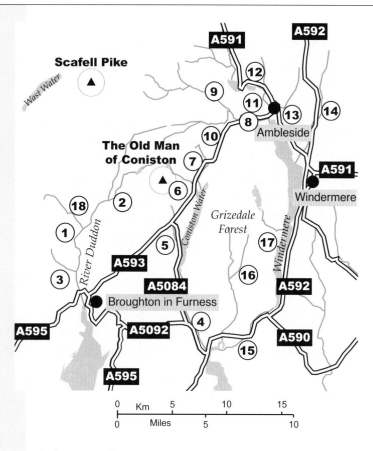

Windermere and SW

Duddon

Introduction   An excellent river in a superb valley, paddleable from source to sea. It splits into three sections and is suitable for a range of abilities. This river has an access agreement so please check with the river adviser for details www.bcu.org.uk/access/riverinfocumbria.html.

Water level   Needs a few hours of heavy rain. The upper section will only stay up for 4-5 hours. The lower and middle sections stay up longer due to the extra water coming from Seathwaite Tarn via Tarn Beck.

Contributor:
Jonathan Hyde

Gauge   Gauge from Ulpha bridge looking downstream; if all the rocks are covered it's at a good level, the lower section can be run with slightly less water, the upper needs the rocks to be well covered and you should bear in mind that it runs off quicker.

Duddon (Birk's Bridge to Hall Dunnerdale Bridge)

Access   Parking and access is at Birk's bridge (234994) a small packhorse style bridge.
Egress on river left just after Hall Dunnerdale bridge, a small path leads to a telephone box (213953), where there is space to park.

Grade   **4(5)**
Length **5.5km**
OS sheet   **96**

Description   The short section above the bridge can be run at certain levels, but it is more usual to put in just below the bridge. The first 500m is grade 3 up to Troutal Gorge (Gd 5), which is easily recognised by the cliff face on river right. Portage river left up a steep bank; it is possible to inspect from a small eddy on river right. *Inspection is essential* as the awkward drop is unrunnable at certain levels. At most levels these falls are run down the slot on the right, but at very high levels go down the middle. It has been run backwards and upside-down but this is not advisable! The next 3km to Wallowbarrow is continuous grade 3/4 at a fairly steep gradient with no serious problems. Watch out for the wire spanning the river at very high levels.
When the valley sides steepen dramatically you are entering Wallowbarrow gorge (Gd 5). After passing a small cliff, break out river right before the massive undercut boulder which appears to block most of the river. Inspect or portage along the footpath, on the right-hand bank. The first drop is run from right to left,

boof the slab and break out after another undercut boulder. The
next section starts on the left. At low levels run the left-hand slot
between two rocks; at medium and above, run the two-tier drop
on the right.

You are now approaching the biggest drop in the gorge. Start this
next section right of centre until a couple of metres before the fall,
where you need to be left of the central rock. Boof the stopper,
then run the fall, angling slightly right, break out on the left. The
last section of the gorge is a grade 4 boulder garden which ends
at the hump-backed bridge. After this, the river changes character
and eases off to grade 3 for the last 2km down to Hall Dunnerdale
bridge. Egress on the left after the bridge or carry on down the
middle section.

Duddon (Middle - Hall Dunnerdale Bridge to Ulpha Bridge)

Grade   **3(4)**

Length **3.5km**

OS sheet   **96**

Access   Access on river left just after Hall Dunnerdale bridge.
There is space to park near a telephone box (213953), from where
a small path leads down to the water.

Egress on river left downstream of Ulpha bridge. There is parking
just before the cattle grid (197930).

Description   A nice steady paddle, no problems until the water
works weir, which is easily spotted by the brick walls lining each
bank. The weir can be shot easily, at any level, on the right-hand
side down the sloping weir face. Alternatively, it *can* be shot down
the fish steps on the left... but be aware of the nasty tow-back.
Please inspect from the boat so as to avoid access problems. It
is grade 3 down to Jill's Folly, where the river widens round a
right-hand bend. A small island in the centre indicates this next
rapid. Run this on the right next to the holly bush and down
between two boulders, where the pinning rock has caught many
paddlers out. It can be run left of the island at higher levels, but
is not as much fun. A continuous boulder garden then leads to
a breakout left, above Ulpha Gorge (Gd 4), recognisable by the
cliff face ahead. At the head of the gorge keep right of the central
rock, except in very high levels when the left-hand side avoids
a nasty tow-back. Inspection from left bank is advisable. Gentle
water leads to the last notable rapid on this section, where the
river widens again through some small islands. Follow the main
flow of water down the left and be ready to use some quick pad-

dle strokes to avoid the rocks. The bottom of this rapid creates a playhole at certain levels. It is grade 3 from here to Ulpha bridge. Egress on river left after the bridge.

Duddon (Lower - Ulpha Bridge to Duddon Bridge)

Grade	**3(4)**
Length	**6km**
OS sheet	**96**

Access   Access on river left downstream of Ulpha bridge. There is parking just before the cattle grid (197930).
Egress is river left after the A595 road bridge, parking 20m up the Ulpha road in a lay-by (199882).

Description   From Ulpha bridge the first 2km has some good grade 3 rapids, but nothing too serious until the river meets the road again and warning is given by the huge rocky outcrop on the left bank. Immediately after this you need to follow the main flow to the left to avoid the rocky ledge spanning the other two thirds of the river. A 100m boulder garden then leads to the next notable rapid. As the river enters the woods you need to be river right, where the river drops down some small steps, (can be run on the left at higher water levels). The river now carries on for 2.5km of interesting grade 3, with some good wave trains down to the most serious rapid on this section at Rawfold bridge (Gd 4). A large central island warns of the start and from here the bridge is visible beyond. Follow the right-hand channel until the river meets again. This is where some strong paddle strokes are needed to cross over to the left where the tongue flows down under the bridge. Immediately after this head for the calmer water on the right, as the main flow washes into the left-hand bank. 100m further is a *potentially lethal* weir! This *can* be run hard left or hard right, but at high levels is a definite portage down the right-hand bank. More fast grade 3 leads to the last grade 4 rapid on this section, where the river widens through some small islands. Follow the left-hand channel to start with, then head right towards the main flow. This will require some tight manoeuvres. Carry on down the central flow to complete this rapid (can be run down the right at higher water levels). The last kilometre down to Duddon Bridge is grade 2; egress under the left-hand arch or carry on through the right arch, where there is a play wave spanning the river. Egress on the left bank.

Tarn Beck

Grade **4/5**

Length **1.2km**

OS sheet **96**

Introduction   A steep burn that runs along the side of the road, making it easy to scout and set up protection. It joins the River Duddon below Wallowbarrow gorge and can be paddled as an extension of the middle Duddon.

Water level   Only runnable after considerable amounts of rain, it is similar to the upper Duddon but holds water longer as it is fed by Seathwaite Tarn.

Gauge   There should be water running in the becks and the rocks below Ulpha bridge on the Duddon should be covered.

Access   Just north of the church at Seathwaite the river is right beside the road (231963). Put in above the narrow slot.
To egress either follow the footpath from the confluence with the Duddon to a lay-by south of Seathwaite (225960), or continue along the final 1.5 km of the upper Duddon (Gd 3) to the bridge at Dunnerdale Hall.

Contributor:

Josh Litten

Description   This section starts with a two-tier fall through a narrow slot, which often looks worse than it is. Several more small falls and narrow shoots follow, the worst of which falls into a small pool with a boulder straight ahead. This fall has a nasty tow-back at high levels,. Following this steep section is another large fall with a shallow plunge pool. The beck flows on and under a footbridge with a series of tight 'S' bends. From here the beck calms down all the way to the River Duddon, but watch out for strainers.

Logan Beck

Grade **5/6**

Length **2km**

OS sheet **96**

Introduction   Lots of steep rapids littered with boulders and some falls.

Water level   High.

Gauge   There should be water running in all the becks running off the hillsides.

Access   From the Duddon bridge head up the west bank and

after a cattle grid bear right and access the beck at Beckstones
bridge (184 903).
Egress at bridge (196898) or continue down the Duddon.

Contributor:
Nigel Timmins

Description A very difficult river that needs full inspection and
safety set up. No detailed description as you will have to inspect
and decide what you shoot and what you portage.

Crake

Grade	**2/3**
Length	**8km**
OS sht.	**96/97**

Introduction The Crake flows from Coniston Water to the sea at
Greenodd and stays 'up' longer than most rivers in the area. For
much of its length the tree-lined river flows through farmland and
provides a mixture of man-made and natural rapids interspersed
with fast-flowing flat sections. This is a classic middle grade river
that is popular with novice paddlers, although overhanging trees
can be a real problem, especially at higher levels.

Water level Moderately wet to wet. The Crake holds its level for
several days after rain. It is not worth doing when it is low.

Gauge If the shingle beach just downstream of Spark Bridge is
covered the river is at a good level.

Access Access from either the car park on Blawith Common
(287901), a 300m carry and 500m paddle, or Brown Howe car park
(291911), a 1.3km paddle to the outflow of Coniston Water.
Egress at either Spark Bridge (306849) or Greenodd petrol station (316826). Please ask! *Do not get out to inspect Bobbin Mill Falls*
as this will cause access problems. If egressing at Spark Bridge
please park and behave sensibly.
This river has an access agreement so please check with river adviser for details www.bcu.org.uk/access/riverinfocumbria.html.

Description From the outflow of Coniston Water, the Crake
flows through Allan Tarn and down under a minor road bridge
to an obvious right angle bend, beyond which lies the most
technical rapid on the river. The 50m long 'S' rapid (Gd 3) has a
particularly magnetic rock at the bottom. Beyond this there is a
small weir that is great for side-surfing and flat spins. Fast, flat
grade 1/2 water leads on down through overhanging trees to a

small sloping weir (no difficulties) just above Lowick Bridge, after which the river becomes more continuous and interesting. Take the left channel at the next island and follow bouncy grade 2 water for the next 1.5km until an obvious man-made weir is reached. This is usually shot right of centre and a series of natural rock steps take you playfully down to the top of Bobbin Mill Falls (Gd 3). The weir can be shot anywhere and then it is a straightforward run down through the left bridge arch. Run the main fall on the left, but be wary of a sharp right turn at the bottom which capsizes many. Egress is just on river right after Spark Bridge or continue on down, taking the left-hand channel past the island. Bouncy water leads on down to a small weir, shot on the right and then 1km of flat water lands you at Greenodd.

Contributor:
Roger Ward

Other important points   Much time and effort has been spent establishing access to this stretch of river. Please use the agreed access and egress points.

Torver Beck

Grade	**4**
Length	**1km**
OS sheet	**96**

Introduction   Short fun section, fairly steep but holds its water for longer than most other becks.

Water level   High water only.

Gauge   Easily inspected from the road bridge and footpath alongside, the rocks must be well covered.

Access   Take the A5084 to Coniston. The road passes close to Coniston Water and very soon after leaving the lake shore you will come to the bridge over the beck. The put-in is a short distance further on at a lay-by on the right (287927), giving access to the footpath opposite, which leads to the river. Egress is just above the first road bridge (291923).

Contributor:
Josh Litten

Description   Many small technical falls with one significantly bigger than the rest. The run starts with a rockslide under a bridge; several small falls, but no major difficulties follow this. About 500m from the finish there is a much larger rocky fall. Below this are more small falls which lead pleasantly to the finish above the bridge.

Church Beck

Gd. **4/5 (5/6)**

Length **1.5km**

OS sheet **96**

Introduction   Flowing steeply down from the Coniston fells this is not exactly your ideal kayak run! The falls have been run, but also make a good 'canyoning' trip. The run from below the falls is fast and technical.

Water level   Low water if you intend to run the falls. High water for below the falls.

Gauge   A strong flow and the rocks covered under the bridge in Coniston is required.

Access   Park near the Sun Hotel (301975) in Coniston. Follow the footpath beside the hotel until you reach the beck, it is then possible to inspect the whole run and decide where you would like to get on.
Egress by the bridge on the road to the lake shore (305974).

Description   The section below the falls is the regular run. Start where the river narrows through a steep-sided gorge, easily recognised by the slate wall with railings that blocks the path. The first rapid on this section is a three-tier drop followed by a fast continuous rapid. A 2m fall leads to a steep section (beware strainers). More fast water leads to the footbridge. The gradient lessens now for this final section through the village to the bridge.

Contributors:
Dan Toward and
Josh Litten

The Falls   Start below the packhorse bridge. This section is a series of 5 technical falls, some runnable, some not (make your own mind up!) Swimming/canyoning this section in low water is a good way to inspect.

Yewdale Beck

Grade   **3(4)**

Length   **4km**

OS sht. **90/97**

Introduction   The upper section is a serious, but exciting spate boulder run. There is one crucial portage at the end of this section. The lower section contains a series of bedrock rapids, but is marred somewhat by a large number of sheep fences across the river.

Water level   Upper section, wet/very wet. Lower section, wet.

Gauge   Upper section: view the river at Tilberthwaite, most of the boulders should be just covered.

Lower section: view the river where it flows under the B5285, the channel here should be deep and fast flowing.

Access   The upper section can be accessed from the car park at Tilberthwaite (313000). Egress for this section is where the river joins the minor road to Hodge Close Quarry. Ensure you can identify this point from the river because a sheep fence lies downstream part way down a grade 4/5 rapid and below here there is a dangerous blocked fall.
The lower section can be accessed from the Hodge Close road bridge (314998). Egress is on Coniston Water (308970).

Description   The beck can be paddled from upstream of Tilberthwaite car park at grade 4/5 (carry upstream as far as you feel comfortable), *capsizing here is not an option as the river bed is quarried slate waste!*
From the car park continuous bouldery rapids lead rapidly downwards, towards a sharp left-hand bend. Around this corner lies a steep rapid (Gd 4) after which the beck continues at a bouldery grade 3, passing through a sheep fence. Egress where the road meets the river on the left bank.
Do not continue past here as breakouts are minimal and an impossible gorge with a sheep fence on the entry rapid lie below. Portage down the road to the Hodge Close road bridge to start the lower section.
The lower stretch is mainly grade 2, and the biggest hazard is a series of sheep fences. After White Ghyll joins from the right, the beck gains interest as it passes over a series of bedrock ledges (Gd 3) before passing under a minor road bridge to deposit you on the lake.

Contributor:
Roger Ward

Other important points   *Missing the take-out for the upper section would have very unpleasant consequences.*

Brathay

Grade **2/3(5)**

Length   **5km**

OS sheet   **90**

Introduction   More people must have paddled on this river than any other in the Lake District. Easy rapids, pleasant scenery and good access must be the reason for its popularity... unfortunately its white water content leaves a lot to be desired! Good if you are learning though.

Water level   Can be paddled at almost any level, but best when it has a reasonable flow.

Gauge   The pool and rapid above Brathay Hall should have a good clear current running through it.

Access   This river really starts at the outflow of Elterwater but access is difficult, so it is far better to start above the lake and get in directly in Elterwater village (328047). Car park next to the river (but you have to be up early to get a space here.) Egress either at Brathay pool (366034) or the north end of Windermere at Waterhead, opposite the large car park (376033).

Description   From Elterwater village (yes, this is the bottom of Great Langdale Beck) the river runs easily and reasonably swiftly into the lake. Keep left and cross the beautiful lake. A twisting flat section leads you to a right-hand bend and sign on the left, warning of Skelwith Force. *Do not* on any account pass this sign, if you do not want to run the falls (Gd 5). They are paddled surprisingly frequently, but it is a nasty drop, particularly in low water, that has eaten its fair share of 'suitors' and even drowned a few! The fall, some 3m below the main drop is an excellent looping spot and again some 'park and play' boaters just come and paddle here. With care you can sometimes park on the road next to the falls. The section below is the only grade 3 and is quite complex, being a series of tree-lined islands. Basically you start on the right, and by the sharp left-hand bend move over to the left. It sounds easy but it is not, be warned!
Below Skelwith Bridge the river returns to type, being flat and easy. The road nears the river and those who only wish to paddle this lower bit sometimes use a small muddy lay-by to access it. As you approach Brathay footbridge, the river begins to speed up and an excellent beginners' ferry glide spot is located here. Another 250m and you come to another rapid, grade 2, best middle left. It flushes out into Brathay pool with reasonable parking and good exit from the river on the right. If you wish to continue, there is a nice small rapid around the corner to the left and under the bridge, and then quiet water leads down to the junction of the Rothay and subsequently into Windermere. Keep left and head towards the public landing spot, car park and perhaps more importantly, tea shops!

Contributor:
Nigel Timmins

Great Langdale Beck

Grade **3/4**

Length **5km**

OS sht. **89/90**

◯◯◯

Introduction   This great little river runs out of one of the best-known and picturesque valleys of the Lake District. The hard section is short, but intense.

Water level   High water is needed to give a fun run down this river.

Gauge   If you can paddle down without scraping at the start, it is a good level.

Access   Access is at the Old Dungeon Ghyll hotel, at the very head of the valley (285060). Unfortunately you now have to pay for parking. Get in by the entrance to the car park across a field on river left and through a gate with a sign saying for canoe access only. Egress is at the village of Elterwater by the car park on river left (327047). Once again you have to pay here, so it might be better to leave your cars for free at the small car park across and above the main Langdale road.

Description   The river is very easy for a couple of kilometres, being channelled in an artificial flood defence system. The view is fantastic though and a pleasant float enables you to enjoy it to the full. It picks up lots of water on the way and is quite wide by the time it gets to Baysbrown bridge (317053), (alternative access) near Chapel Stile. There is now an excellent stretch of rapids, dotted with rocks making some great little breakouts. A footbridge follows and things ease as you approach a large sloping weir. This can easily be shot, normally, middle right. Go round a right-hand bend, and be ready to break out right, as you are now above Pillar Falls (Gd 4). This is a tricky little drop normally done down the right-hand side. Some large projecting rocks middle left are not pleasant, and you do not want to get trapped on these! (The scene of an epic 999 TV programme). Below lie a couple more grade 3 rapids that can be quite hard at this grade, a short but intense section of water that seems much longer once committed to it. Take out at the bridge or continue easily across Elterwater and into the Brathay… remember that Skelwith Falls lie just below.

Contributor:

Nigel Timmins

Other important points   If Great Langdale Beck is up, head towards Little Langdale Beck for a second helping, as this will also be at a good level, and is similar in standard.

Little Langdale Beck

Grade	**3(6)**
Length	**2km**
OS sheet	**90**

◯ ◯ ◯

Introduction   A short easy beck, with a desperate grade 6 fall or easy portage. It is close to Great Langdale Beck and it is recommended that you do both on the same day.

Water level   High water is required.

Gauge   If the river is eminently paddleable at the finish bridge it is on.

Access   Access is down a narrow single-track road to a ford, 600m from the hamlet of Little Langdale (316028). No parking down here, so you will have to leave the car back in the hamlet after dropping the boats off. Finish at the road bridge (330030).

Description   The river starts easily, apart from a couple of sturdy sheep fences across the river. These fortunately succumb to a determined approach next to the bank.
As you enter the trees the fun starts. Some short grade 2, before a double-tiered fall of grade 3, then more easy water before another narrow shoot of grade 3 below a little building on the left. More grade 2 water and you come to a sharp right-hand bend with a small weir on it. Get out here as Colwith Force (Gd 6) lies below. This three-tiered fall of some 16m has been 'done' and one wonders in awe at those who paddle such a thing. Most however will take the easy portage trail on river right.
Get in below the falls for one more tricky grade 3 fall, before all too soon the road appears. You can carry on below, into Elterwater and the Brathay, but the river quickly eases around the corner and about 4 sheep fences are encountered… not really worth it.

Other important points   At the time of writing (November 2002) a large tree lay in the force, making a desperate fall impossible. Make sure you do not miss the breakout at the little weir above the force.

Contributor:
Nigel Timmins

Rothay

Grade   **2(3)**

Length **6km**

OS sheet **90**

Introduction   Flowing from Grasmere to Windermere this is a superb little river, ideal for novices. It runs through the middle of perhaps the best-known part of the Lake District, Grasmere and Rydal Water. Starting on these highly scenic lakes, it flows down through a beautiful wooded area and nimbly misses the tourist-infested town of Ambleside before finally finishing in the most famous lake of the area, Windermere. The only downside of this pleasant trip is the difficult/limited parking at the top.

Water level   Wet, but can hold its level well, due to Grasmere.

Gauge   The best spot is probably at Pelter bridge (366059); if there is a good current coming through the boulder-strewn rapid above, it is at a reasonable level.

Access   Access onto Grasmere is difficult and parking very limited, being only a small lay-by on the left (travelling towards Ambleside) just before the end of the lake (343063). The road is busy and you have to lower your boats carefully over the wall. The easiest access is just above Rydal Water at a large car park (348065). Like all car parks in this busy part of the Lake District you have to pay. Egress is best down on Windermere at Water-head public landing spot and once again a large 'paying' car park is opposite.

Description   At the outflow from Grasmere is a small weir and then some lovely grade 2 rapids lead you down to Rydal Water. Keep left and cross Rydal Water, passing Heron Island on your right and down to the outflow, where the water picks up speed and crashes down a very boulder-strewn rapid, grade 3 and normally bumpy. As you pass under Pelter bridge the river returns to a pleasant grade 2. Stock Ghyll enters from the left and there are then a couple of nice rapids/weirs, the second of which has an excellent surfing wave for beginners. Then things quieten down and you pass the Brathay, entering on your right, and soon enter Windermere with the landings and car park over on your left.

Contributor:

Nigel Timmins and
Katie Timmins

Other important points   Good tea shops, with yummy cakes!

Scandale Beck

Grade **5+/6**

Length **2km**

OS sheet **90**

Introduction   A steep 'creekin' beck in the modern idiom, steep, boulder-strewn and continuous... fantastic!

Water level   Wet, but not too much water or it starts to get a bit too much, possibly grade 6.

Gauge   Peer over the upstream side of the bridge on the main A591- if you can easily float over the shallow rapids, then it is time to gird your loins and head off uphill.

Access   As you leave Ambleside on the A591 heading towards Keswick you come to a small roundabout with a turning to the right, up a steep hill. Take this and after negotiating the first steep left-hand bend, take the left turn into Sweden Bridge Lane. Drive up this as far as you can (378053). Not far enough! Dump the boats off and drop back down into Ambleside to park, as you cannot park anywhere on this lane. Then follow the track for 2km up to High Sweden bridge (379068), a beautiful packhorse bridge. You can also access the river by taking the same lane, but swing off left when you see the sign to Low Sweden bridge. This takes you to Nook End Farm and the bridge, but once again there is no parking up here. There is a good walking track, leading up the true right bank. Go over Low Sweden bridge and up around the steep bend; when you see a small fence, head over to it and you will pick up the track. Follow this past several walls until it runs out. This is not as high up as entering from the other side, but a bit of 'bush whacking' will get you almost as high. Egress is best either at Low Sweden bridge (375055) or right down on the A591 (372052). You can load the boats in the entrance to Rydal Hall and the bus stop, but you must not park here.

Description   Start below the nasty, narrow falls downstream of the bridge, with about 200m of really nice, pleasant falls that can be run on sight. Watch out for a harder boulder-ridden drop as the beck drops into a small vertical-sided gorge. Easier water follows but at the end of this open section lays the start of some very hard paddling. (Note the small track on river right finishes about here.) A difficult but superb section follows before a slabby fall and a further two-tier drop just above a small footbridge. Below lies a pipe bridge, and between the two lays a large tree right across

the river (February 2003). A small island is encountered then a long fast section into a fall, slab and difficult right turn. Two large drops lie below and the beck is quite wide here and very boulder-strewn. All this is seen looking upstream from Low Sweden bridge. There is a fall under the bridge and you burst out through a curtain of ivy! Below is more extreme paddling with about 3 large falls and lots of smaller bouldery sections. Things ease as you approach the track heading towards Rydal Hall and you can relax now as you get swept round a bend to the A591 road bridge and the finish. You can probably continue to the Rothay but few will have the energy!

Other important points   You can easily inspect this entire river, mostly from the right-hand bank and generally set up safety cover as well, without too much trouble. Trees are a major problem however and it would be well worth clearing what you can first, whilst inspecting.

Contributor:
Nigel Timmins

Parking is a major headache in Ambleside and the roads approaching this beck. Therefore it is best to drive back down into the large 'pay and display' car park in Ambleside opposite the college, after dropping your boats and gear off.

Stock Ghyll

Grade   **4(5)**

Length   **1km**

OS sheet   **90**

Introduction   A full on steep run! Continuous from start to finish.

Water level   High water run only.

Gauge   Easily inspected from the bridge in Ambleside, the weir just above the main bridge needs to be well covered.

Access   Follow the signs 'To the Waterfall' from the centre of Ambleside. Park near the footpath to the waterfall, and walk along the south side of the ghyll to the put-in below the falls (383045). A rope is needed to descend the steep ghyll side to the water, or put in below the 2m weir by the footpath.
Egress at the main 'pay and display ' car park opposite Charlotte Mason College (376047).

Description   The top section from the main waterfall to the weir is a constant grade 4, very fast and steep, no technical lines. Portage the 2m weir as the plunge pool is shallow. Another 200m of continuous grade 4 leads seamlessly into a technical grade 5 rapid.

Contributor:
Josh Litten

Other important points   Be ready for some strange looks as you carry your kayak through the town centre!

Troutbeck

Grade	**4**
Length	**3km**
OS sheet	**90**

Introduction   A classic! It is more often in condition than many used to think. Its only downside is it's far too short! A superb gorge and continuous rapids ensures interest is maintained. It is however narrow and often tree-strewn, so beware.

Water level   Wet. This river runs off a small catchment area, and therefore does not hold its water. If it is raining hard however, it is worth a look.

Gauge   If you can float when you put on, it is on. The more water however the better.

Access   Access is gained just off the A592 where it crosses the river (413027). There is a nice little parking area on river right. The best egress is down at the swimming pool in Troutbeck village off the main A591 (402003), follow the signs. It is best to park next to the recycling bins, and walk across the wooded area to check the river out and the egress. Alternatively you can paddle down to the lake, but ensure you turn left once on Windermere to reach Millerground landing stages. These are accessed from the parking spot on the A592 (403986).

Description   This short but intense trip starts easily enough. A kilometre of grade 2 and 3 allows you time to warm up. You then reach the entrance to the 'pipe' gorge where the river bends sharp left. You will now be wishing you'd inspected this from the overhead pipe bridge (407016) as you can't see what is ahead from the river. You can get to the bridge from the main road, via a public footpath or you can with difficulty inspect on river left from a small breakout just before the gorge starts. A couple of steep drops lead you into a few hundred metres of superb rapids, a truly splendid section but watch out for trees blocking it. Shortly after the gorge, more difficult but fun paddling ensues,

and near a house on river left is an island with a rocky shoot. The section below is also particularly bad for trees, and has had trees spanning the river here for many years. The river eases a little to grade 3, with a weir that is easily shootable. The next weir isn't, and is best shot on the right, but watch out for the boulders below! A series of steps in the river follow and form a continuous grade 4 section (which is again hard to inspect) right down to Troutbeck Bridge, again superb. To continue on down to the lake is for masochists, so get out at the swimming pool.

Contributor:
Nigel Timmins

Other important points   Please be discreet changing near the swimming pool because if we lose this egress spot we will all have to become masochists!

Leven

Grade **3(4)(6)**
Length **3.5km**
OS sheet   **97**

Introduction   This is the river that flows out of Windermere. It's short, exciting, and often paddled despite the restrictive access agreement. It mostly consists of boulder-strewn rapids but a couple of bedrock ones provide the greatest interest.

Water level   It does keep its level very well, being fed by the longest and biggest lake in the Lake District.

Gauge   If the overflow channel on the left below Newby Bridge has water flowing down it, then you are in for some good paddling.

Access   Access the river from the minor road just downstream of Newby Bridge (368863). *Not* however, during October to December inclusive, because of the spawning beds; during this period get in from the field next to the brick shoot. Egress at the end of the river race section, by crossing the field on river left to a gate just above the woodyard and minor road leading to Backbarrow bridge (356855). Egress the lower river by the bridge, river left on the B5278 Haverthwaite road (345835).
This river has an access agreement so please check with the river adviser for details www.bcu.org.uk/access/riverinfocumbria.html.

Description   This first section of river is on the famous Leven Test section (a race for all comers that used to be organized by Eric Totty of Lakeland Canoe Club). You very quickly come to the brick shoot weir, with a simple shoot down the centre, however watch out as the main current when in flood quickly pushes novices towards the left-hand side of Mill force, a 2m drop just below. In fact the fall is quite straightforward and provides an exciting drop, or you can more easily take a staircase down the right-hand side. Flat water brings you to some nice little drops with playful stoppers. You soon reach a much larger fall with a rocky shoot down middle left and then a couple of large drops normally run on the right. A rocky section with a small fall on the right marks the end of this short fun run. Take out in the field on the left, having inspected the take-out first.

If you intend to run the next section be fully aware of what you are taking on. A large sloping 2.5m weir can be shot in a number of areas and then fast water leads into the fall right underneath Backbarrow bridge (Gd 4). The drop is always spectacular and powerful… though I have seen complete novices run this and get away with it. Mind you, I have also heard of a number of well-known paddlers getting 'compromised' on it! Fortunately there is a large pool below to collect the pieces.

Most sensible paddlers will take out now, because below lies a huge and nasty weir (Gd 6) that has been shot, but is not recommended.

30m below is another fall which is well worthwhile. However it is very difficult to access the river again. Careful exploring through the derelict buildings normally finds a launch spot. Once these get redeveloped though, things may be very different.

The fall and subsequent stopper is big, but normally has a clean shoot right in the middle. Inspect first, because once you are on the water it is hard to see the line. Standing waves lead to a very low footbridge, which you can normally limbo under. Immediately below is a small weir often shot on the right in high water. This then leads down through some amazing huge waves with a small rocky fall lying in wait under the A590 road bridge. Below lies yet another large weir, this time easily shootable in a number of places. A very short section of easy water then leads to an island. Ensure you take the left-hand channel as the right has a low bridge and metal stakes in it. The left channel is narrow and quite exciting in its own right. Some more islands lie below, but the river is getting easier and a couple of small stoppers can be played in before you arrive at the take-out bridge. Egress on river left below the bridge.

Contributor:
Nigel Timmins

Other important points   This is a very important fishing river and should only be paddled on the arranged dates that Lakeland Canoe Club organize.

Small Becks of the Area

Some small becks that are not often paddled due to low water, trees or fences.

Grizedale Beck

Grade	**5**
Length	**0.5km**
OS sheet	**96**

Contributor:
Nigel Timmins

Introduction   An extremely short and steep beck. Its only saving grace is it's right next to the road so it can easily be inspected and photographed.

Water level   High or relatively low, it is a compromise. Low it is rocky and bumpy but at least you have time to think. In high flows it would be a very fast descent.

Access   Put in at the road bridge (338913) and take out at the bridge below the falls (339909).

Cunsey Beck

Grade	**2/3(4)**
Length	**2km**
OS sheet	**96**

Contributor:
Roger Ward

Introduction   A short tree-lined beck with the only real challenge at the end, where the river flows through a 100m long mini-gorge. Inspect this on river right *before paddling* as there is nowhere to break out once in the gorge and it is sometimes blocked with trees.

Water level   High/flood.

Access   Access upstream of Eel House bridge (368941).
Egress on Lake Windermere 600m north of the outflow (383942).

Crosby Ghyll

Grade	**5/6**
Length	**2.5km**
OS sheet	**96**

Introduction   An extremely steep beck with numerous big falls, its saving grace is that it is pool drop in nature. Very rarely paddled, partly because it is difficult to get the right water level and partly because it is near suicidal!

Water level   High water is required.

Gauge   Needs to be clearly in flood at the start bridge.

Access   Start where the road over to Eskdale crosses the river at a bridge (188951).
Egress at the minor road bridge north of Ulpha (202937) just before it joins the Duddon.

Description   Starts pleasantly with a section of grade 3 with one grade 4 drop. A bridge has a sheep fence that needs portaging and a 3m fall below. Another sheep fence follows that also needs portaging. A small bridge marks the start of the real difficulties with some big drops and a portage. This is followed by more difficult falls before the take out. Desperate!

Contributor:
Nigel Timmins

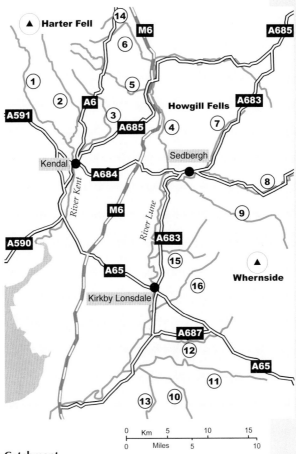

Kent and Lune Catchment

Kent (Upper)

Grade **3(4+)**

Length **8km**

OS sheet **97**

Introduction   A good run featuring fairly easy water in between some large weirs.

Water level   Fairly wet, it holds water a day or two after rain.

Gauge   The rapids below either of the two access point bridges should be feasible.

Access   Put in above Scroggs bridge (467995) or Staveley (473978). Egress in Burneside (506995).

Description   Put in discreetly above Scroggs bridge. Above and below the bridge are two rocky islands, both with choices of 1m drops (Gd 3+). Easy water leads to Staveley Weir, 3m in height with a steep sloping face (expect to bounce a bit!) followed by grade 3 water under the bridge. Next is Wilf's Weir, an easy 2m sloping face and the river eases as Cowan Beck joins it on the right. Now the river becomes a really pleasant grade 2/3 (beware of a chain fence after the sewage works), until after passing under a footbridge ponded water is reached. Below is Cowan Head Timeshare rapid, (Gd 4+), starting with a 2m weir. This testing 100m section of water is very serious as inspection is awkward (private) and bank protection is impossible between the vertical timeshare walls. Portage is simple if quite a long way on river left along the Dales Way footpath. The river continues swiftly to a large vertical 3m weir above Bowston, which would be dangerous in high water and could be sneaked down an overflow channel on the far left. More swift water leads to another large weir split by an island with most of the flow going down large fish steps on the right and a long easy slab to the left of the island. The river flows under factory bridges at grade 2 and soon reaches Burneside bridge.

Other important points   The river could be gained at various points higher in the Kent valley which has a small road, but there are access issues and little gradient. At the top of the valley flowing out of Kentmere is the Top Kent, apparently a beck-style run at grade 4+ requiring a walk in.

Contributor:
Peter Carter

Kent (Middle)

Grade	**1/2**
Length	**6km**
OS sheet	**97**

Introduction   An easy river suitable for novices in canoe or kayak.

Water level   A reliable section that can be paddled at 'normal winter levels' or higher.

Gauge   If it is paddleable at the put-in it is OK.

Access   Put in at Burneside bridge (506995) where a jetty has been installed, although only really suitable for flood levels! Egress in Kendal (517915).

Description   Small and swift initially, the river is joined by the Sprint, passes beneath a footbridge and then is joined by the Mint at a large pool with life rings. Passing under a railway and then two road bridges, the river becomes canalised through Kendal and leads to Gooseholme weir, a 2m drop with a box step in the middle. *This is very dangerous in high water*; look out for a concrete ledge which runs on river right for 100m or more upstream of the weir and allows (in normal flows) for easy inspection or portage. The canalised section through town has many small weirs which produce little surf waves and stoppers to play on if not washed out. Egress after Romney bridge (K shoes), or continue for a kilometre to flat water above Scroggs weir.

Contributor:
Peter Carter

Kent (Lower)

Grade	**4/5**
Length	**6km**
OS sheet	**97**

Introduction   This is one of the area's classics. It is often paddleable and has seen successful open canoe descents, at least to above Force Falls. Usually grade 4 but grade 5 in high water.

Water level   This section can be paddled at low levels, holding water for some time after rain and becoming more powerful, with fewer, much bigger rapids and 'funny water' in flood.

Gauge   Looking at the river at Sedgewick bridge will show the level and character of the gorges (unless washed out). Normally a powerful entry rapid enters a narrow gorge; if very high the water may be level with rock slabs on river right or even over the slabs. At these levels the 'L' shaped drop will be very dangerous and it

is likely the river will be flowing over the rocky 'island' between Force Falls and the fish steps on river right(which is also the recommended line in such flows), and then all this lower gorge section will be grade 5.

Access   Access in Kendal (506995) or at Scroggs weir (513906). Egress at Sedgewick bridge (507868) or the end of a minor road (507864).

Description   The last few of the little weirs leaving Kendal provides a nice warm up before sadly littered banks lead to flat water above Scroggs weir, a large easy sloping weir. Easy water leads to Prizet bridge after 3km (possible access but no parking). This chute is the first of the rapids, (Gd 3), leading into a delightful, easy mini-gorge. Some more easy rapids soon lead to Gunpowder Gorge, a longer harder rapid at the site of an old weir which has some metal spikes surviving, and just about warrants grade 4 for the main drop on a right-hand bend. Below are 100m of grade 3 rapids ending this excellent section. The river is easier now, passing under a footbridge to a vertical weir, which is dangerous in high flows. Inspect and portage if necessary on river right, *not on the left through the garden.* Plenty of speed on the far right should get through the stopper and 400m below is a road bridge above which is another rapid (Gd 3/4), very similar to but more powerful than the one at Prizet bridge. This leads into a short gorge and under the bridge to the 'L' shaped drop (Gd 4), and best run as far left (as far downstream) as possible (very dangerous in flood, portage if in doubt). Below is a wooded island with weirs across both channels. Traditional canoes are recommended to egress on right up wooded banks. Kayaks should continue down the weir of the left channel past the island to the grand finale: Force Falls, grade 4 with a 3+m drop into a huge pool. A thrilling end to a brilliant river.

Contributor:
Peter Carter

Other important points   There is a specific request not to continue down the remaining 5km of river to the sea, (shingle rapids, very bushy and a major cattle fence… not the best the area has to offer!)

Sprint

Grade **4/5**
Length **8km**
OS sht. **90/97**

Introduction   At the right level the Sprint is one of the best white water trips in Cumbria, with several bigger rapids linked by continuously interesting fast-moving white water. The Sprint rises at the head of Longsleddale valley and after a flat, but fast-flowing section it maintains your interest the whole way down to the take-out at Sprint bridge.

Water level   Wet/very wet.
Gauge   If the bend below Sprint bridge is paddleable, the river is high enough. The weir gauge just upstream of Sprint bridge should read above 2 to make the trip worthwhile.

Access   Access at Docker Nook (509015) or further up the valley where the road comes close. Parking is very limited at Docker Nook and the farmer is currently not very friendly towards paddlers. It may be better to drive further up the valley to where the river comes close to the road and there are better opportunities for parking.
Egress at Sprint bridge (513960).

Description   From the put-in, fast and generally flat moving water leads down to the 'S' bends (Gd 4) which start just by the bridge at Cocks Close. The 'S' bends are probably the most technical rapid on the river and demand good boat skills to survive. A vertical weir follows which is shootable at most levels. Bouncy grade 3 rapids lead on down to Garnett Bridge Falls (Gd 4) where a move from right to left part way down sees you through the narrow gorge below. The river now cuts deeper into the valley and signs of civilisation are few as the river continues on its way with grade 3 rapids to keep the interest. The next grade 4 rapid involves a steep shoot through the bedrock and a punch out through the stopper at the bottom. A few more small rapids lead down to a grade 3/4 through bedrock, with curling waves trying to capsize the unwary before the last drop, which is run either side of the boulder. A kilometre below the next road bridge is a broken weir, generally run on the right, from where a stretch of grade 3 over rock shelves leads down to Sprint Mill Falls (Gd 4). This is a difficult rapid with a sizeable drop, generally run right, then left, then right, after which a pipe bridge is passed under with a final easy fall by Sprint Mill cottages. Fast-flowing water

Contributor:
Roger Ward

continues, over a small weir and down to the take-out. You have just completed one of the classic paddling trips of Lakeland.

Other important points Although a grade 4 at 'normal' levels, at high water the Sprint can quickly become grade 5, and due to its continuous nature a swimmer and their equipment would be difficult to rescue.

Mint

Grade **3+(4)**
Length **10km**
OS sht. **97**

Introduction This is a sister river to the Sprint which, though slightly easier, is equally good. It is always interesting with some super bedrock falls and slabs, the best of which is saved for the end.

Water level Six hours of rain are needed after a dry spell to make this paddleable. It is not worth doing if it is low as there will be much bumping and scraping.

Gauge The best spot to check the level is at Laverock bridge (536952), a rapid exists just upstream of the bridge. If there is a clear channel here the river will be worth doing.

Access The roads up to the start are small and narrow so please drive with care and consideration. Start at Rossil bridge (554996) next to the old packhorse bridge, and finish in Morrisons car park (522943), next to the recycling bins.

Description For a couple of kilometres, the river is small and badly overhung by trees, but it provides a pleasant warm up. A small weir can be shot easily and then a little way down, after a sharp right-hand bend, you encounter the first of many grade 3 sections. This is known as the fish steps and is quite a steep rapid, formed by steeply angled bedrock steps. Care is needed, more in low water as you can get stuck on some of the projecting steps. In higher water it all flushes through but can be quite powerful. Patton bridge follows (the road crosses the river here but it is not a good access or egress point), and then a long, very pleasant section of grade 2/3 follows. A strange girder bridge is encountered that used to hold a sheep fence and around the corner lies another taxing grade 3. The easiest line is down the right-hand bank but it can be shot in a number of places. Further down again, the river enters an easy but short and pleasant gorge, before more continuous grade 2 rapids are encountered.

Below a pipe bridge a nasty vertical weir interrupts this fine river trip. It is approximately 1.5 metres high with a shoot middle right. *Do not on any account take this line, as a bar at water level would decapitate you.* It is very difficult to see this from above. Better to shoot the weir near the left-hand bank where the plunge pool is quite deep. However at high levels a large boily stopper forms and it would be wise to portage this weir on river left in these conditions. A short way on, you come across a messy factory and caravan storage area on river left, and this marks the start of Meal Bank Falls. There is easy water round the corner and under the bridge and then in front of you lies an enormous piece of concrete on river right. Most of the water is channelled to the left with a substantial fall and stopper below (Gd 3+). Shoot just right of centre and you should be OK, take it on the left if you like being back looped! A second but more natural series of falls lies in wait 100m below (Gd 3+). These are quite technical but the best line is just left of centre. More pleasant little rapids follow and you soon arrive at Laverock bridge. It has reasonable parking and is a good egress point, but it would be a shame to get out here, as a superb rapid waits below. An easy section is followed by a weir that is easily shot, but just below this lies a superb little gorge and bedrock falls (Gd 4). Again these are quite technical but there are one or two small crucial breakouts that enable you to run this section without getting out of your boat to inspect. Further down is a small measuring weir, possible stopper with long tow back. The supermarket and your car are now just a short way down on your left. Get out just above the bridge on your left where there is a small track, back to the recycling bins and car park.

At its grade it is a fantastic little river, definitely not to be missed!

Other important points   This river can be started much higher up, from the A6 road bridge, but it does have a couple of tricky falls and numerous fences so is questionable as to its worth. Like most of the rivers in this area it is an important fishing river, it will be a brave (read stupid) paddler who does this river during the prime fishing season!

Contributor:
Nigel Timmins

Lune (Tebay to Rawthey Confluence)

Grade   **3/4**

Length   **6km**

OS sheet   **97**

Introduction   A 'cracker' that is well known to many paddlers. It has easy access being next to the M6, has a number of paddleable sections, good rapids that can be attempted in most water levels, and of a medium grade. For these reasons it is popular, but like everything popular it has caused numerous problems by its very popularity. Canoeing at present is opposed on the main section of river, but a good access agreement does exist on the lower section to Devil's Bridge.

Water level   Medium to high levels are best.

Gauge   If you can easily float down at the start (wherever you are) then the river is in an ideal condition. Do not paddle this if it is going to be a scrape from the start, leave it to a better day... it will be worth it.

Access   Access and egress can be made at any of the following points:
Tebay bridge (614028)
Crook of Lune (620963), (normal start)
Sedbergh road bridge, A684 (632923)
Killington road bridge, B6256 (622908), (normal finish)
Rawthey confluence (628897)
The Crook of Lune has access problems, but if you are careful you can reduce the problems on this 'honey pot' area (we are not the only people using this site). Drive down the narrow road to the river and unload your car. *Do not* on any circumstances leave your car here. Drive back up to a parking area above the viaduct and leave your car there, or better leave it on the small road next to the 'main line' railway. It is only a 5 minute walk back to the river and saves canoeists getting a bad name. Please try and alleviate this problem on this section of the Lune.

Description   Although there is good sport to be had at Tebay, where the river runs through a mini-gorge and falls (Gd 4) there then follows a fairly mundane section, not worth doing except in very high water. The usual access point is the Crook of Lune (see access notes). 2km of fairly fast but straightforward water leads to a footbridge over the river. Here lies the first major interest, Hole House gorge (Gd 3) the first rapid starting just above the foot-bridge and extending well below. This used to be an excellent first

What you can do in a kayak... Lower Irthing

Playing on the Greta

Jackfield Rapids, River Severn

Swarkestone Bridge, River Trent

Jackfield Rapids

Jackfield Rapids

Slalom on Chester Weir

Playboating on Chester Weir

division slalom site, and you can see why. The final narrow gorge is exciting but normally straightforward.

You then pass under an old railway viaduct with the odd 'bridge jumper' whistling past you! There is now a section of mostly quiet water, till just above the Sedbergh road bridge. Here lies an awkward fall (Gd 3) with a magnetic rock for the unwary. Some way below the bridge the rapids start up again and culminate in the hardest rapid (Gd 3/4), a narrow slot on river right which drops several metres. The fall can easily be portaged on river left, but this has caused numerous access problems. Far better is to shoot it, either 'blind' or with only one person inspecting it, so as to not upset the landowner. More pleasant rapids lead eventually to the normal take-out at Killington road bridge, 6km from the Crook of Lune.

Below lay 2 weirs, both needing care. The first is straightforward but can have a massive holding stopper on it in high water and the second, Stangerthwaite weir, is huge and complex with spikes and lumps of concrete all over the place. Most shoot it middle left over a projecting 'V' shaped apron, or portage on the right (difficult). The third major gorge lies below at grade 2/3 and is very pleasant, finishing at the junction of the Rathey. Get out here either across the field on the left or slightly further down in a more discreet area also on river left and follow the steep track up to the lay-by on the main road.

Below here the river is only grade 2 but is very pleasant, particularly as an open boat trip. The hardest rapids are just before Devil's Bridge. There is an access agreement from Rigmaden Bridge down to Devil's Bridge. Please contact the river adviser and do not put this agreement in jeopardy.

Other important points   A number of rivers join the Lune. Borrow Beck which is excellent can be paddled into the Lune and if so the Lune will also be high, and you can get out at numerous places depending on the length of trip you want. Beck Foot, the little stream running down next to the road from the railway viaduct at the Crook of Lune put-in, has been done at grade 4 but is small and not recommended due to the access problems in this area.

Contributor:
Nigel Timmins

Lune (Rigmaden Bridge to Kirkby Lonsdale)

Grade **2**

Length **10km**

OS sheet **97**

Contributor:
Nigel Timmins

Introduction   The river is only grade 2 but is very pleasant, particularly as an open boat trip. The hardest rapids are just before Devil's Bridge.

Water level   Medium to high levels are best.

Gauge   If you can easily float down at the start the river is in an ideal condition.

Access   Access at Rigmaden Bridge (615848) and egress at Devil's Bridge (616782), Kirkby Lonsdale.
There is an access agreement from Rigmaden Bridge down to Devil's Bridge. Please contact the river adviser www.bcu.org.uk/access/riverinfocumbria.html and do not put this agreement in jeopardy.

Borrow Beck

Grade **3+(5)**

Length **8km**

OS sht. **90/91**

Contributor:
Peter Carter

Introduction   A remote and wild spate run with an exciting set of rapids in the lower wooded section. Well known due to its inclusion in the old 'Rivers of Cumbria' guide.

Water level   Wet, needs lots of rain and it doesn't stay up for long.

Gauge   Can you paddle round the first bend without excessive rock-bashing?

Access   Park in a lay-by with a phone and walk down to the river (553038). Egress is at Low Borrowbridge, park on the bend (610013).

Description   The river is fast, shallow and bouldery (Gd 2) for the first 5.5km with a couple of fences, the second on a bridge after 2km. On reaching the second bridge, the valley steepens and becomes grade 3. It then enters a wooded area and is instantly grade 3+ with small drops, leading to a drop choked with a tree (Nov 2002) and not far below is the main fall of 2.5m (Gd 5). After this, continuous small rapids with one notable narrow chute (Gd 3/4) lead down past the road bridge to a weir under the motorway and on to Low Borrowbridge. Egress on right just above the confluence with the Lune.

Other important points   The run can be extended by driving up to Hause Foot (550055) and putting in on Crookdale Beck, reputedly a grade 4.

Birk Beck

Grade **3(4/5)**

Length **8km**

OS sht. **90/91**

Introduction   A small beck with an exciting upper section, due to the large Docker Force and a couple of smaller falls. Unfortunately things ease off below Scout Green, before getting very flat beyond Greenholme, although if you do the full trip in high water, the beck and then the River Lune will whisk you rapidly on your way.

Water level   Fairly wet, perhaps runnable with a little less water than some of the other local becks.

Gauge   At Scout Green the river level can be judged as it runs adjacent to the road. If you can float it is on.

Access   If paddling Wasdale Beck you can continue down this; (3km of 4/5 but this may not have enough water in it). Alternatively park by the railway bridge (585095) and walk 400m along a bridleway to get in at the lower bridge, just below two fences. For a shorter trip get out at the junction of Bretherdale Beck and walk up the footpath to Dorothy Bridge (599053). For a full trip, continue into the Lune getting out either at Roundthwaite, (609031) or if you have time at Old Tebay bridge at the falls.

Description   The beck is swift and twists around some bends, to a small drop leading to a horizon line, which ensures you get out above the 4m high, fairly vertical Docker Force (Gd 4/5). An awkward portage regains the beck in a deep pool below the falls. The beck splits around an island, which causes some bashing and then after 500m there is another horizon line. This 3m fall is much more straightforward with a small drop leading to a slab and drop into a pool (Gd 3/4). A series of slabby rapids in a tiny gorge lead under a bridge to the final fall, a slab dropping 2m into a pool (Gd 3) and under the footbridge to Scout Green. The beck is now easier (Gd 2) with occasional small slabby rapids until Greenholme is approached; here some bushy islands and sharp turns could cause problems. As you pass under a bridge there is a left-hand bend with a rocky reef and a possible take-out up a path

Contributor:
Peter Carter

just after the junction with Bretherdale Beck .
Continuing down is fast grade 1/2 water leading to the Lune after
1.5km. The Lune is fast but provides a few deeper eddies and
leads under the M6, the railway and the M6 again until Roundthwaite Beck joins on the right and a nice surf wave provides a
good egress point.

Other important points   The keen can continue carefully round
the corner passing the notorious weir under the railway bridge
and then to Tebay Falls (Gd 4) on the Upper Lune, to get out
below the gorge at the bridge.

Rawthey

Grade   **4**
Length **14km**
OS sht. **97/98**

Introduction   A fantastic river running off the southern Howgills
towards Sedbergh. It has a bit of everything, starting as a small
stream with technical falls, a spectacular conglomerate gorge and
finishing as quite a big river before emptying into the Lune.

Water level   Fairly wet. It needs a good 6 hours of rain to bring
this river up and unfortunately it does not last very long.

Gauge   Any of the bridges in Sedbergh will confirm if this river
is paddleable. Can you get down without scraping?

Access   Start at Rawthey bridge (713978) or just before at some
large lay–bys and finish either at the A683 road bridge (678923),
or the A684 road bridge (665919) on the outskirts of Sedbergh, or
continue at a more leisurely pace to the road bridge near the Lune
confluence (628896).

Description   High up, the river is narrow and bedrock predomi-
nates, requiring constant manoeuvring. There are many small
drops but one in particular at certain water levels has held paddlers who dawdle over it. Surf the stopper at your peril!
On down and you come to a footbridge with a good-sized fall just
above, shoot centre right. The river now eases and you get a good
view of Cautley Spout high on the right, a popular waterfall walk.
Beware though, as after the river takes a large loop, a large complex fall is waiting for you below. It is a 3-tier fall, with a narrow
shoot on the right, which can be gained in medium water but is

more difficult in high water. In those conditions it is usually better to blast down the centre… always exciting!

You are now in a gorge and some good paddling ensues. It gradually eases and the gorge walls fall back for a time. Just below a bridge and small weir, the river enters another gorge, with four quite hard falls, the last being the crux. A large waterfall then enters from the right and the geologists amongst you will find this section of gorge a fascinating place. Fortunately it is all straightforward, and leads easily to the first of two take-outs, at road bridges. Just below the first bridge you pass the Clough and you can easily see the last fall on that river. Easy water leads to the next bridge and egress point. For those who wish to continue (the super fit amongst you!), easy water leads to a small fall at the next narrow bridge. A couple of awkward weirs and you then pass under the railway viaduct with another awkward fall some 500m below. This is a two-tier fall starting on the left and finishing on the right. Beware, because in high water the stoppers can be enormous. Easy water then leads to the final bridge and confluence with the Lune.

Contributor:
Nigel Timmins

Other important points   You can start higher than the suggested put-in by a bridleway adjoining the forest (727967) which you follow to the river. This gives some serious paddling, culminating in a gorge of grade 5/6.

Clough

Grade   **4/5**

Length   **14km**

OS sheet   **98**

○ ○ ○

Introduction   Yes I know its been said of many rivers, but this is one of the best! Get the right water level and you are assured of a great trip. There can hardly be any flat water on this river and there are frequent drops to keep your interest and adrenalin levels high.

Water level   Fairly wet, it only drains a small area and does not hold its water for long.

Gauge   To check this river out, you unfortunately have to drive some way up the valley, but as soon as you see the river, you will know whether it is on or not, you can either float or you can't.

Access   There are numerous possibilities, depending on the length of trip and amount of water flowing:

Minor road on the left after you come out onto the open moor
(698913) having left Sedbergh.
First road bridge (714907).
Small lay-by with concrete seat (751897) or just upstream of here
opposite Dandra Garth Farm.
Next road bridge (768903) or better, up by the left turn to Grisedale.
Garsdale Head (784918).
Egress on the Rawthey at the A684 road bridge (665919) just out-
side Sedbergh.

Description   If there are tons of water you can start as high as
Clough head… you are in for a 'full on' paddle though! Obvious
falls can be seen from the road, though one of the most difficult
cannot and it is worth inspecting on the way up. Stop just after
the road bridge (768903) next to the '8 mile milestone marker'.
The falls are just above the bridge and around the corner, a difficult two-tiered drop. Nice paddling below, till you come to a blind
drop at a small bridge (762900) 'Long House'. It is fortunately
straightforward at about 1.5m high. Good water all the way to the
next road bridge and then some limestone steps mark the start of
a harder section and gorge. The most difficult section can again
be inspected on the way up. To do this, go down the small minor
road to a bridge (698913). A narrow fall above the bridge leads to
a constriction below. Below that is another fall, which often sports
a huge stopper. This whole section can be grade 5 in high water.
Things ease a little for a while but more falls follow, with a quite
large weir/fall near Hallbank that is awkward. The final fall just
upstream of the Rawthey confluence is big, at 2m and normally
shot middle left. A grand finale to a great river.

Contributor:
Nigel Timmins

Dee

Grade	3(4)
Length	3km
OS sheet	98

Introduction   An interesting little river that unfortunately has a
difficult fall/portage, so making for a fairly short upper trip.

Water level   Very wet.

Access   The best access point is at Stone House bridge (770858),
though it is feasible to start higher. Egress *must be made* at the
parking spot identified on the OS sheet (864 743).
You could get on below Dent (707873) for an easy trip down to the

Rawthey, about grade 2/3.

Description   A very small technical river, the majority of it can be inspected from the car as you drive up the valley above Cowgill. Above Stone House bridge are some fairly big drops and these will only 'go' in really high water. Most people start at Stone House bridge with good parking next to it. Downstream the river runs over beautiful bedrock slabs with a water-worn groove down the middle… quite unique! Below the bridge in Cowgill the river begins to move away from the road and inspection is much harder. Fortunately it is fairly easy but you are strongly advised to have inspected the take-out at the parking spot (864743). At the parking spot the river enters a small gorge with a neat little fall above the footbridge. Ensure you can land on the slabs below (river right) as there is a fairly tricky fall of about 3m lying in wait. Either land on the slippery slabs before the fall and exit the river, or shoot the fall (grade 4) and get out river right about 20m downstream via the 'cavers' footpath. This must all be checked beforehand as it is not obvious from the river. *Do not on any account carry on downstream*, unless you are training for extreme rivers, as the fairly innocuous easy section of river suddenly enters a gorge about 200m further on. This gorge however starts with a difficult fall that is probably shootable, hard left, but lands you in a box canyon above an un-shootable drop. You might be able to land on the left above this fall, but the fall is large and lands on a rock with vertical pinning potential. To portage this lot would be very difficult, just climbing out would be hard!

A shame as the river then *seems* to be fairly easy all the way to Dent. The river below Dent can be paddled, but it is fairly easy at first, Grade 1/2 and then a short section of 2/3 before it joins the River Rawthey.

Other important points   Dent is a beautiful little Dales village with a central cobbled street. So small in fact that when you drive into it, you feel you should not be there. The roads above Dent are very small with many blind bends and corners… drive slowly please.

Contributor:
Nigel Timmins

Hindburn

Grade	**4(5)**
Length	**8km**
OS sheet	**97**

Introduction   A small river with continuous interest, drops, slides, weirs, and many boulder-strewn rapids, but quite a few tree problems.

Water level   Very wet conditions are needed to make this river runnable.

Gauge   At the finish in Wray on the B6480 is a small measuring weir. This needs to be completely covered with at least an inch of water flowing over it.

Access   Get in high on the river above Lowgill at the bridge (650640). Take out in the village of Wray or more discreetly just downstream on the B6480 road bridge. Here you will find a small car parking spot on river left just above the bridge (604680).

Description   Fast water leads off and you encounter many difficult rapids. One is a series of rock-slides which makes for quite committing paddling. The most dangerous is some way down marked as a fall on the OS sheet (623675). Upstream of this is a small bridge. Get out here and inspect and/or portage on river right. The fall is a two-tier drop. The first is straightforward at about a metre but the second is a steep, stepped fall of about 3m. Best shot on the right but as often is the case, getting this is difficult (Gd 5). If you want to portage this get back on well below the fall via a small track. Below are a couple of smaller falls and drops and the river then rushes on round some sharp bends into Wray and the egress bridge.

Contributor:
Nigel Timmins

Wenning

Grade	**2**
Length	**12km**
OS sht.	**98/97**

Introduction   A rarely paddled river that runs through a quiet rural landscape. It does need a lot of water, but why it has been so neglected is not clear.

Water level   Fairly wet conditions are required as the river is broad and shallow in places.

Gauge   The river does need to be in a mild flood to make it paddleable and this can easily be checked at Clapham or the bridge further down. If you can float easily down the rapid below either of the bridges then it is at a good level. Do not bother if it looks like it might be a bump and scrape.

Access   There are a number of access points but one of the best is at Clapham (733678). Easy parking and access over the bridge from the station and upstream of the bridge. Also at the next bridge down (693683), here there is a rough track leading into the river…a possible ford? There is very poor access in High Bentham but a pleasant spot is found in Low Bentham opposite the Punch Bowl Hotel. It might be politic to visit the pub. Egress in Wennington either onto the 'green' just before the bridge (617700), or just upstream of the village at a small parking spot next to a bench with a small path leading down the river.

Description   You start quietly enough but the flow increases in speed and there are a number of excellent little rapids with numerous small weirs creating the most challenging sections. Beware though as some of these are made up of wire baskets that are falling to bits. As you approach Low Bentham there are two larger weirs. The first is vertical and probably best portaged (at least in an open boat) with the second some 20m below. This is angled on the right and has a number of fish steps on the left. It can be shot on either side but *do not* shoot in the middle, as some nasty spikes stick up at the base of the weir. A further 3km of fairly easy water brings you to the small village of Wennington with the best egress on river right just upstream of the village. Below lies more easy water with egress either in Hornby or the River Lune (though you will have to paddle a fair distance to find an egress point).

Contributor:
Nigel Timmins

Greta

Grade	**2(3)**
Length	**10km**
OS sht.	**97/98**

Introduction   A pleasant river running out of Ingleton that is not often paddled. A shame, as below Burton the river is great for playing on in short boats.

Water level   Needs to be high, to be at its best.

Gauge   If the rapid below the (half-way) bridge in Burton in Lonsdale has a clear route down it, it is at a good level.

Access   Get in either in Ingleton on the A65 road bridge by an iron bridge (difficult parking as you cannot park next to the bridge), or far better (though it makes for a fairly short 4km trip) from a small lay-by on a minor road, just upstream of the Burton in Lonsdale bridge (655719). Egress is at Greta bridge, just before the Lune (611726). Best to get out on river left just below the bridge. Parking is limited here, only room for 2 or 3 cars.

Description   A pleasant grade 2 trip, through fairly remote country. From Ingleton it is all fairly easy, but once you reach Burton things improve dramatically, as the river now runs over wide bedrock slabs. Under the bridge is an excellent little play wave. But don't despair, as there are many more below on this fairly continuous fun section. About 2km down you come to a much larger fall of about 1.5m (Gd 3) just before the river swings rightward. This can easily be shot on river right or left. Below is an awkward reef, with a rock sticking up in the main channel creating some 'boily' water. A rocky shoot past an island can be awkward, but in general things now revert back to an easy grade 2 and you are left with a pleasant run into the finish. A superb river, easy but continuous good fun!

Other important points   Above Ingleton are some superb waterfalls that have been 'run'. A detailed description is not given, as you will need to walk up and inspect them. Good to do if the river is too low when you get here, as it will provide you with useful information for a later visit.

Contributor:
Nigel Timmins

Roeburn

Grade	**3/4**
Length	**4km**
OS sheet	**97**

Introduction   A very small river that needs plenty of water. If you hit it lucky, this is a wild ride through a very remote gorge.

Water level   Very, very wet, as it needs lots of water.

Gauge   Drive up the river just above Wray and check it out, it will be obvious if it is 'on'.

Access   Get in high up on the river near Winder Wood (600638). Egress either in Wray or more discreetly down at the B6480 road bridge on river left, just upstream of the bridge (604680).

Description   This river is superb and drops extremely quickly at over 100ft per mile with no flat bits! Trees are however a major hazard so great care is always needed. It starts fast and just continues with rapids and small falls. There is one larger fall that is difficult to inspect. This is where the river bends left and enters a small gorge with a ledge of about 1.5m, shoot it hard on the left. A large concrete wall marks the point where the small road just upstream of Wray meets the river, but it is probably best to continue through Wray and get out below the village on the B6480 road bridge.

Contributor:
Nigel Timmins

Wasdale Beck

Grade	**5**
Length	**3km**
OS sheet	**90**

Introduction   A steep, boulder-strewn, alpine style river, Wasdale Beck is a great spate river which rarely comes into condition. All significant drops can be inspected and portaged if necessary.

Water level   Very wet. This is a spate run requiring a lot of water… the more the better.

Gauge   When looking at the falls near Shapwells Hotel the drops should all look runnable. If in doubt don't bother because a low level run is very tough on boats!

Access   Park in the lay-by on the A6 Shap road, 1800m before the turn to the Shapwells Hotel (561082). Egress at Shapwells Hotel (578095). Please park carefully at Shapwells; because it is rarely paddled this has never been a problem provided the usual etiquette is shown. Let's keep it that way.

Description   The initial sections of the beck are steep, continuous rapids through boulder fields requiring quick reactions and the definite need to keep pointing downstream to avoid broaches. After passing under the first bridge the river steepens even more to the first significant rapid.
Large boulders in the river signal the need for an inspection (for most). The river bends to the left with a lot of the volume heading right. The best line is on the left, boofing over a large boulder and some skilful slalom work.
From here on there is rarely a dull moment. The next major rapid is marked by a rocky outcrop on river right. Several small drops

and boulder dodging lead to a larger drop requiring a boof move over a boulder that spans nearly half the river, taking care not to go too far left into an undercut mud wall. Directly below this is a sheep fence, which normally can be paddled round with care. The final rapid can be inspected when you park at Shapwells Hotel… an excellent series of rock steps forming an impressive finale. It is worth considering having protection on both banks here, especially in very high water levels when the drops form some quite impressive stoppers. The first drop is a weir that is pretty straightforward (although some speed will be required to avoid a pin on several submerged rocks) best taken left or right. A short section leads to 3 rock slabs/drops best taken left of centre with a bit of speed. Egress immediately below on river left before a large sheep fence.

Contributor:
Ian Wilson

Other important points   There are several sheep fences across the river which, depending on their state of repair, may require portaging. There are also several footbridges that may require portaging at very high flows.

Small Becks of the Area

Some small becks that are not often paddled due to low water, trees or fences.

Barbon Beck

Grade **3/4**

Length **3.5km**

OS sheet **97**

Introduction   A wild limestone beck that is fairly easy, but it is difficult to catch with enough water in it. Although the upper section is next to the road, the lower and more serious section is not!

Water level   Very wet, the river needs to be in a good flood condition.

Gauge   Check it out at the finish; if the river is clearly paddleable it is worth driving up to the start.

Contributor:
Nigel Timmins

Access   Get on from the small mountain road where the road and river meet (657828) and finish below the village of Barbon just upstream of the main road bridge, A683 by a large lay-by

Leck

Grade **3/4(5)**

Length   **4km**

OS sheet   **97**

Introduction   A superb wild river starting high up in the limestone fells above Ingleton.

Water level   Very wet.

Gauge   Check out the level in Cowan Bridge; if you can easily float then it is worth the drive and carry down to the start.

Access   Access is difficult and the best spot is to leave your car on the minor road high above the river and take the unmade track down past Smithy House Farm and start at the footbridge near Whittle Hole (658797). Best to egress the river in Cowan Bridge river left, just upstream of the bridge on a footpath. Parking is difficult here, the best place being on the right just after the bridge, heading towards Ingleton. Beware though as the road is extremely busy.

Contributor:
Nigel Timmins

The West

Contents

High Peak

Midlands and Borders

Introduction

This area of central and western England, although geographically quite large is unfortunately not overly blessed with white water. The rivers/sites described here do not fully detail what is on offer within the region, but do indicate the varied nature of the rivers and streams that make up the paddling within the area. The legal access to moving water is notoriously poor within the Peak District National Park. Even some of the major rivers such as the Dove and Derwent have limited if any access to them. This situation has not improved in the twenty years or so since I first paddled in this area. Roll on the revolution.

Luckily, outside the National Park the rivers Severn and Trent provide easy white water at any water level, with few if any access issues.

For the more adventurous among you, the high peakland moors are littered with small, steep, spate streams and brooks which, in the right condition will provide a unique experience and a few first descents. Where possible I have tried to indicate the location of a number of unfinished projects, which may entertain people in their search for something new.

Bill Taylor

West Regional
Coordinator for the
Guidebook

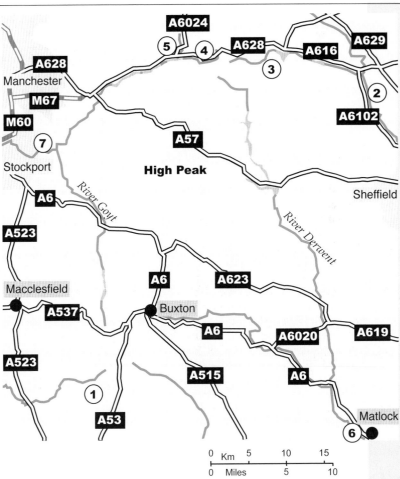

High Peak

Dane

Grade **2/3**

Length **3.5km**

OS sheet **118**

Introduction   This section of the River Dane can provide excellent sport when bank full. Unfortunately, it rises and falls very quickly, and a few hours after the rain has finished sees the river return to its boney normality. If that is the case walk the 1km from the put-in to see the impressive Luds Church (marked on the 1: 25000 OS map) an unusual gritstone geological feature. Returning to the river, a well-used footpath on the southern bank provides both inspection options and a walking return to the starting point if needed. This section of the Dane passes only two or three buildings on its route but the river can be popular with local fly fishermen; unfortunately its small size means that close contact if anyone is fishing is nearly always the case!

Water level   Wet to very wet conditions are required.

Gauge   At both the put-in and take-out of this section the river should look 'up' and peaty in colour. Most rocks should be covered when looking upstream from the bridge in Danebridge (Wincle).

Access   The best put-in is at the car park on river left 600m above the Gradbach YHA, launch directly from the car park (998662). This can be found off a tight turning leading down to the Youth Hostel from the 'B' road that links the villages of Flash and Algreave. The best egress is on river left above the bridge in Danebridge/ Wincle (find a usable exit before paddling).
The nature of the access situation requires a discrete approach; parking and changing in this small, sleepy Peak District village is not recommended.

Description   In the right conditions the first 100m should be fast and shallow, overhanging trees and the odd stock fence the only real issues. Under the footbridge at the YHA the stream should slowly become more interesting. On river left the Black Brook comes in, swelling the Dane before the gritstone walls close in and the start of the mini-gorge. The next 1km or so provides the best sport, a series of small falls and shoots (up to grade 3 depending on water levels) set among impressive rock architecture towering above both banks. Paddlers should be on active lookout for trees. The rock walls slowly fall away and the river down to Danebridge and the egress runs at an interesting grade 2+.

Other important points   In biblical rain this section can be started higher up at Three Shires Head. The run can start with the 1m fall under the bridge; again, trees, barbed wire and stock fences need to be taken into account. This section runs at a technical grade 2/3. The other upper headwater of the Dane starts above Flash Bottom (great name). This has been paddled from just below Under Hill Farm and involves running a blind culvert, a number of rock ledge falls of up to 2m and considerable tree and undergrowth issues. This is recommended only for the adventurous.

Both Black Brook, flowing in from Gradbach woods, and Clough Brook have been run, the former at grade 3+ after hours work with rope and chain saw, and once in a year rainstorms. Walk up from the footpath junctions (990658) until you have seen enough. The latter can be accessed from the A54 just west of Algreave and joins the main river after the gorge section. It runs at grade 2 with logjams in the lower part.

Contributor:
Bill Taylor

Don

Grade	**2/3**
Length	**8km**
OS sheet	**111**

Introduction   The Don is paddleable from Deepcar down through Oughtibridge before it meets the industry of Sheffield. It then flows through the industrial surroundings of Sheffield and Rotherham, where at times it forms part of a navigation. There is some touring potential as it continues from Rotherham to Conisbrough and on to Doncaster, after which it is a flat fenland river.

Water level   Wet to very wet conditions are required.

Gauge   The river needs to look full when you first gain sight of it at the access point.

Access   There is access to the river from a path up the left bank from a minor road (292981) in Deepcar. It is possible to walk up the path and put in higher but only after heavy rain. It may also be possible to start much higher above Penistone. Take out river right by the footbridge across from the Middlewood Tavern on the A616 which provides a possible parking spot and convenient watering hole.

Description   From Deepcar the Don flows through a pleasant wooded gorge below Wharncliffe Rocks, with one interesting

Contributor:
Martin Burgoyen

grade 3 rapid. There are a couple of weirs, one a vertical weir at Wharncliffe Side that is best portaged on river left. The river opens out above Oughtibridge where there is a slalom course, and possible take-out. Oughtibridge marks the start of more weirs, which need inspection and care. More collapsed weirs form rapids (Gd 2/3) below the British Tissues works. Take out river right by the footbridge across from the Middlewood Tavern.

Little Don or Porter

Grade   **3**

Length   **5km**

OS sheet **110**

Introduction   This upper section of the River Don needs both a sense of commitment and adventure. It is not to be taken too lightly as it has been the site of a broken leg and a miserable walk out.

Water level   Very wet, only possible after prolonged heavy rain.

Gauge   This section starts high up near its headwaters, and therefore to prevent a long and disappointing walk the surrounding peat should be well sodden. It really needs to be raining during the walk in.

Access   This short section is accessible from the lay-by at the top and highest part of the Woodhead Pass (174004) on the A628 Barnsley to Manchester road. It is a half-mile walk southwards through the heather, and hopefully heavy rain to the Loftshaw Brook, which later becomes the Porter or Little Don.
Take out just before Langsett reservoir (198007) and walk up the forest track to the main A616 road and lay-by (201012).

Contributor:
Martin Burgoyen

Description   Put in wherever you first see the river. Though only a few metres wide at its start, it is paddleable in spate. It has tight sections with some small drops and problems with overhanging trees. Breakouts are a novelty. Take out just before the reservoir.

Other important points   Below here there are more reservoirs, with the next suitable access at Deepcar on the Don.

Etherow

Grade	**4**
Length	**3km**
OS sheet	**109**

Introduction   A classic short run that is visible from the main road above. A rocky gorge about halfway provides the best of the excitement. The grade is given due to the nature of some of the bedrock and the horrible nature of a possible swim. The grade 4 tag is probably a little harsh, but it is one of those runs that a competent grade 3 paddler would struggle on.

Water level   Only possible after prolonged heavy rain. It is best to wait for a few very wet days, and when this section is bank full it will provide you with a real blast.

Gauge   There is a gauge on river right directly before the weir which can be found 100m upstream of the bridge below the egress. The gauge should read 4+ or above for the stream to be in condition.

Access   The access is found on the busy A628 via a pull-in, just west of Salter's Brook bridge (137002).
A minor road gives good access to the take-out (117998), which is probably best done above the small weir, and before the river disappears under the old railway line and into Woodhead Reservoir.

Description   After starting upstream of the bridge the first few hundred metres are an easy warm up for what lies ahead. The odd stock fence may need to be portaged. Any breakout needed on the first section is of the 'grab grass tussock and hold on' variety. As the river bears round eastward in line with the road the fun begins. The small valley tightens around the steepening gradient and propels you downward at impressive speed for such a little river. Side streams on the left bank help add some power to the drops, a number of which need to be paddled under power as they end in rock walls. Black Clough entering from river left has 100m of fun in spate condition (Gd 3+). The take-out is above the weir (it can be shot on the right) and the footpath on river left leads you back across the bridge up the track and back to the main road.

Contributor:
Martin Burgoyen

Hayden Brook

Grade   **4+**

Length   **2km**

OS sheet **110**

Introduction   Hayden Brook is one of those runs that is more inspected than paddled. Its advantage is that its level can be assessed from the road as the river spills out into Woodhead Reservoir. When caught in condition it provides a narrow, wild, fast ride with plenty of opportunities for banged elbows, involuntary rock splats, and the knowledge of needing to get out well before Hayden Falls.

Water level   Biblical, look for animals walking around in twos!

Gauge   Look upstream from Hayden Bridge on the A6024 (099007). The boulder garden upstream should be runnable.

Access   The access is via the parking spot on the A6024 Holmebridge road (098022).
Park up and walk 250m due west down towards the river. The put-in is where you feel happiest and is dependent on the water levels. Inspection of the section down to where the new plantation starts is prudent. It is important to check the location of the 6m Hayden Falls (Gd 4+ and a possible portage). There is little chance of seeing it coming when the section above is in nick and your full attention is on the here and now. Egress for the trip is at Hayden Bridge. The original bridge and remnants of the old road are 10m upstream of the new road. Take out upstream of the old bridge before the flume and tunnel under the A6024, parking is available at a number of single car pull-ins.

Description   The higher put-in is 100m below where Stable Clough enters from river left. There is a small flat area on river left directly below an exposed peat cliff.
There are 100m of grade 3 before Thorleys Gorge, a jumble of rock and boulders that offer numerous pinning opportunities at grade 4. (It has been run at grade 5 when the level was best described as 'mental'). Be warned, this not a place to be upside down. The mêlée is soon over and the river returns to a fast grade 3.
After 400m or so of rockslides and small drops Hayden Falls is reached. Above there is a small stream flowing in from river left, which might be spotted; a few more drops bring you into sight of a dry stone wall on river right. Get out above the wall on river left where you can. Hayden Falls (Gd 4+) is a 6m fall with a step

Contributor:

Bill Taylor and
Sue Pinner

halfway down. The plunge pool (a possible lower starting point, or re-access after portage) *is of limited depth and landing is problematic and possibly painful.*

Below, 250m of grade 3 brings you to Capri Falls (a mark two with blue paint work!). This is preceded by a number of holly trees on both banks. The river here turns right over a series of one metre falls. In full flow this blurs into an impressive rapid where reactive paddling is the order of the day (Gd 3/4). Pre-inspection should have warned you of the fence post running across the river... it can be ducked.

The river now enters a plantation and a bridge is soon reached. The flow eases off a fraction before landing you at the old bridge and your egress.

Derwent

Grade	**1/2**
Length	**6km**
OS sheet	**119**

Introduction The Peak District River Derwent could be a classic, easy white water touring river if it was not for the local access situation. Although all of it has been paddled, and some sections can provide good sport up to grade 3, the really feasible sections for paddling are limited. The stretch described here runs from Darley Dale Bridge to Matlock Bath. It provides some simple white water in a beautiful if overcrowded valley. The river is a typical limestone waterway with dippers, wagtails and the smell of wild garlic as your constant companions.

Water level Wet to very wet. As with all limestone bedded streams the river dries quickly. A few hours after the storm event has passed will see the river return to thin levels.

Gauge A visual check at the start or finish should indicate the condition of the run.

Access The access can be found at the bridge north of the village of Darley Bridge on the B5057 as it crosses the river. The nearby pub, The Square and Compass, provides good food and access to the river can be gained from the pub car park after permission has been sought from the landlord. Put in below the bridge on the right-hand side. Egress is at the bottom of the Matlock slalom course via steps on river right.

You can shorten the trip and get to the best water by using the

car park and access to the river at Artist's Corner (297596), it's a pay and dismay! On busy days it may be worth parking there for the egress and walking your boat back up on the road from the slalom course finish. The slalom course can be spotted from the A6 as it passes Matlock Bath. The course is used for training and lower level competitions. Best check with local paddlers or access the local club's website at www.matlockcanoeclub.co.uk.

Description   The river starts at a gentle pace and as you leave the noise of the roads the trees close in and you have a chance to enjoy the scenery. The first rapid is found under the left arch of the old railway bridge (after 3 km). The run into Matlock itself produces a few minor rapids and the bridge in the town is best taken via the left arch. The river down to Matlock Bath begins to pick up, and the sight of Pic Tor up on the left bank and a railway bridge indicates the start of the best water. The slalom course and egress is soon reached with the central rock exhibiting some form of magnetic power for novices. Egress via the steps on river right.

Contributor:
Bill Taylor

Goyt

Grade   **2/3**

Length **2.6km**

OS sheet **109**

Introduction   The Goyt starts high up by the Cat and Fiddle pub west of Buxton. The section described here is much lower down and from Marple Bridge to the egress at the Manchester Canoe Club (MCC) site (949901). The river has a number of weirs that can become dangerous in high condition. If in doubt portage. The rest of the trip provides pleasing grade 2 (3 in very high water) paddling in a surprisingly leafy environment considering its location.

Water level   Wet, it needs rain. A check at either access or egress should give you an indication.

Gauge   Check out the first weir in Brabyns Park (next to the Environment Agency hydrological station). There should be a reasonable depth on the shingle rocky rapid below the weir.

Access   The river trip can be lengthened by starting higher up at New Mills, or even the base of Fermilee Reservoir in very wet conditions. Both trips will involve the shooting/portaging of a number of weirs, some of them possibly dangerous. The trip from the Fermileee Reservoir can involve some access problems with landowners.

The normal access is via Brabyn Park. It can be found off the A626 just west of Marple Bridge train station, there is parking and access in the park; put in above or below the weirs which are within the park.

Egress is via the MCC base, on Dale Road, that is taken from the A626 opposite the Railway pub just to the west of Rose Hill train station. Dale Road ends up being no more than a farm track, as long as you are going downhill keep with it. Parking here is limited; contact the MCC www.manchestercanoeclub.org.uk.

Description   After putting in at Brabyns Park two weirs can be encountered, dependent on where you put in . The first, by the EA's measuring station, is usually shot via the middle ramp. If high and the tow-back looks unpleasant use the side slides. Portage on left if required.

The second weir is a horseshoe type, which can be punched at most normal levels. Again portage left if in doubt. The river continues with a few rocky rapids and the odd fallen tree being the only major issues. This section is an excellent introduction to moving water at normal levels. A heavier rapid and a sweeping right-hand bend brings you to the egress and the MCC site. The slalom poles are the give away.

Take out on river left and walk up to the club site and onto the road.

Contributor:
Bill Taylor

Other Possible Options in the High Peak

There are all manner of small streams and cloughs (a local name for Peakland rivers) which can provide short but entertaining sport in the right conditions. Most of the following have been paddled to varying degrees of completion and enjoyment:
Crowden Great Brook, the next valley west from Hayden Brook, down to the YHA hostel.
The Goyt, from above the reservoirs from Foxhole Hollow waterfall to the Errwood Reservoir with some portages.
The upper Etherow 1km above the put-in described in the guide.
Blackden Brook north of Edale as it flows off Blacken Moor and into the River Ashop.
The River Derwent above the north arm of Howden Reservoir, walk up until you get bored.
The Alport from the waterfalls by Glerthering Clough down to Alport bridge.

Contributors:
Sue Pinner and
Bill Taylor

The River Ashop that runs alongside the A57 as it climbs from the reservoirs up to the pass, put on as the water level allows.
The feeder streams that flow into the reservoirs south of Saddleworth Moor, both Birchen and Holme Clough have waterfall stunts if that is your kind of thing.

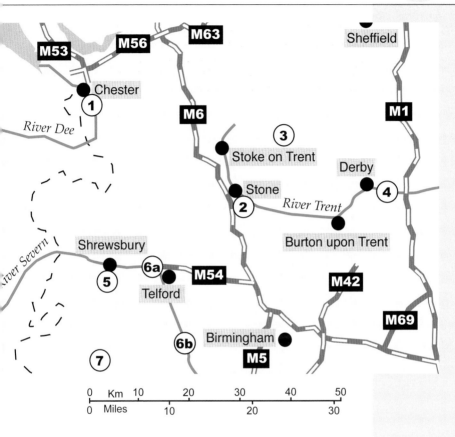

M53
M56
M63
Sheffield

Chester
① **M6**
River Dee

M1

③
Stoke on Trent

Derby

Stone
② **River Trent**

④

Burton upon Trent

Shrewsbury
⑤ 6a **M54**
Telford
M42

M69

6b Birmingham
⑦ **M5**

```
0    Km  10        20        30        40        50
0    Miles        10        20        30
```

Midlands and Borders

Chester Weir, River Dee

Playspot

OS sheet **117**

△ ③ ○

Location   The lowest weir on the River Dee in the city of Chester.

Characteristics   A series of partially retentive stoppers and (at the right state of tide) a surfable wave.

Introduction   This site has a number of advantages in as much as it always has enough water flowing over it to make it worthwhile. With basic tide knowledge it can provide a number of usable and variable conditions and there is also limited parking and easy access.

Water level   There is a minimum level that must flow over the Chester Weir by statute of law but, on average, it takes 30 cumecs. Various reservoirs in Wales are managed to guarantee this flow so there is almost always enough water. You need to plan the time of your visit in relation to the tides; high tides will change the nature of the weir and sometimes completely submerge the weir so that it becomes invisible. Plan to be there a couple of hours after High Water so that you can work the weir as the tide drops. To work out the time of HW Chester add 1 hour and 5 minutes to HW Liverpool or 52 minutes to HW Dover (see www.hydro.gov.uk/easytide.html).

Gauge   Visually check from the Old Town Bridge in Chester itself, but it can be used at most levels (see above).

Access   There is limited parking to the south and below the weir (407658). A footpath runs alongside the river on the south bank. There are two other options: one is to fight for a parking space (not literally!) when you turn down a narrow lane to the river by the roman amphitheatre which leads to the river. The other option is to get in at Sandy Lane which can be found off the B5130 as it heads out of the city towards Farndon; there is parking for large groups and a pleasant, placid 2km paddle down to the weir itself.

Description   Chester Weir, according to the history books, is part natural with the rest being built originally sometime in the 10th century. Modern paddlers will find it running diagonally from river left to river right. The main weir face, when shootable, is taken in the middle and through areas of weakness in the tow back. Of most interest to paddlers is a series of salmon steps on river left; each of these forms a sort of stilling pool, providing a partial holding stopper. The normal way to shoot the weir is to paddle diagonally into the top pool from the left-hand side of the top of the weir. *(There are some small metal bolts which, although not dangerous can catch and hold a plastic boat at the top of the weir; these are visible and can be avoided).* Below the last stilling pool a blockwork groin provides a breakout on river left. Because of the nature of the tide the central sloping weir can be played in at the right levels. As the high tide falls away it provides an excellent surf wave for a limited time; this can turn into a holding stopper as the tide drops further.

Contributor:
Bill Taylor

Other important points   The old roman bridge below the weir provides eddies behind the pillars and can be used for a basic introduction to white water. There have been reports of blue-green algae on this lower section, therefore best to check in summer.

Stafford and Stone CC, River Trent

Location   The site can be gained via the main Stoke-on-Trent to Stafford road, the A34. Just after leaving the A34 for Stone on the A520, take the first right after the bridge and into the car park next to the site.

Playspot
OS sheet **127**

Characteristics   80m of 'user friendly' grade 1/2 white water.

Introduction   This is the site of the famous Stafford and Stone Canoe Club. The club itself has been the home of a number of well-known slalom paddlers over the years. This short section of the River Trent running alongside the club hut has had money spent on it over the years, by agencies such as the now defunct NRA and is managed by the club mainly for slalom training. The water itself provides a safe, contained location to work on and improve technique and introduce people to moving water. There are issues of the quality of the water especially after heavy rain!

Water level   Can be paddled at any level, but best when the water level allows the features and eddies to form fully. In high level the site can be washed out.

Access   Competitions and slalom training take precedence here

so contact the club for details. Up-to-date contact details can be found on the BCU website www.bcu.org.uk.

Description   The site is 80m long. The normal put-in is just after the stone bridge on river right. A small warm-up pool leads to a gentle downstream 'V' and eddies both left and right. Halfway down, a mid-stream boulder (constructed out of bricks) provides options river left and right; more well formed eddies lead to a larger collecting pool at the bottom. Steps on river left lead up to the footpath and a return to the top of the site.

Contributor:
Matt Berry

Other important points   Although described as a site, a flat water trip in the form of a loop can be made, by travelling for as long as you care downriver, and eventually carrying across fields or via bridges to the parallel Trent and Mersey Canal. A number of options can be worked out by the study of the appropriate OS map.

Churnet

Grade   **1(3)**
Length **1.5km**
OS **118/119**

Introduction   The Churnet is one of those paddles that probably is not worth travelling very far to do, but if you are in the area and it is raining hard then…
The description here is of the short loop using the canal as the way back and incorporating the best of the few features.

Water level   Wet/very wet.

Gauge   The river should be looking brown and busy. A short walk along the canal would provide a good indication of the conditions.

Access   There are a number of access points. The best one for the trip described here is via a rough road and track, which can be found off a 'C' class road, which in turn is found from the A522 south of Wetley rocks. The 'C' road is followed towards Consall Hall; before reaching the hall a road/track is taken on the right-hand side, which leads down to the access, locally called Consall Forge, and a pub (000491). The river runs through lowland farmland and a nature reserve and access can be problematic.
If you wish to extend the trip (mostly at grade 1) put in at Cheddleton and a nice pub (982521), and/or take out at Dimming Dale

and the Forestry Commission car park (063432). The upper sections allow you to make a return trip via the Caldon Canal as the river and canal are either one and the same or run parallel.

Description   The description here is for the shortest trip that provides the two elements of white water. After putting in at the small parking place on the west bank of the canal, paddle using the canal past the pub on the left bank and under the bridge. Continue on 100m or so until you hear or spot the overflow shoot leading down, right and under the railway. This fall is some 3m high at a steepish angle. In very high water it provides an unpleasant boxed-in stopper, which will stop most boats dead and allow little option for escape. In normal paddleable levels it shoots the paddler from the canal via the dark tunnel into the adjacent river.

The river at this point is small and may suffer from fallen and overhanging trees. The occasional sweeping bend and rocky rapid interrupts the flow. Before long the river drops away out of sight and breaks the horizon. The only clue to this feature is some distant noise of the fall and the sight of a small wall on river left. In very high water there is little chance for a pause in an eddy before the fall is taken. Inspection is possible only from the left bank. Paddle the sloping drop (3m) starting left and heading right. An eddy is to be found on river left at the bottom of the drop. The trip is terminated here. Paddle a few metres further downstream until you can carry up the left-hand bank, over the railway line and back on the canal. A short paddle back leads you to the overflow and eventually back to the access point.

Contributor:
Matt Berry

Trent (Twyford to King's Mill)

Introduction   An agreeable lowland paddle with two grade 2 sections to add a little something to the trip. The advantage of this section is that it can be paddled at any level, the Trent often holds its water days after the rain has stopped. In addition the countryside is pleasing and the bird life various.

Grade   **1(2)**
Length   **12km**
OS **128/129**

Water level   Paddleable at any level. When brown and over the banks the River Trent can produce some interesting eddy lines at King's Mill providing some opportunities for freestylers and squirt boating.

Access   Is via a small lane, which leads down to the north bank of the river at Twyford. This dead-end lane is found off the main Willington to Barrow upon Trent road, the A5142. A shorter trip (6km) can be done by starting at Swarkestone (nice pub). Egress is via another dead-end lane leading to King's Mill and a larger pub. You gain this from the crossroads in Castle Donnington and the B6540. Parking at King's Mill can be problematic, as the landlord has in the past requested that paddlers should not take up the space meant for customers. Best to ask before parking and make sure you provide some custom.

Description   The Trent is our third longest river and as this section is some way from its headwaters high up in the western Peaks, the trip starts at Twyford at a gentle pace. The paddle down to Swarkestone is easy grade 1. On a sweeping left-hand bend the observant will spot some rock caves in a field on the river right. The first bridge is Swarkestone itself. The stone bridge is one of the longest in Britain, at some quarter of a mile long. The river is usually taken via the far right arch. Below the bridge are simple grade 2 rapids and a number of eddies for breaking in and out. The river is now swifter than in the first 6km, and in high water a number of the sweeping bends may require a careful line. After 2km or so you will pass an old railway bridge that often collects trees on its supporting pillars. A further 3.5km and the sight of a steep forested bank on river right signals the start of King's Mill rapids. The flow heads left and small rocky constrictions add to its speed. An old overflow weir on river right hails back to the days when this site was the furthest upstream lock on the river. The river then turns left providing a simple grade 2 rapid and the egress point is on the right-hand side.

Other important points   This section can be paddled as a loop (you will need the OS maps). On the bank opposite the egress and the pub is a footpath that leads to a track and the Trent and Mersey Canal. This is then paddled westwards back to Swarkestone (and a 800m carry along the footpath or road back to the river), or continued to Twyford and a 1.25km portage.

Contributor:
Bill Taylor

Shrewsbury Weir, River Severn

Playspot

OS sheet **126**

Introduction   A large weir, which in very, very high water produces a classic surf wave. Normally the weir produces an unpleasant drop and tow back which cannot be recommended. The weir *can be dangerous* in any conditions but perfect in very high water. It is included in the guide because at the right levels with the right standard of paddler it is a good site. If you are in any doubt, see any tow back along the face of the weir whatsoever, or cannot recognise if it is safe, *go home.*

Water level   Needs to be very, very high (in extreme flood). Fortunately the River Severn at this point floods a number of times a year, therefore if it has been very wet in Mid Wales it is worth checking to see if the weir is in nick.

Gauge   Visual, the river needs to be pushing through the railing on the left bank by the weir itself, for the wave to form properly.

Access   There is a right of navigation on the river at this point. Access and egress is via limited parking (502130), river left downstream of the weir and to the south of Castle Fields. Finding the access is difficult unless you have an OS map, or have local knowledge.

Description   The wave when formed produces anything from a breaking wave to a big glassy green thing. The whole repertoire of moves can be made; if you are up for it you don't need me to tell you what to do.

Other important points   A few years ago, I was surfing the wave late one spring evening; it was getting dark and I was thinking of calling it a day. Just as I was turning to steer the boat back to the bank a 10m oak tree, complete with root system, a mass of branches and a full canopy, came steaming over the weir. It crashed into me knocking me off the wave and capsizing me. 200m, and six nervous rolls later I was still disentangling myself from the branches, only to be knocked over again and back into the heart of the tree. It was a long walk back to the car... Watch out for debris!

Contributor:
Bill Taylor

Severn (Jackfield Rapids)

Grade **2**

Length **2.5km**

OS sheet **127**

Introduction   The River Severn is one of our great open boat and kayak touring rivers, but provides little in the way of white water. The best section, described here, is known as Jackfield Rapids; it can be paddled as a 'park and play' or as a short trip.

Water level   Almost any level, gets washed out at high flows. The Severn at this point will hold its water for a week or so.

Access   For the short 2.5km trip put in at the 'pay and display' car park (665037) beyond the Ironbridge Gorge museum, and not the one at the museum. The car park is found at the western end of the main road running along the river and through the town of Ironbridge. You pass the museum turning, go over a mini-roundabout and take a sharp left. Launch via the car park into the river. Egress is via a path found on river left by the Jackfield Rapids, which leads back up to a 'C' road that runs alongside the valley on river left. There are a few small lay-bys on the road. Please don't block the Canoe Club main access and change out of view from the locals.

There is a right of navigation on this section of the River Severn from Pool Quay some 60 miles upstream of Jackfield to where Gladder Brook enters the river below Bewdley and before Stourport, some 25 miles below Jackfield.

The access to and site of the actual rapids is managed and owned by Telford Canoe Club who lease the river's right bank. They will allow groups to access the site (better parking), use their toilets, and camping site for a fee. Up-to-date contact details can be found on the BCU website www.bcu.org.uk.

Contributor:
Bill Taylor

Description   The river starts gently at normal levels. The section down to the town provides a few minor rapids and the islands are usually passed on the left. You pass under famous bridges, both old and new, and soon run into Jackfield Rapids; a number of eddies on river left provide opportunities for inspection should it be required. The main shoot provides defined and usable features and the rapid is blessed by a large collection eddy on the river left below the main action. This marks the site as an excellent one for improving basic white water skills, coaching or spending summer evenings being inventive with eddy lines.

Other important points   The section above the town is match fished and this will restrict the number of eddies you can work. The river will flood, sometimes at very high level; the trip in these conditions may not be technically much more than grade 2 but the river will be powerful, eddies confused and the river in the trees. A swim would be long, cold and unpleasant.

Severn (Bridgenorth to Bewdley)

Grade	**1 (2)**
Length	**11km**
OS sheet	**138**

Introduction   This is a popular section of the River Severn that has the advantage of being paddleable at any water level. A return from Bewdley to the start can be made via the Severn Valley Railway (which runs from May to September on most days; outside those months it only runs weekends). Check with the Tourist Information Office based in Bewdley on 01299-404740.
The river provides easy touring through a pleasant valley with little white water that can be by-passed by a selective choice of routes.

Water level   Any.

Access   There is a right of navigation on this section of the river. Access in Bridgnorth is via the car park and the slipway at Severn Park (719933) just north of the main town. The park itself is accessed via a roundabout on the east side of the river as the road heads north towards Dewley (A442).
Egress is just under the town bridge in Bewdley via steps on river right (787753). There is parking nearby.

Description   The nature of the river will depend on the volume of water in it (read the notes on the Jackfield Rapids section) but normally it is a quiet paddle in enjoyable countryside. In high water the eddy lines can cause the inexperienced problems. The only white water of any note may be found at Eyemore rapids (Gd 2) which are some 8km into the trip. In the summer months it may be that the route on the right of the island is too shallow. Below the island there may be some additional standing waves.
Within 3km Bewdley is reached, the right arch of the bridge sets you up for the egress via the steps on river right.

Contributor:
Bill Taylor

Teme (Downton Gorge)

Grade   **2/3**

Length **12km**

OS sheet **137**

Introduction   The River Teme has its headwaters in the hills of Powys and then runs east toward the English Midlands. The section described here is the Downton Gorge, a grand name for a pleasant grade 2/3 paddle on the Teme as it is squeezed between the limestone hills of Bringewood Chase to the south and Downton Common to the north.

Water level   Needs to be wet.

Gauge   The wooden jetty at the Linney car park (506746) needs to be covered.

Access   The access is problematic to say the least. Please check with the river adviser Karl Bungey on 01684 574546, or e-mail teme@activeoutdoors.co.uk before even thinking about planning a trip. Get on the river via the footpath river right (435720) as the 'C' road crosses the Teme 800m west of the hamlet of Burrington. Parking for 2 or 3 cars. Egress is at the Linney playing fields (the start of the lower Teme trip) at (506746).

Contributor:

Shaun Taylor

Description   The first 2km are flat. You pass under a couple of old bridges before the first broken weir at Hay Mill. It is best taken on the right. There are impressive limestone cliffs on river left. Before Castle bridge there is a horseshoe weir which is again taken river right.
By Bringewood Forge you may find a small playwave if conditions allow. The paddle down to the confluence of the River Onny is grade 1/2. 600m after the joining of the Onny you come across a 45° angle weir with a fish ladder. The ladder can hold novice paddlers and their kayaks so be careful. A further 3.5km sees you at the take-out.

Teme (Lower)

Grade   **2+**

Length **4km**

OS sheet **138**

Introduction   The section of the River Teme flows through and passes the Shropshire town of Ludlow. It provides a pleasing paddle in a surprisingly green valley considering it passes through the town itself. This section has the added excitement of a variety of weirs along the way.

Water level   Wet/very wet.

Gauge   From the main road bridge in Ludlow (513742) that takes the B4361 across the river, looking towards the river left there is an old Environment Agency gauge. It should read 51 or thereabouts. From here the horseshoe weir directly below the bridge can be inspected.

Access   Getting on for this section is best done from the Linney playing field (506746), below the castle on river left and above the town itself. There is a pay and display. In the winter this car park is often closed. If you wish to miss the first weir there is a lower access point via the Millenium Gardens directly below the weir and at the start of the narrow road that leads you to Linney playing fields. Egress is via a steep muddy slope, on river left just above the bridge on the A49; parking there is limited. If you paddle under the railway bridge which is directly after the A49 bridge you have gone too far. There is a second egress point which lengthens the paddle by 1km and by one unpleasant weir. Portaging the weir itself needs the landowner's permission, so check with the BCU river adviser (see previous section). Egress is again on river left via a track leading to the village of Ashford Carbonell. A sweeping right-hand bend and a gravel bank 250m below the weir signals the take-out.

Description   The first of the four weirs is within 20m of putting on. It is a diagonal 1.5m weir running from river right to left. Below the weir the first of the two town bridges is soon met, after this the second diagonal weir is soon sighted. At most levels the far right is the best line. After shooting this, or portaging on the left via a tree-fest, the river quickly runs under the second town bridge and to the top of the horseshoe weir. At decent levels the last section should be an enjoyable grade 2.

The horseshoe weir has a fish ladder at its apex. The ladder itself has walled sides which will not fit a kayak or open boat. Best to leave it to the fish and select whichever side has the least tow back and smoother ride. The fourth weir (of the broken variety) is found on a sweeping right-hand bend. It can be taken at most points in the obvious gap, (this weir is due to be rebuilt in the near future). The rest of the paddle will be grade 1/2 at the best levels.

Contributor:
Bill Taylor

Other important points   The four weirs in the first 1km can be suspect at higher water levels. Best to check out the horseshoe weir from the river left by the petrol station before getting on.

Hydrology for the Paddler

What is hydrology and how does it relate to the paddler?
Hydrology can be defined as the scientific study of water above, on and below the surface of the Earth. A basic understanding of this subject can help paddlers spend less time peering over bridges looking disappointedly at boney river beds, and more time in a boat, getting the best out of England's notoriously fickle rivers.

The importance of the Catchment Area
Thinking paddlers should consider certain landscape characteristics just as much as the weather conditions and the state of the river in front of them. These characteristics need to include the topography, geology, vegetation cover and land-use of the *catchment area* supplying water to the river system. All water that flows in a river fell as rain, sleet or snow, within the catchment area servicing the river's system. Areas of high ground act as drainage dividers separating one catchment from another. On entering a catchment area, the water may take a variety of routes, most of which will deliver it into the main river channel.

Measuring the Discharge
The distance from the headwaters of the section you intend to paddle will influence the amount of water it contains. If there is a large proportion of the catchment area above you the river will be higher for longer, and peak at higher levels than sites further upstream. This is due to the greater amount of water arriving at your access point to the river channel, delivered by all the tributary streams that spill into the river above your location, and from other paths such as overland flow, ground seepage and direct precipitation into the channel. The amount of the water and how long the river stays up can be technically referred to as the *magnitude* and *duration* of the flood flow. These two characteristics define the volume of water in the river, which is termed its *discharge*. Discharge is measured as the number of cubic metres of water passing through a cross-section of the river per second (such a unit is called a *cumec*); as an example the average release for Holme Pierrepont slalom course is 28 cumecs, for the Nene site it is 5 cumecs . The discharge is related to the size of a channel and the speed of the water flow within it. The same discharge can be accommodated in a small channel (shallow and narrow) by a fast flow, or in a larger channel (wide and deep) as a proportionally slower flow. The speed of a river is termed its flow *velocity* and is also determined by two factors, first *discharge*, as explained above, and secondly channel *gradient,* i.e. the steepness of the river bed.

Flashy and Delayed Flows
Most headwaters are found in upland areas where high rainfall can be expected and the steeper slopes will encourage faster run-off. If you intend to venture into these upper reaches for your day's sport it is important that you are taking your boat off the roof rack whilst it is still raining. Such sections of river are characterised by a rapid rise and fall in water level. This condition is referred to as *flashy* and results from the interplay between three factors: (i) the high speed of run-off from surrounding hills, (ii) the steep gradient of the river bed (increasing the speed of river flow) and (iii) the small proportion of catchment area above your launch point. In this case it needs to rain long and hard for the river flow to reach a

sustained high magnitude and duration.

Conversely, sites that are some considerable distance from headwaters exhibit a belated but longer rise and fall around a higher peak discharge. Such conditions are referred to as *delayed* and result from the greater volume of water which can be collected in the upstream catchment, coupled with the long distance that some of this must travel to reach the section. A comparison of the River Sprint and River Kent, of the south-east Lakes, will help illustrate the two conditions described. The Sprint, a tributary of the Kent, has a limited catchment area, therefore to find it in worthwhile condition it needs to be raining hard and continuously as you step into your spraydeck. On the Kent itself, some of the more interesting water is over 30km downstream of the Sprint confluence; this lower section is therefore fed by a much larger catchment that includes other tributaries such as the River Mint. These waters therefore tend to exhibit delayed characteristics influenced by what happened further upstream a number of hours ago as well as what is actually happening there and then.

Stream Ordering

A useful method of estimating the expected discharge of a particular section of a river is to employ techniques known as *stream ordering*. The technique most useful to the paddler is Shrieve's method. The only essential skills required for this task are basic numeracy and the ability to read an OS map. The first step is to locate and identify all the tributaries that feed into the section you wish to navigate. Then, starting at the most upstream point, begin to number all headwaters with a '1'; these are *first order streams*. As you reach a confluence between two first order streams, the river downstream takes on the value of '2', becoming a *second order stream*. Then, as you continue to work towards your access point, after each confluence the channel downstream is given the combined value of the two upstream sections. Therefore the channel downstream of a confluence between a second order stream and a third order stream will take the value of a fifth order stream. As the order of the section relates to the number of streams which feed into it, the higher the order the greater the discharge which could be expected. Although this method appears self-explanatory, it is important to remember that the numerical value given to the section you are considering does not relate to the length of tributaries upstream, simply their combined numbers. Although Shrieve's method is not foolproof it is a good rule of thumb.

Influence of Drainage Density

Drainage density can be explained simply as the amount of channel found within a river's catchment area. In catchments of high density there are many feeder streams in a relatively small space; this allows precipitation to reach a channel quickly via any of the possible routes. This tends to produce a flashy flow. A notable example would be Borrow Beck draining the south side of Shap Fell in the Lake District. At the other extreme a river like the Ribble has a low drainage density. In this example there are only a few tributaries spread within a large area and therefore the time taken for inclement weather to result in canoeable conditions will be delayed and the peak flow will not be as high. Human intervention can affect these general trends by the use of gripping (those herringbone shaped patterns that you see dug into the hillside) and the excavation of drainage ditches, such as those often found in peat moorland. These features produce an unnatural increase in drainage density and therefore channel flow, which is exactly what the landowner intended them to do. This feature has altered the condition of Peak District rivers considerably in the last twenty or so years.

Catchment Shape

The shape of the catchment area will affect the nature of the flow. A drainage basin which is long and thin will tend to lead to a delayed response, whilst a rounded catchment tends towards flashy conditions.

Geological Influences

The geological influence is especially marked in rugged terrain where there is more rock exposed. Some rock types are described as *impermeable;* these do not allow any precipitation to soak or seep in, instead making it run over the surface. Such water will tend to quickly drain into rivers. The Upper Duddon in the Lake District and River Dart in Dartmoor are good examples, being flashy rivers flowing on igneous rocks. Other rock types allow water to enter into them. These rocks are described as *permeable* if the water enters via jointing and bedding (cracks), as is the case with many limestone river catchments. Alternatively, if the rock soaks up water into its pores, as with some sand and gritstones, it is described as *porous*. The River Goyt in Derbyshire flows on such rocks. Whether the underlying rock type is porous or permeable, the water will take longer to reach the river channel once it embarks on a subterranean route. However, there is variation between water moving relatively quickly through a well-developed limestone cave system and slow movement within the limited pore spaces of a well-cemented sandstone.

Significance of Soil Type

Where a soil cover overlies the geology of an area, some of the water will infiltrate into the ground as it makes its way towards the river channel. The rate of loss into the ground will vary with soil type and structure; for example, water will easily pass into a porous sand-based soil but will find it harder to enter a more impermeable clay-based soil. As before, water which takes an underground route, will be delayed in its eventual arrival into the river channel. After a period of dry weather, even a porous soil surface can become hardened, acting like a sealant and keeping the water flowing over the ground surface, until the hard crust has been softened by the rain.

Once within the soil, water could pass downslope as *throughflow.* Alternatively, where there is a permeable rock layer below, some of the water can percolate into the underlying geology.

During prolonged rainfall, water may not be able to enter into a normally permeable rock or soil structure due to saturation. If this saturation point has been reached, often indicated by free-standing pools of water in nearby fields, then despite the characteristics of the soil and rock type water will flow overground and rapidly enter the channel. So any lucky paddler who witnesses sheets of water flowing over a hillside after several days of continuous wet weather should grab the nearest floating object and head for the most convenient access point. A good example of the influence of soil type is the upper River Lune that is often in 'nick' sometime after other rivers have returned to their boney normality.

The Influence of Precipitation Type

If rainfall is hard and heavy, a porous soil will not be able to absorb the water at the rate at which it is falling. Therefore a greater proportion of the rainfall will flow overland promoting a flashy response. At the other extreme, precipitation falling as snow will have a much greater delay between initial fall and river response, perhaps in the order of months. River flows can be especially high when the thaw of snow amassed over a winter period is triggered by heavy spring rainfall.

Vegetation and Land Use

Finally, we turn to consider the influences of vegetation and land use. Large expanses of woodland within a river's catchment area will have a marked effect on water flow. The first effect is precipitation *interception* by leaves. Forests are known to catch up to, and in the case of some of the broad leaf trees in excess of, 50% of rainfall. This delays the speed of water entry into the river by temporarily halting its progress until it drips to the ground or runs down a stem or trunk to the forest floor. It also has the beneficial effect of keeping the rivers at a paddleable level for longer once the river is up.

At the same time this allows greater opportunity for evaporation to occur, thereby preventing some of water from ever reaching the ground. The actual rate of evaporation is determined by meteorological factors; a simple example would be the influence of temperature, evaporation rates reaching their maximum on a hot summer's afternoon. Other forms of vegetation will have the same effect but to a lesser degree; for example cornfields intercept 35% of rainfall and grass cover 10% to 20% depending on its length. Another vegetation-related water loss is due to uptake of water from soil into root systems. Human influences are very important here as vegetation change is very often initiated by farming and forestry practices and there is the matter of seasonal changes in vegetation cover to take into account. On balance, the benefits of interception (longer lasting and more predictable paddleable levels) far outweigh the losses to evaporation.

Urbanization

A further human influence that can have a marked effect on river hydrology is the amount of urban development within a catchment. The increased sealing of the ground surface by impermeable concrete and tarmac, together with the routing of rain water quickly into rivers by sewer and drain systems can lead to increased flashiness. This can actually provide some exciting urban gutter runs. A completely opposite influence has been the calming effect of dam and reservoir construction on river regimes. A notable example of this is the River Tees, which was famous before the construction of Cow Green Reservoir for its flash floods locally called *freshes*. These days the variations in water level are more subdued and largely a result of the peculiarities of the local water authority as they release water from the reservoir rather than the fickle Pennine weather.

Summary

The above factors have been identified as important considerations for any paddler wanting to get the best out of English rivers. These, along with the commitment to closely follow weather patterns and take note of local river conditions, not only will see you spending more time in your boat enjoying that stolen (but predictable) classic run and less time on wild goose chases and frequenting tea shops, (which is of course a sport in its own right).

Have a nice wet one.

Contributors:

Dr Ian Drew
(Senior Lecturer in Physical Geography and Hydrology at Manchester Metropolitan University)

Bill Taylor
(BCU Level 5 Coach and Senior Lecturer in Coaching Science at Manchester Metropolitan University)

Acknowledgements

This guide wouldn't have been possible without the efforts of so many people. Paddlers have provided river descriptions and photos, checked countless draughts, commented on grades, walked down rivers and paddled runs to check that important point. Others have provided advice, help and support in all kinds of ways.

A big thank you to you all. This guide is both richer in character and more accurate for your efforts.

Alistair Yates	Karl Bungey
Andy Levick	Katie Timmins
Bill Taylor	Laurence 'Hoopla' Harris
Chris Pierce	Lee Pimble
Chris Thorley	Louise Royle
Chris Wheeler	Mark Rainsley
Colin Litten	Mark Wilkinson
Dan Scott	Martin Burgoyen
Dan Toward	Martin Burgoyne
Dan Townsend	Matt Berry
Dave Luke	Mike Devlin
Dave Shawcross	Mike Tinnion
Dave Watkinson	Muzzy
David Pearson	Nick Bolland
Desperate Measures	Nigel Timmins
Drummond Outdoor	Nookie Equipment
Franco Ferrero	Nottingham Mafia
Heather Rainsley	Perception Kayaks
Ian Drew	Pete Breckon
Ian Wilson	Pete Cornes
Ingrid Mathews	Pete Wood
J. D.	Peter Carter
Jan Weatherill	Phil Ascough
James Farquharson	Rob Arrowsmith
Jamie Drummond	Rob Yates
Jasmine Waters	Robert Cunnington
Joan Ferrero	Roger Ward
Jonathan Hyde	Russ Smith
Josh Litten	Shaun Taylor

Shrewsbury Canoe Club
Simon Westgarth
Spanner and Clwyd
Steve Balcombe
Steve Childs

Stephen Timmins
Stuart Miller
Sue Pinner
Tony Pizacklea
Wednesday Club

Special Thanks

A special thanks is due to the regional coordinators and editorial team, Bill Taylor, Chris Wheeler, Franco Ferrero, Mark Rainsley, Mike Devlin, Nigel Timmins and Robert Cunnington, who bore the brunt of the effort involved in producing this guide.

Special thanks are also due to Pete Wood for the artwork and design of the guide.

Photo Credits

Front Cover	Andrew Waddington
Pages 33, 34, 36, 69-72	Mark Rainsley
Page 35	Heather Rainsley
Pages 105-108	James Farquharson
Page 141	Chris Wheeler
Pages 142-144 top	James Farquharson
Page 144 bottom	Dan Scott
Pages 177-179	Andrew Waddington
Page 180 top	Rob Cunnington
Pages 180 bottom, 213, 214	Andrew Waddingon
Page 215	Pete Breckon
Page 216 top	Rob Cunninigton
Page 216 bottom	Rob Arrowsmith
Page 249	NIgel Timmins
Page 250	Mike Tinnion
Page 251	Ian Wilson
Page 252 top	Nigel Timmins
Page 252 bottom, 285 bottom	Mike Tinnion
Page 285 top	Nigel Timmins
Page 286 bottom	Mike Devlin
Page 286 top, 287	Lee Pimble
Page 288	BCU Library

Index

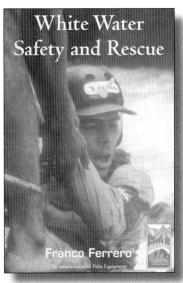
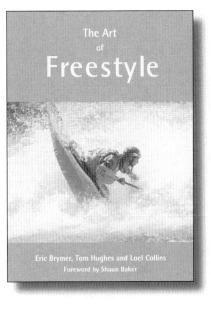

Also available from
Pesda Press

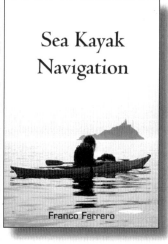

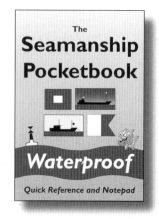

www.pesdapress.com